Vegetarian

FOR A NEW GENERATION

Vegetarian

FOR A NEW GENERATION

Seasonal Vegetable Dishes for Vegetarians,
Vegans, and the Rest of Us

LIANA KRISSOFF

PHOTOGRAPHS BY RINNE ALLEN

STEWART, TABORI & CHANG | NEW YORK

Published in 2014 by Stewart, Tabori & Chang
An imprint of ABRAMS

Library of Congress Control Number: 2013945654

ISBN: 978-1-61769-040-2

Editor: Elinor Hutton
Designer: Chin-Yee Lai
Production Manager: Erin Vandeveer

The text of this book was composed in Jubilat, Gotham, Helvetica and Samantha Upright.

Printed and bound in the United States

10 9 8 7 6 5 4 3 2 1

ABRAMS
THE ART OF BOOKS SINCE 1949

115 West 18th Street
New York, NY 10011
www.abramsbooks.com

for THALIA

Contents

Making
Meals

everyday plates

Following are a few ways to put some of the simple recipes in this book to use in easy, satisfying meals, the kind of vegetable plates you could throw together on a weeknight. I've paired dishes that might not be obvious partners, to give you an idea of their versatility—why not serve falafel with corn on the cob? I've also taken care to ensure that not too many burners will be going at once, that you can take advantage of prepared ingredients from the freezer or refrigerator (pesto, cooked grains or beans, and so on), and that some dishes can be made in advance.

vegan
- Sugar Snaps with Walnuts, Basil, and Cranberries
- Quinoa
- Slow-Fried Sweet Potatoes
- Avocado Puree

- Asparagus with Roasted Strawberry Vinaigrette
- Porcini Risotto
- Generous shavings of hard cheese

- Green and White Beans and Small Turnips and Arugula Pesto
- Refried Lentils
- Cheddar-Seed Crackers
- Red Pepper and Apple Jam or Carrot Marmalade

vegan
- Dry-Fried Green Beans with Garlic Chips and Peanut Sauce
- Long-Grain Brown Rice
- Miso-Crusted Chinese Eggplant

vegan
- Herby Falafel with Tahini-Pomegranate Sauce
- Lemon-Pepper Sautéed Cucumber
- How to Eat Corn on the Cob

- Spinach, Herb, and Ricotta Dumplings
- The Perfect Caponata
- Sweet Corn Polenta

- Healing Stew
- Millet-Parmesan Cake
- Arugula Pesto

- Swiss Chard and Ricotta Frittata
- Crunchy-Topped Broiled Tomatoes
- Salad greens with Tangerine Vinaigrette

vegan
- Basic Black Beans with Epazote
- Green Riced Cauliflower
- Curly Kale Pakora
- Quick Pickled Beet Stems

vegan
- Cauliflower (blanched and cooled) and white beans (cooked and cooled) tossed with Tangy Cashew-Herb Dressing
- Seedy Quinoa Cakes (using flax seeds)
- Roasted Carrot and Daikon with Japanese Spices

- All-Purpose Urad Dal
- Broiled Masala Cauliflower
- Seared Okra with Basil and Tamari

- Buttermilk–Celery Root Puree
- Sweet Wine Mushrooms
- Roasted broccoli with garlic
- Classic Aioli

- Spaghetti Squash, Pesto, and Cherry Tomatoes
- Salt-Wilted Kale (Parmesan variation)

three-course seasonal menus

These meals are a little fancier than the ones on the preceding page, and follow a slower, more formal procession from appetizer to main course to dessert. You might want to invite some friends over and call it a dinner party. Since many of the recipes make smallish portions, consider increasing the quantities if you're serving more than a few people, or toss together a simple green salad or offer a loaf of good bread and wedges of cheese alongside the main course.

SPRING vegan

- Creamy Cashew-Asparagus Soup with Pea Shoots
- Spring Vegetables with Lentils and Quinoa
- A Chocolate Something

SPRING

- Tender Lettuce, Orange, Pistachio, and Feta Salad
- Artichoke Hearts with Brown Basmati Rice and Dill
- Lavender-Oat Shortbread, with fresh berries and soft whipped cream or vanilla ice cream

SPRING

- Sugar Snap Peas (or raw asparagus) with Curried Feta Dip
- Bitter Greens Soup with Mom's Italian Wedding Croutons
- Quickie Blueberry-Beet Sorbet

SUMMER vegan

- Double-Tomato Soup with Curried Nuts
- Twice-Roasted Eggplant and Red Pepper, with Seared Okra with Basil and Tamari
- Sesame-Oat Fruit Crisp (use coconut oil)

SUMMER

- Simple, Spicy Cucumber Soup
- Poblano Casserole, with Long-Grain Brown Rice garnished with fresh cilantro and grated cotija or crumbled feta, and a green salad with Chipotle-Cumin Dressing
- Mango sprinkled with lime juice, salt, and ground cayenne

SUMMER

- Zucchini Flans with Lemon Cream Sauce
- One-Baking-Sheet Tomatoes and Chickpeas, with pan-fried polenta
- Frozen watermelon blended with a few unfrozen pieces and a squeeze of lime juice

FALL vegan

- The Perfect Black Bean Soup
- Sweet and Spicy (and Well-Done) Hash, with warmed corn tortillas or Chickpea Flour Crêpes
- Stewed Stone Fruit with Maple "Cream"

FALL

- Basic Roasted Butternut Squash Soup (plain, or the variation with Greek yogurt, walnut oil, and Aleppo pepper)
- Garlic-Sautéed White Beans and Winter Greens, with Red Lentil Sauce-Absorber
- Easy Little Cheesecakes with Anise-Grenadine Peaches

FALL

- Parsnip Nuggets, with Classic Aioli
- Leek and Mushroom Broth with a Little Egg Salad, with crusty dark bread or Garam Masala Cheese Crisps
- Apples sautéed with butter, maple syrup, and cinnamon, with vanilla ice cream

FALL AND WINTER vegan

- Shaved Kohlrabi with Lemon and Mustard
- Multivegetable khoresh
- Date Snacks and sliced fresh pears

FALL AND WINTER

- Roasted Mushrooms and Arugula with Goat Cheese Polenta
- Thalia's Cabbage Soup
- Banana-Cardamom Bars

to eat standing up, with drinks, or with friends

Here's a list of the recipes that would make especially good party food—porch-sitting noshes, outdoor fire-pit accompaniments, or Friday-after-work cocktail snacks. Serve just one or mix and match.

- Spring Onion Tart with Potato Crust (cut into small squares)
- Iced Radishes with Blue Cheese–Walnut Butter, with Cheddar-Seed Crackers
- Persian-Style Eggplant Dip
- Herby Falafel (make them bite-size)
- Chaat Party
- Curly Kale Pakora
- Coconut-Kale Chips
- Parsnip Nuggets or roasted radishes, with Classic Aioli
- Rustic Tortilla Espagnola (cut into small squares)
- Chickpea Crêpes (add a good pinch of cracked black pepper to the batter)
- Tanya's Brown Lentil Salad, with tortilla chips
- Date Snacks, with sliced hard cheese
- Spicy Fried Giant White Corn

*A SELECTION OF BEAUTIFUL SALSAS—SOME HOT,
SOME MILD—WITH FRESH TORTILLA CHIPS:*

- Classic Fresh Chopped Tomato Salsa
- Last-Minute Blended Salsa
- Thick Roasted Tomato Salsa
- Fresh Tomatillo and Avocado Salsa
- Salsa de Semillas
- Grilled Sweet Corn and Feta Salad
- Basil and Seared Pineapple Salsa
- Scotch Bonnet Chile and Mango Salsa

Introduction

There are countless reasons people turn to a vegetable-based diet, but the ones I find most compelling are the more prosaic: They lend themselves well to a wide variety of culinary interpretations and cooking methods—they can be spiced, sauced, buttered, sautéed, grilled, steamed, you name it. They're less calorie dense than meat, dairy, and grains so overeating is less of a concern. Vegetables are easy to shop for, especially if you're open to using whatever's in season, and they're easy to store. With a few exceptions, in comparison to other sources of nutrients, vegetables are pretty inexpensive. Finally, if eating locally is a goal, it's currently much easier in most parts of the country to obtain good produce from nearby farms and gardens than it is to source a quantity of local meats and fish that would sustain a meat-centric lifestyle.

This mindset matches the continuing evolution of our country's eating habits as more and more people embrace not only less-resource-intensive diets but the variety and ease of vegetable-based cooking. The very makeup of the typical American dinner plate is changing: The ideal square meal, visualized as a round plate divided into sections, is no longer half meat. And the typical "vegetarian plate" is no longer a bowl of rice and token-protein tofu. Every chef-driven restaurant worth its salt now offers beautifully composed vegetable-based meals in which the guiding factors are flavor, variety, and ingenuity. These are meals that are as appealing to meat eaters as to vegetarians or vegans, and the recipes in this book will help you put together such delicious and interesting plant-based meals easily and regularly, whether you're a vegetarian or not. And just as Americans are beginning to question the primacy of meat, our culinary reliance on wheat—in the form of bread, pasta, crusts, and cakes—is being challenged too; these recipes are all gluten free.

Cultures all over the world have practiced vegetarianism since the beginning of recorded history. This is most notable in India, where about a third of the population is vegetarian and there is a long tradition of plant-based eating. The food systems of regions where the predominant religions are Buddhism or Hinduism—whose adherents believe in a principle of nonviolence that extends to animals—can be rich sources of inspiration. In the United States, vegetarianism as an organized movement—with books and official organizations supporting it—only really began to take off in the mid-nineteenth century, concurrent with and heavily influenced by the Second and Third Great Awakenings. The cookbooks published at the time reflect vegetarianism's association with temperance and Christian asceticism, with the idea that we should be "eating to live" and not the other way around, that "perverted tastes" and seasonings that provoke "appetites already deeply sensuous" are at best obstacles in the path to health and well-being and at worst abominations. *Nature's Own Book*, a short volume describing the Sylvester Graham–inspired, mostly vegetarian dietary practices at the Temperance Boarding-House in New York City, advises us: "Black and red pepper, mustard, and such kinds of seasonings . . . should be totally, and utterly excluded from the table and from the kitchen." (And this advice is repeated throughout the book, in case you might have misunderstood.) Perhaps the first full-on vegan cookbook published in English, by Russell Thacher Trall (a founder of the American Vegetarian Society), is titled *The Hygeian Home Cook-Book; or, Healthful and Palatable Food without Condiments* (1874); it includes a chapter devoted to "Mushes." But not only were vegetarians usually encouraged to eat "plain" foods, they were sometimes advised not to eat too many actual vegetables—remember that the notion that foods contained vitamins, nutrients other than proteins and fats, and so on, was at that time still quite new.

It has taken a while, and it has involved some detours through textured vegetable protein and hash brownies, but order a "vegetable plate" at a reasonably decent American restaurant today and you could be rewarded with some of the best, most creative, most interesting dishes the kitchen is turning out—and vegetables themselves will be very much the chief article. No longer content with bland, warmed-over steamed vegetables or bowls of rice jumbled with a few vegetables and various proteins, vegetarians and those of us who thoroughly enjoy meals that tend to be mostly meatless expect not only black and red pepper and mustard but cumin, cardamom, coconut milk, cilantro, fresh ginger, and Mexican oregano. And on our plates we expect to see mostly fresh vegetables.

Today, the vegetarian impulse in this country has for the most part become divorced from organized religion; instead the emphasis now tends to be on personal physical health and well-being. When it comes to avoiding the major diseases, eliminating meat intake altogether might not be the elusive silver bullet (some studies suggest that

there may be a link, if a tenuous one, between a meatless diet and lowered risk of death from heart disease; similar studies have pointed to a lower risk of developing type 2 diabetes; cancer studies are less conclusive), but it's clear that if there are any health benefits of following a vegetarian or vegan diet, those benefits can also be had, at least in part, by a diet that is, well, *partly* so. Initiatives that encourage people to simply eat more vegetables and less meat have been gaining ground, with more and more people adopting "Meat-Free Monday," "vegan until six," or "temporary vegetarian" routines. A long-term incremental or even part-time or temporary approach to vegetarianism is entirely doable for most people. It's easy to try out on a temporary basis, and allows for flexibility and the need to be accommodating to our own varying circumstances and situations.

I've come to be cooking and eating more vegetables for a reason that might seem counterintuitive at first blush: Last summer, my family and I moved from Georgia to Nebraska. Beef country. The local one-off mom-and-pop grocery stores in our neighborhood, all with real live butchers, take great care in offering meat of the absolute best quality, aging it in the store and handling it with the level of respect a food that comes from an animal deserves. When the meat is as good as this, I don't need as much of it—and I don't feel the need to get too darn creative when I do cook with it—to feel like I've truly enjoyed myself in the kitchen, nourished myself at the table, and in general made the very best of things. And so I've found that my attention, as a curious and reasonably adventurous home cook and avid consumer of good food of all kinds, has naturally—and quite happily—shifted to vegetables. Even in beef country, it isn't at all difficult to find amazingly fresh vegetables and luscious fruits, most of them locally grown and sold not only from roadside stands and farmers' markets and through farm-run CSAs but in independently owned and operated grocery stores. It's probably pretty easy where you live too, and I hope that these recipes will inspire you to seek out the bounty—whether you find truly great tomatoes at your regular supermarket (it happens), or mild, herbal green garlic at the city farmers' market, or bright, firm tomatillos at the Mexican grocery store just across town—and take full advantage of it.

What I'm not attempting to do here is present a path to vegetarianism, veganism, or a gluten-free diet. There are a lot of other books whose authors have much more direct experience in that area than I do, and I'd encourage you to supplement your reading with those if you're interested in instituting a dramatic lifestyle change. I'm not a nutritionist and I'm not concerned about how much protein or calcium you're consuming. You won't find giant bowls of beans and barley or protein-rich tofu and chickpeas added to a dish for no reason except that the dish would lack an essential nutrient otherwise. Of course, use your judgment and adjust the recipes or plan your daily or weekly meals to ensure that you're getting the sustenance you need: If you are vegetarian, put an egg on it or add a wedge of cheese to your plate; if you're vegan, add a handful of chickpeas, toast some walnuts and have them on the side, pull some dal or beans from the freezer, eat more kale tomorrow. And of course, if you're omnivorous, these dishes all make beautiful accompaniments to small portions of simply cooked, good-quality meat or fish. These dishes should be taken for what they are: delicious (I certainly hope), easy to prepare, and relatively healthful. And there are some treats, too—sweets and a few straight-arrow potato dishes—because we all need traditional comfort foods now and then.

This is a book, quite simply, for anyone who loves vegetables—those who, for whatever reason (and there are many), would like vegetables to play a larger role in their home-cooked meals. It's also a book for those of us who prefer to cook and eat with the seasons, enjoying asparagus in as many ways as possible while it's pea-sweet and plentiful, tomatoes when they're at their absolute best, kohlrabi when it's most tender and crisp. I hope that those of you who are looking for ideas for expanding your options for plant-based meals will find some inspiration here.

SEASONALITY AND VARIETY

As your cooking experience broadens to include more vegetables and more kinds of food from different food traditions, you'll feel more confident snapping up a big bag of super-fresh baby bok choy from the grower's table at the market even though it wasn't on this week's shopping list. (Shopping list? What's that?) You may become a more thoughtful consumer, as I have over the years, and start to notice as soon as certain vegetables come into season. You'll know in April, for example, to start scouring your cookbooks and clipped recipes or jotted-down ideas for new things to do with asparagus, or morels, or strawberries. You'll know that you should replenish your fresh ginger and garlic supplies because pea shoots might be available this Saturday and they're *so good* sautéed with ginger and garlic. As poblanos or Hatch chiles start to take over the produce stands in late summer, you'll be ready with a fresh bag of charcoal to grill bushels of them at a time to sock away in the freezer. If you haven't yet internalized a basic understanding of the growing seasons, or if, like me, you sometimes get a bit scatterbrained and indecisive when presented with a wealth of produce, check out the little seasonality chart at the end of this book, or jot down a few recipes from the appropriate season's chapters before you leave home. And if you're heading to an Asian, Indian, or Mexican grocery store for the first time, you might want to skim through the lists on pages 000, 000, and 000 and take note of ingredients to keep an eye out for—not just unusual fruits and vegetables but more common produce that is likely to be cheaper and of better quality there than at a regular supermarket, as well as pantry staples, spices, and seasonings that'll come in handy as you cook through the recipes here.

Some people can get along very well eating the same few things every week, every month of their lives, and I admire and occasionally envy that approach—and maybe one day that's how I'll choose to eat. It would certainly leave more time and brain space for other pursuits! But if you're reading this book, you're probably a bit like

me, and believe that variety is the key to any diet you'll actually enjoy and thrive on. Paying attention to seasonality builds in some variety on its own, and approaching those ingredients with global influences adds even more potential for culinary diversity. You can hardly be bored when you're making an Indian chaat for a tangy, cooling summer supper one day and the next you're serving blistery, spicy green beans with a rich tamari peanut sauce or epazote-scented black beans and rice. My hope is that this book helps expand the scope of your culinary experience with common members of the plant kingdom.

MAKING RECIPES INTO MEALS

As long as we're rearranging the American plate to maximize the role of vegetables, let's also go ahead and do away with the idea of one main dish and accompany-

ing side dishes, shall we? The spring, summer, fall, and winter recipes that follow are essentially starting points for creating delicious, easy, satisfying meals. There are a fair number of dishes here that can be meals in themselves—most of the soups and the hearty casseroles, for example, need little else to complete them—but the majority of the dishes are best when paired creatively with others that complement or contrast with them in interesting ways. For the most part, the recipes yield smallish quantities and are simple enough to fit into many different kinds of meals; they're also easy enough to accomplish that you shouldn't feel taxed if you're making several dishes at once.

As is true with most recipes, the number of people each will serve is highly subjective and open to interpretation. I've given a range for most of the dishes here—for example, "Serves 2 to 4," where the lower number might be accurate if you're serving the dish with one other item, the higher number if you're serving it with several other dishes. If you're serving the dish as an appetizer or starter salad, say, you'll just make each serving a little smaller to accommodate the larger number of people in the range given. In determining how many people each recipe serves, I've taken into account the "richness" of the dish—you wouldn't (necessarily) want a huge plate dominated by something very creamy or cheesy, for example. Dishes that are hearty one-dish meals and don't need much accompaniment aside from maybe a simple green salad are indicated with a serving line that reads "Serves _ as a meal."

I've also included some recipes for dishes based on pantry staples like rice, lentils, dried beans, and grains (all gluten free, of course), and these all make excellent sauce-absorbers and plate fillers. Plain old brown rice or simmered red lentils are fine, but I've given a few slightly more flavorful options for pairing with the

vegetable dishes in the rest of the book. The basics are designed to be made in advance in larger quantities and stored in the refrigerator or freezer so they're easy to heat up and spoon alongside your vegetables whenever you need them.

Toward the end of the book you'll also find a bunch of spice mixes, concentrates, and make-ahead flavor boosters you can stash in your pantry, fridge, or freezer to use as easy shortcuts weeks or months down the road. Because you're probably already familiar with the concept of freezing chopped herbs or chiles, ginger-garlic paste, roasted poblanos, marinara sauce, pesto, and stock—all well worth doing, of course—the make-aheads here might expand your options a bit: Japanese-style spice mixes, red curry sauce and vegetable stock concentrates, a few quick springtime refrigerator pickles (cold, crisp pickles are always welcome on the table), some go-to salad dressings both creamy and vinaigrettey, and even a selection of fruit-based concentrates and drinking vinegars for mixing into seltzer or cocktails.

Finally, just because it's nice to have something a little sweet at the end of a special meal, or something crunchy to snack on with drinks, I've thrown in a few simple, relatively healthful sweets and treats.

NOTES ABOUT THE RECIPES

- Regarding vegetable size, assume **medium-size** unless "large" or "small" is indicated in the ingredients list. Let's consider a medium-size onion of any variety to be about the size of a baseball, and a medium-size shallot about the size of a stretched-out golf ball. That said, these recipes are pretty forgiving, so use what you have and adjust as necessary.
- Pay attention to **indicators of doneness** in the recipe directions—cook "until the onions are translucent," for example—and use those as guides more than cooking times, which will depend on the size and weight of your pan, your heat source, the quantity of vegetables in your pan, and how finely or coarsely you've chopped the vegetables.

- As always, taste often. I like my food pretty darn salty, sour, and spicy, so use your judgment and add **salt, citrus** and **vinegar,** and **fresh** and **dried chiles** to taste.
- And speaking of heat, in a lot of recipes I'll call somewhat generically for fresh **hot green** or **red chiles.** If you want your dish to be spicier, use serranos, or leave the seeds and white membranes in a jalapeño; if you want a milder chile flavor, use seeded jalapeños, or even a jalapeño-size part of a poblano or yellow-green Anaheim chile.
- Use **kosher salt** unless the recipe calls for another kind of salt.
- Use **virgin** or **extra-virgin olive oil**—if you have both, use the former for cooking and the latter for dressings. If you want to buy only one at a time, go for a midrange extra-virgin; it withstands the heat of cooking just fine, in my experience.
- In cases where I want a neutral, light-flavored vegetable oil, I almost always use **canola** or **grapeseed oil.**
- If the recipe does not call for a specific kind of onion, any will do—**yellow, white, red,** or **sweet onions.** In dishes where the onion will remain raw, I usually use sweet or red onions; in most cooked dishes it doesn't really matter.

NOTES FOR VEGETARIANS, VEGANS, AND THE GLUTEN FREE

All of the recipes, of course, are truly vegetarian, but if your diet is strict you might want to check labels of any prepared ingredients carefully to make sure they don't contain products you prefer not to use.

- **Cheese** is sometimes made with animal-derived rennet, but just about any style of cheese now can be found without rennet. Look for "microbial enzyme" or "vegetable rennet" in the ingredients list.

I've indicated which dishes are essentially vegan, meaning that they contain no eggs or dairy products, but if you are vegan you should be aware that some of these recipes might contain ingredients that are eschewed by some strict practitioners:

- **Honey,** which some vegans do not eat, appears occasionally, and it can be replaced one-to-one with agave nectar or maple syrup in these recipes without adverse effects.
- **Sugars** are used sparingly in these dishes, but they do crop up. Because the purification of some types of sugar involves the use of bone char, strict vegans might wish to substitute unbleached cane sugar or dehydrated and granulated cane juice, though the flavor and consistency of some dishes will be different.
- **Wine** and **wine vinegar** are used in some of the dishes I've labeled vegan. Some wines have been filtered using animal products and are thus not considered strictly vegan by some. You can find lists online of specific wines that are vegan and seek out those.

Similarly, if you have celiac disease and are strictly gluten free, please read labels and use your judgment when preparing food. Several ingredients I've used in this book are sometimes gluten free but sometimes not:

- **Miso paste** is made primarily of fermented soybeans, but it sometimes contains barley, which contains gluten. Read the label carefully.
- **Tamari** is a wheat-free fermented soy sauce, but not all tamari is certified gluten free. Look for "gluten free" on the label.
- **Oats** are basically gluten free, but many oat products have been contaminated by gluten-containing wheat either because the oats in the fields were grown close to wheat or because the oats were processed on the same equipment as gluten-containing grains. If you're especially sensitive to gluten, buy prepackaged oats and oat flour whose labels specifically state that they are certified gluten free.

SPRING

greens

Tender sprouts and bitter greens, wild weeds and crisp heading lettuces—many of these, while often available throughout the year, are at their sweet peak in springtime, and this is when dishes made from them seem to be most welcome on our tables. The delicate leaves of mâche, watercress, and butter lettuce, also known as Bibb or Boston lettuce or the odd-sounding butterhead, are best dressed simply in a slightly sweet, not too tart vinaigrette that lets the green's mild nature shine through, while crunchy, almost juicy lettuces like romaine and iceberg and the inner parts of green-leaf and red-leaf lettuces can take on more burdensome plate-partners: tart or creamy dressings (see pages 258 to 260 for a few of each), chunky vegetables, grains and beans. If you're not sure yet about bitter greens like pale, white-stemmed escarole, curly endive, frisée, or dandelion greens (pick them from your yard before the flowers appear, and they'll be at their tenderest), spring is the time to try them, as right now they're a little sweeter than usual and more friendly to sensitive palates.

A LETTUCE TIP

Many folks insist that you shouldn't wash your lettuces until just before you're ready to serve them, but I don't think a day or half-day makes that much difference. I'll rinse them gently in cold water in a large bowl—the salad-spinner bowl, if it's available—with the leaves either pulled from the head or left attached if they're loose enough that water can circulate around them. I'll let the water settle for a few minutes so any grit can sink to the bottom, then lift out the greens, drain, and spin dry. (If you don't have a salad spinner, just drain as well as you can, then carefully gather the leaves in a clean kitchen towel or pillowcase and swing it—do this outside, or in the tub or shower stall—to extract the excess water.) If the leaves are very fragile, I'll wrap them in a paper towel before putting them in a clean container or plastic bag and putting them in the crisper drawer of the refrigerator. Do tear or cut them only at the last minute, if possible, so the edges don't oxidize and turn rust-colored.

Bitter Greens Soup
with Mom's Italian Wedding Croutons

SERVES 6 AS A MEAL

One of my favorite meals growing up was what my mom called Italian wedding soup—though after I ordered it in a Pittsburgh Italian restaurant with a high level of western-Pennsylvania cred, I realized that my mom's version isn't exactly canonical. (Similarly, once when a waiter at an Indian restaurant started to describe mulligatawny as a "thin soup," my mom interjected, "Not when *I* make it.") The most important feature of my mom's Italian wedding soup is the croutons, which are unlike any croutons I've had anywhere else: bright yellow-green and eggy, sometimes crisp and sometimes a little chewy, depending on how long they happened to stay in the oven, and loaded with minerally parsley. She uses regular wheat flour in hers, but I've found oat flour to work just fine, and it gives the little squares the barest hint of sweetness, which plays nicely off the bitter greens in this soup.

FOR THE CROUTONS

Oil, for the baking sheet

6 large eggs, separated

Salt

¼ cup (25 g) oat flour

1 cup (100 g) finely grated Parmesan cheese

½ cup (40 g) chopped fresh flat-leaf parsley

FOR THE SOUP

2 tablespoons olive oil

1 onion, diced

2 ribs celery, diced

3 cloves garlic, chopped

Salt and freshly ground black pepper

5 cups (1.2 L) vegetable stock

1 large head escarole or curly endive, chopped, or 4 cups (240 g) chopped dandelion greens or arugula, or a combination

1 cup (145 g) shelled fresh or frozen peas

1 cup (175 g) cooked quinoa or white beans (page 228 or 226; optional)

½ large lemon

MAKE THE CROUTONS

Preheat the oven to 350°F (175°C). Lightly oil a large rimmed baking sheet.

Put the egg whites and a pinch of salt in a large bowl and whisk until soft peaks form. In another large bowl, whisk together the egg yolks and oat flour. Using a rubber spatula, stir a bit of the whites into the yolk mixture to lighten it, then gently fold in half of the remaining whites. Add the cheese, parsley, and the remaining whites to the yolk mixture, and fold them in until just combined. Spread the batter ¼ inch (6 mm) thick on the prepared baking sheet—it's okay if the edges are uneven as long as the thickness is consistent; the mixture won't cover the bottom of the baking sheet completely. Bake until golden brown all over, about 20 minutes. Turn the oven off.

Use a metal spatula to transfer the spongy bread from the pan to a cutting board (cut the sheet into quarters first, if necessary). Cut the bread into ¼-inch (6-mm) squares. Use the croutons soft, as is, or return the squares to the baking sheet and place it in the cooling-down oven until they are dried and crisp, 15 to 30 minutes more. (You can make these up to a day in advance and keep them in an airtight container. Re-crisp them in a 350°F/175°C oven for a few minutes, if you like.)

continued

In a large pot or Dutch oven, heat the oil over medium-high heat until it shimmers. Add the onion, celery, garlic, a pinch of salt, and a few grindings of pepper. Cook, stirring frequently, until the onion and celery are very tender and beginning to brown, about 8 minutes. Add the stock and bring to a simmer. Add the escarole and fresh peas (if using frozen peas, do not add them at this point) and return the stock to a simmer. Cook until the ribs of the escarole are tender, about 5 minutes. Add the quinoa or beans, if using (as well as the frozen peas, if using), and cook just until heated through, about 3 minutes.

Ladle the soup into wide soup bowls and squeeze a bit of lemon juice over each serving. Top with croutons and serve.

Tender Lettuce, Orange, Pistachio, and Feta Salad

SERVES 2 TO 4

I can't imagine a better lunchtime salad to welcome early spring than this one—colorful, tart, and fresh, with bites of juicy citrus recalling the cold winter days when it seemed the house always smelled of torn orange or clementine peels. If it's too early for your farmers' market, look for a head or two of pretty, tender butter lettuce (aka Boston or Bibb lettuce) at a good grocery store. The ones with the roots still attached can be surprisingly fresh.

1 orange

2 tablespoons red wine vinegar

½ teaspoon agave nectar or honey

Salt and freshly ground black pepper

¼ cup (60 ml) olive oil

⅛ small red onion, very thinly sliced

2 small heads (about 8 ounces/225 g) butter lettuce or other tender lettuces, torn into bite-size pieces

¼ cup (30 g) shelled salted or unsalted pistachios, toasted

3 ounces (85 g) feta cheese, crumbled

Finely grate the zest of half of the orange into a large bowl. Add the vinegar, agave nectar, ½ teaspoon salt, and a few grindings of pepper, and whisk well. Set aside.

Segment the orange: Cut off the top and bottom of the orange with a sharp knife, stand it upright, and cut off the peel and pith to expose the flesh. Working above a separate bowl to catch the juices, cut between the membranes to release the orange segments into the bowl. Squeeze the empty membranes and peels over the bowl to extract any additional juice, then discard them.

Reserving the segments, add the orange juice to the bowl with the vinegar mixture. Add the oil in a thin stream to the vinegar mixture, whisking constantly. Add the orange segments and onion.

Pile the lettuce into the bowl with the dressing, add the pistachios and cheese, and toss well. Serve immediately.

Stir-Fried Lettuce
with Chiles, Rice Stick Noodles, and Sprouts

SERVES 2 OR 3 AS A MEAL

VEGAN

Surprisingly, you cannot say there's nothing in the fridge for supper when you have wilting lettuce. I always seem to have one or two bags of romaine hearts, for example, that I can't bring myself to make into a salad—if you do too, then start soaking some noodles and you'll have a fully satisfying meal in less than half an hour. A quick stir-fry with chiles and a simple, salty tamari-based sauce highlights the vegetal, bitter quality of a sturdy lettuce like romaine, and the high heat brings the languishing leaves back to life.

7 ounces (200 g) rice stick noodles, about ¼ inch (6 mm) wide

About 4 cups (1 L) boiling water

1 ½ tablespoons tamari

1 tablespoon shaoxing (Chinese cooking wine), dry sherry, or vermouth

Freshly ground black pepper

2 tablespoons vegetable oil

2 cloves garlic, minced

2 fresh hot chiles, seeded and thinly sliced

2 heads (about 12 ounces/340 g) lettuce (preferably a sturdy variety like green- or red-leaf or romaine, or a combination), roughly chopped

2 cups (140 g) very fresh mung-bean or other sturdy sprouts

2 to 3 pinches sesame seeds, toasted in a skillet

Put the noodles in a heatproof bowl and cover with the boiling water. Let them soak for 10 minutes, then drain in a colander, rinse under cold running water, and drain well.

In a small cup, combine the tamari, shaoxing, a few grindings of black pepper, and 2 tablespoons water.

In a large, deep sauté pan or wok, heat the oil over medium-high heat until it shimmers. Add the garlic and cook, stirring, for 30 seconds. Add the chiles, then pile in the lettuce and noodles and drizzle with the tamari mixture. Cover the pan and cook for 1 minute. Then, using tongs or a metal spatula, turn the lettuce and noodles until they are thoroughly combined—this will take some doing, but keep at it—and the lettuce wilts, about 2 minutes more. The noodles should be tender but still quite chewy. Taste and sprinkle in a little more tamari if needed. Transfer to a serving bowl, put the sprouts on top, and sprinkle with the **sesame seeds**. Serve hot.

Cool, Creamy-Dressed Lettuces with Hot, Spicy Lentils

SERVES 4 AS A MEAL

My friend Eric Wagoner, who runs an internet-based farmers' market in Athens, Georgia, is one of those people who takes pictures of the food he's cooking, eating, or about to eat and posts them online. If everyone I knew did this I'd quit the World Wide Web altogether, but I have to admit that when Eric posts a picture—often featuring the freshest local produce, meat, and/or dairy—it has a nine-inten chance of being wildly inspirational. He went through a salad phase recently, and, naturally, so did I. He will put anything and everything in a salad,

piles and dollops of the craziest damn things, which you know just have to be delicious together.

This Eric-inspired salad uses crisp, crunchy romaine, which will hold up to the hot lentils spooned on top of it, in combination with a slightly more tender lettuce, which will wilt a bit, bringing the hot and cold elements of the salad together. Scooped-out chunks of creamy avocado play a vital role, as does the tangy, cilantro-flecked dressing.

continued

FOR THE DRESSING

- 1 cup (240 ml) sour cream or thick plain yogurt
- ¼ cup (60 ml) buttermilk
- ½ cup (10 g) fresh cilantro, minced
- 2 scallions, minced
- Salt

FOR THE LENTILS

- 1 teaspoon hot paprika
- 1 teaspoon ground cumin
- 1 teaspoon dried oregano, preferably Mexican
- Salt
- 2 tablespoons vegetable oil
- 1 onion, diced
- 2 cloves garlic, minced
- 1 tablespoon tomato paste
- 2½ cups (550 g) cooked French green lentils (see page 225)

FOR THE SALAD

- 4 small ripe tomatoes, chopped, or 1 pint (565 g) cherry or grape tomatoes, halved
- 2 Hass avocados, peeled and chopped
- Juice of ½ lime
- Salt and freshly ground black pepper
- 2 romaine hearts, cut or torn into bite-size pieces, chilled
- 1 head red- or green-leaf lettuce, cut or torn into bite-size pieces, chilled
- ½ cup (65 g) grated extra-sharp cheddar cheese (optional)

MAKE THE DRESSING

Whisk together the sour cream, buttermilk, cilantro, scallions, and ¾ teaspoon salt. (The dressing can be made up to 3 days in advance and stored in the fridge in an airtight container. Taste and season with more salt just before serving, if necessary.)

MAKE THE LENTILS

In a small bowl, stir together the paprika, cumin, oregano, and ¾ teaspoon salt and set aside.

In a large sauté pan, heat the oil over medium-high heat until it shimmers. Add the onion and garlic and cook, stirring frequently, until translucent and golden, 5 to 7 minutes. Add the tomato paste and spice mixture and stir for 1 minute. Add 1 cup (240 ml) water and the lentils and cook, stirring constantly, until the lentils are heated through and thoroughly incorporated into the spice mixture, about 2 minutes. Taste and season with more salt, if necessary. Remove from the heat, cover, and keep warm.

MAKE THE SALAD

In a medium bowl, toss together the tomatoes, avocados, lime juice, and salt and pepper to taste.

Put the lettuces in a huge bowl and drizzle with about half of the dressing. Toss to coat evenly, adding more dressing if necessary. (You may not need all of the dressing.) Divide the lettuce among serving plates, top with spoonfuls of the hot lentils and the tomato-avocado mixture, then sprinkle with the cheese, if you'd like. Serve immediately.

asparagus, artichokes, and peas

These three vegetables—asparagus, artichokes, and peas—are my family's favorites, the Holy Trinity of spring produce. Sweet peas planted well before the last frost, local asparagus just cut from its crowns, and the mineral, almost meaty luxury of young artichokes are all easy to love. No vegetables are more springlike. (Except, perhaps, fresh fava beans, beloved by every person who has ever thought or written about food in any meaningful way . . . except me. I do hope to one day join the fava-loving brotherhood, but until the event of my conversion that vegetable will be conspicuously absent from my table.)

The first time my husband, Derek, tasted a spear of raw asparagus that my daughter and I had grown ourselves (it was one of about six we harvested that first season), he exclaimed that it tasted just like the fresh peas of his childhood. I'll often combine the two vegetables in an attempt to re-create that exceedingly fresh, sweet, grassy flavor. English peas, which to my mind are best swiped with your tongue straight from the pod, need very little enhancement, but they do pair awfully well with asparagus and artichokes. Now's also the time to start looking for fat, succulent sugar snap peas in farmers' markets—they are so much better than the packaged ones available in grocery stores year-round, and are a standby easy snack. While fresh English and sugar snap peas will keep, loosely wrapped, in the refrigerator for a few days, they are best eaten immediately after harvesting, if possible. Fresh artichokes, especially young ones or any variety other than the large globe type, are unfortunately not too common at farmers' markets outside California, but keep an eye out for them in better grocery stores. A fresh, untrimmed artichoke will keep for at least a week in the refrigerator.

Asparagus with Shiitake Cream

SERVES 4 TO 6

Fresh marjoram—with its faint anise fragrance—has been steadily working its way up in my mental ranking of herbs for a few years now, ever since I had a pizza that came to the table with big handfuls of it piled atop melting Emmentaler and sizzling garlic. I'd always just considered it to be a lighter-tasting, more delicate version of oregano, to be used if you want a less powerful oregano flavor—but who would ever want that? I've since come to appreciate marjoram specifically for its distinctive floral character. Paired with earthy, finely diced shiitakes (each little morsel absorbing some of the infused cream), sweet spring asparagus, and just a tiny bit of lemon, marjoram really comes into its own. If you can't get your hands on it, though, go ahead and use a few torn sprigs of oregano instead—the tenderest tips you can find.

The Porcini Risotto (page 220) is a near perfect accompaniment to this dish: Cook it first and keep it warm, then cook this asparagus and serve them together.

With Porcini Risotto (page 220)

3 tablespoons unsalted butter

2 large shallots, minced

Salt and freshly ground black pepper

4 ounces (113 g) shiitake mushroom caps, diced (about 2 cups)

1/2 cup (120 ml) dry white wine

1 bunch asparagus (about 1 pound/455 g), bottoms trimmed, cut into 1-inch (2.5-cm) pieces

1/4 cup (60 ml) heavy cream

1 to 1 1/2 tablespoons torn fresh marjoram leaves

Fresh lemon juice (optional)

In a large sauté pan, melt half of the butter over medium-high heat. Add the shallots, a pinch of salt, and a couple grindings of pepper. Cook, stirring frequently, until the shallots just start to brown at the edges, 3 to 4 minutes. Add the mushrooms and the remaining butter and cook, stirring frequently, until the mushrooms have released some of their liquid and are starting to brown, 4 to 5 minutes. Add the wine and cook until it has reduced by about half, about 2 minutes. Add the asparagus, cream, and marjoram and cook, stirring frequently, until the asparagus is just tender and the cream has reduced and thickened slightly, about 3 minutes. Taste and season with salt and pepper and a squeeze of lemon juice, if needed. Serve hot.

Asparagus with Roasted Strawberry Vinaigrette

SERVES 4

VEGAN

Tart-sweet strawberries, mashed together with a little balsamic vinegar and a pinch of sugar, make a simple, bright, and flavorful dressing for roasted asparagus. If you can find fresh morels, roast a couple handfuls of them with the asparagus for an especially fancy dish that could serve as a main course with some pureed celery root or garlicky mashed potatoes alongside.

1 bunch thick asparagus (about 1 pound/455 g), bottoms trimmed

2 tablespoons olive oil

Salt and freshly ground black pepper

6 ounces (170 g/about 8) strawberries, hulled

1 1/2 tablespoons balsamic vinegar

Pinch of brown sugar

Preheat the oven to 400°F (205°C). Set a rimmed baking sheet in the oven while it heats.

Put the asparagus in a shallow bowl and drizzle with the oil. Sprinkle with about 1/4 teaspoon salt and a couple of grindings of pepper. Rub the asparagus spears all over to coat them with the oil. Transfer the asparagus to the hot baking sheet. Roll the strawberries in the oil left in the bowl and sprinkle with about 1/4 teaspoon salt and a grinding of pepper. Quickly transfer them to the baking sheet with the asparagus. Don't wash the bowl. Roast until the asparagus is tender and the strawberries are collapsing and leaking juices, about 15 minutes. Using tongs, transfer the asparagus to a serving platter.

Scrape the strawberries and all their juices into the oil remaining in the shallow bowl. Using a fork, mash the strawberries into a smooth paste, then mix in the vinegar, brown sugar, and salt and pepper to taste. (You can also do this in a mini food processor for an extra-smooth consistency.) If the vinaigrette is too thick, add a teaspoon or so of water.

Spoon the vinaigrette over the asparagus and serve hot.

Creamy Cashew-Asparagus Soup with Pea Shoots

SERVES 3 OR 4

VEGAN

Tender, sweet, succulent pea shoots, which are the small, early sprouting parts of the pea vine with a few leaves attached, used to be available only to those lucky enough to be or know a farmer or gardener, but happily they are becoming easier to find. They will keep for a few days in the crisper drawer, ready to toss into salads or to use as garnishes. I also get them at Asian grocery stores when they're in season, saving the smallest, most tender shoots to serve raw and lightly braising the rest.

This bright green, steaming-hot soup is enriched not with cream but with raw cashews, which are simmered in stock and then blended with the vegetables until very smooth. If you have 1/2 cup (120 ml) of cashew cream (see page 259) handy, you can use it instead of the 1/2 cup (60 g) cashews: Just simmer the vegetables, put them in a blender with 1 1/2 cups (360 ml) of the cooking liquid and the cashew cream, and proceed as directed.

1 1/2 cups (360 ml) vegetable stock

3/4 cup (90 g) raw cashews

1 bunch asparagus (about 1 pound/455 g)

4 ounces (113 g) sugar snap peas

Salt and freshly ground black pepper

2 cups (1 ounce/28 g) sweet pea shoots

3 teaspoons olive oil

1 teaspoon fresh lemon juice

In a large saucepan, bring the stock, 1 1/2 cups (360 ml) water, and 1/2 cup (60 g) of the cashews to a boil, then lower the heat and simmer for 15 minutes.

Meanwhile, trim off and discard only the very bottoms of the asparagus, leaving the tough portion of the stalks intact. Coarsely chop the stalks. Remove any tough strings from the peas. Add the asparagus stalks and peas to the saucepan, bring the mixture back to a boil, then lower the heat and simmer until the vegetables are just tender but still bright green, about 5 minutes (the woody parts of the asparagus stalks won't get tender but will be fine once blended and strained).

Using a slotted spoon, transfer the cashews, asparagus, and peas to a blender, then add about 2 cups (480 ml) of the cooking liquid from the pan. Blend until very smooth, then blend some more. Set a sieve over a clean saucepan and strain the soup, pressing the solids with a heatproof spatula to get as much of the soft puree as possible through the sieve, leaving behind only a fibrous pulp, which you can discard or compost. Be sure to scrape all the puree from the underside of the sieve into the saucepan. Rinse out the blender with another ½ cup (60 ml) of the cooking liquid and pour it through the sieve into the pan as well. Season with salt and pepper to taste. Set aside.

In a medium bowl, toss the pea shoots with 1 teaspoon of the oil, the lemon juice, and a pinch of salt and pepper.

In a small sauté pan, heat the remaining 2 teaspoons oil over medium-high heat until it shimmers. Add the remaining ¼ cup (30 g) cashews and a pinch of salt. Cook, stirring constantly, until golden, about 1 minute, then transfer to a paper towel to drain.

Reheat the soup over medium heat, stirring, until heated through. Ladle the soup into serving bowls and top with the pea shoot salad and hot fried cashews. Serve immediately.

Artichoke Hearts with Brown Basmati Rice and Dill

SERVES 2 OR 3 AS A MEAL

CAN BE VEGAN

Fragrant basmati rice and grassy dill, with plenty of black pepper, pair beautifully with the somewhat briny artichoke hearts, whether canned, frozen, or freshly steamed. These are simple, pure flavors, comforting and hearty, especially on a chilly spring day. Adding a dollop of tangy labneh or Greek yogurt makes a surprisingly rich dish.

1 cup (185 g) brown basmati rice

1 tablespoon olive oil

½ large onion, thinly sliced

Salt and freshly ground black pepper

6 ounces (170 g) frozen or canned artichoke hearts, defrosted and/or drained, or 4 globe artichokes, trimmed, quartered, and steamed (see page 34)

1 tablespoon chopped fresh dill

Labneh or other thick plain yogurt, for serving (optional)

Put the rice into a medium saucepan and add water to cover by about 1 inch (2.5 cm). Bring to a boil, then lower the heat and simmer briskly, uncovered, for 15 to 20 minutes. Drain the rice in a sieve, rinse under cold running water, and drain again. (The parcooked rice can be stored in an airtight container in the refrigerator for up to 3 days.)

In a large, deep sauté pan, heat the oil over medium-high heat until it shimmers. Add the onion, a pinch of salt, and a few grindings of pepper. Cook, stirring frequently, until the onion is very soft and golden, about 8 minutes. Add the artichoke hearts, parcooked rice, 2 cups (480 ml) water, and ½ teaspoon salt. Bring to a boil over high heat, then lower the heat and simmer, stirring occasionally, until the rice is tender and most of the liquid has been absorbed, about 20 minutes, adding up to ½ cup (120 ml) more water if the pan becomes too dry before the rice is tender. Taste and season with more salt and pepper, if needed. Stir in the dill. Serve with a bowl of labneh for dolloping on top, if desired.

Fresh Artichokes Braised with Sweet Peas

SERVES 4

VEGAN

Until the first time I came into a big bagful of perfectly fresh and not-too-expensive artichokes, I couldn't imagine them anything but steamed whole and eaten leaf by leaf, the front tooth–scraped petals piling up in a bowl that's always just a little too small between my daughter and me. The trimming and de-choking and the sheer quantity of detritus you end up discarding for just a handful of edible heart can be discouraging, it's true, but trust me: Fresh artichokes with their long, meaty stems still attached, steamed until just tender (you can do this a day in advance) and then gently braised in good homemade stock with super-sweet peas, are so worth the effort. The delicious simplicity and beauty of the dish merits a place in the center of a dinner-party table, perhaps with the Roasted Carrot Salad with Spicy Lemon Dressing on page 41 and a boldly spiced brown basmati rice like the one on page 219.

½ lemon

4 globe artichokes

1 tablespoon olive oil

2 shallots, thinly sliced

1 ½ cups (8 ounces/225 g) fresh or frozen shelled English peas

½ cup (120 ml) vegetable stock

Salt and freshly ground black pepper

Pinch of sugar

Squeeze the lemon into a large bowl of water; reserve the squeezed lemon half.

Prepare the artichokes, rubbing the lemon half over the cut surfaces as you work: Cut the top third off—a sharp serrated knife works well here. Working around the artichoke, pull off and discard the leaves, a layer at a time, until the leaves are very pale green, then stop. Using a paring or chef's knife, trim the tough fibrous parts of the base and stem and the dried end of the stem. Cut the artichoke into quarters (leaving the stem attached if possible) and use a spoon or paring knife to scrape out the hairy, spiny choke at the center. Drop the prepared artichoke quarters into the bowl of lemon water. Continue with the remaining artichokes.

In a large saucepan, bring 1 inch (2.5 cm) of water to a boil. Drain the artichokes and put them in a steamer basket; lower the basket into the saucepan, cover the pan, and steam for 15 minutes. Remove the steamer basket from the saucepan and set aside. (The steamed artichokes will keep in an airtight container in the refrigerator for up to 2 days.)

In a large sauté pan, heat the oil over medium-high heat until it shimmers. Add the shallots and cook, stirring, until softened and beginning to brown, about 5 minutes, lowering the heat if they brown too quickly. Add the artichokes and cook, stirring occasionally, for 5 minutes. Add the peas and stock and cook, stirring occasionally, until the peas and artichokes are tender, about 5 minutes more. Season with salt, pepper, and sugar to taste, and serve hot.

Sugar Snaps with Walnuts, Basil, and Cranberries

SERVES 2 TO 4

VEGAN

If you have a special bottle of nut oil, this dish, with its uncomplicated flavors and just a quick turn in a hot pan, is a fine place to use a drizzle or two (if you use an oil other than walnut, use the corresponding nuts in place of walnuts). Sautéing with nut oil and finishing with a squeeze of lemon juice gives sweet, crisp sugar snap peas a buttery gloss, and the basil heightens the overall sweetness of the dish.

1 tablespoon walnut or olive oil

12 ounces (340 g) sugar snap peas, strings pulled off if necessary

1/2 teaspoon salt

Juice of 1/2 small lemon

1/3 cup (35 g) walnut halves, toasted and chopped

1 tablespoon minced dried cranberries

1 large sprig fresh basil, torn

Freshly ground black pepper

In a large sauté pan, heat the oil over medium-high heat until it shimmers. Add the sugar snaps and salt and toss well. Cook, tossing and stirring frequently, until the peas are bright emerald green and just heated through but not yet floppy, 4 to 5 minutes. Squeeze in the lemon juice and add the walnuts, cranberries, basil, and a few grindings of pepper. Toss well, and serve hot.

Variation

To make more of a one-pot meal, use a deep pan, slice the peas in half before sautéing so they're easier to incorporate when you add a grain, increase the quantity of oil, salt, walnuts, and basil a bit, and fold in 2 1/2 to 3 cups (250 to 300 g) cold cooked brown rice (page 228) or quinoa (page 228) after the rest of the ingredients, turning with a spatula until it's heated through.

Sugar Snap Peas with Curried Feta Dip

SERVES 4 TO 6 AS AN APPETIZER

I like to use Bulgarian feta in this dip for the walloping tang, but regular French- or Greek-style feta is fine too—though you might wish to add a squeeze of lemon juice. If you're lucky enough to come across super-fresh asparagus, it's great for dipping too: Just rinse off a bunch, trim the ends, and pile it on a platter—yes, raw—alongside the sugar snaps.

5 ounces (140 g) Bulgarian feta cheese

1/4 cup (60 ml) plain Greek yogurt

1 fresh hot green chile, seeded and chopped

1 tablespoon olive oil

1 teaspoon good-quality Madras (hot) curry powder

Pinch of ground cayenne

About 1 pound (455 g) sugar snap peas, strings pulled off if necessary

In a mini food processor, combine the cheese, yogurt, chile, oil, curry powder, and cayenne and process until smooth. Taste and add more cayenne if needed. Scrape the mixture into a small bowl and serve with the sugar snaps for dipping. (Alternatively, to serve as a side dish, toss the peas with enough dressing to just coat them.)

young roots and new potatoes

Gardeners usually overplant their plots of root vegetables, which in late spring or early summer then need to be thinned out. The thinnings are wonderful in and of themselves: tender baby beets and true baby carrots, not the regular carrots that have been shaved to baby size and are sold year-round in plastic packages. Also in spring, you'll find an array of beautiful radishes: not just the small, perfect ruby spheres but long, slender French breakfast radishes, black radishes (with their creamy white insides), watermelon radishes (green outsides, streaky pink insides), and more. Raw, they need nothing more than some coarse salt, and maybe some soft butter, but they're also welcome thinly sliced or julienned in light salads of tender greens. Or roast them to mellow their bite and bring out their sweet side. (Don't neglect the radish or beet tops, even if they are a bit bug-eaten: Roast them along with the roots, or sauté them with olive oil and salt.)

New potatoes are actually those that are pulled up from the ground around the potato plant in spring and early summer before they've matured, while the rest of the tubers underneath the plant are left to mature. New potatoes have thin skins that don't need peeling, and sweet, dense flesh. These are wonderful cooked and put into salads (the Warm Roasted New Potato Salad on page 45 shouldn't be missed), or just steamed and tossed with fresh herbs and butter.

Self-Glazed Carrots

SERVES 2 TO 4

This has to be the easiest way imaginable to cook carrots: Start them out in a cold pan with a glassful of water and a chunk of good-quality butter and just let them boil away; when you hear them suddenly switch from bubbling to sizzling, they should be perfectly tender. The little bit of liquid left in the pan emulsifies with the fat to coat the carrot coins in a light glaze. To make this vegan, simply replace the butter with olive or virgin coconut oil—it works just as well.

6 medium carrots, preferably slender ones (see Note), peeled if necessary, cut into ¼-inch (6-mm) slices

1 tablespoon unsalted butter

½ teaspoon salt, or to taste

Grated zest of ½ orange

A few sprigs of carrot tops (optional)

Put the carrots in a large sauté pan with the butter, salt, and 1 cup (240 ml) water. Place over high heat and cook, uncovered, stirring occasionally, until the water has evaporated and the carrots start making a sizzling sound, about 12 minutes (about 9 minutes after the water begins to boil). Add the orange zest, and toss for about 30 seconds. Taste and season with more salt, if needed. Sprinkle with a few torn sprigs of carrot tops, if you like, and serve hot.

Note: Multicolored carrots are great here, but the beautiful dark purple variety will gray the glaze a bit, so if cooking for the color-sensitive you might wish to use either all purple carrots or swap those out and save them for a different dish. Also, if you're lucky enough to have tiny real baby carrots, the ones not much thicker than a Sharpie, you can leave them whole rather than cutting them up.

Variation

Use vegetable stock instead of water, and add a pinch of saffron threads, a few drops of honey, a cinnamon stick, and some hot red pepper flakes. When the stock has evaporated and the carrots are tender, stir in a few tablespoons of coconut milk or heavy cream.

Roasted Carrot Salad with Spicy Lemon Dressing

SERVES 2 TO 4

There was a beautiful Moroccan carrot salad—juicy grated raw carrots with harissa, mint, and feta—making the rounds on the internet a couple of years ago, after Deb Perelman posted a reader's recipe for it on Smitten Kitchen. I learned at least two things from that dish: that carrots are absolutely amazing if they're paired with something a little tangy or spicy (or both) to offset their natural sweetness, and that feta can be crumbled into and tossed with anything to make it infinitely better. You'll see the results of the latter throughout this book. Here's a fairly obvious riff on the dish, with nearly caramelized roasted carrots, lots of lemon juice, and some heat. This would also be great made with peeled and chopped beets instead of the carrots.

8 ounces (225 g) thin carrots, trimmed, scrubbed, and cut into 1-inch (2.5-cm) lengths

2 tablespoons olive oil

Salt and freshly ground black pepper

1 tablespoon harissa (page 252) or ½ tablespoon *sambal oelek* (hot red chile paste)

1 tablespoon fresh lemon juice

2 tablespoons chopped fresh flat-leaf parsley

1 teaspoon chopped fresh mint

Preheat the oven to 400°F (205°C). Set a rimmed baking sheet in the oven while it heats.

Put the carrots in a medium bowl and drizzle with 1 tablespoon of the oil. Sprinkle with a pinch of salt and a grinding of pepper and toss to coat with the oil. Put the carrots on the hot baking sheet in a single layer and roast, shaking the pan once or twice so they cook evenly, until tender and lightly browned in spots, about 20 minutes. Do not wash the bowl.

In the bowl, whisk together the harissa, lemon juice, ½ teaspoon salt, the remaining 1 tablespoon oil, the parsley, and the mint. When the carrots are done, transfer them to the bowl with the dressing and toss to coat. Taste and season with more salt and pepper, if needed. Serve warm.

Iced Radishes with Blue Cheese-Walnut Butter

SERVES 6 TO 8 AS AN APPETIZER OR HORS D'OEUVRE

Snap up a handful of different radishes at the morning farmers' market, chill a bottle of rosé, do the opposite with a stick of butter, and you'll be well on your way to a sophisticated late-afternoon snack. A loaf of crusty dark bread and a dish of unusual pickles would be nice to set on the coffee table too, followed by a substantial grain- or bean-based salad with a lemon-mustard dressing.

12 ounces (340 g) mixed radishes (French breakfast, watermelon, black), scrubbed

About 3 cups (720 ml) ice water

½ cup (1 stick/113 g) good butter (preferably homemade), softened

2 ounces (57 g) cream cheese, softened

2 ounces (57 g) blue cheese

Salt and freshly ground black pepper

½ cup (45 g) walnut halves, toasted and cooled

Slice the radishes or cut small ones in half. Put them in a bowl and cover with the ice water.

Put the butter, cream cheese, blue cheese, a pinch of salt, and a grinding of pepper in a mini food processor and pulse until smooth, scraping down the bowl several times. (Alternatively, mash everything well in a bowl with a fork.) Transfer to a medium bowl.

Chop the walnuts and stir them into the butter mixture. (Or leave them in large pieces and serve them alongside the radishes and butter.) Transfer the butter mixture to a ramekin for serving.

Drain the radishes, pat dry, and arrange on a serving platter. If preparing the radishes in advance, lay them out on a serving platter, cover with a damp paper towel, and wrap the whole plate with plastic and refrigerate for up to 3 hours. Serve with the ramekin of blue cheese–walnut butter for spreading on the radishes.

Roasted Baby Beet Salad
with Arugula and Blue Cheese Vinaigrette

Why would you make a mustardy vinaigrette and whisk in soft blue cheese till it breaks down and gets all strange-looking? Why not? It's delicious, and possibly even better than the more common buttermilk and sour cream–based dressing, so who cares what it looks like? I really love the contrast between the tangy, salty dressing and the sweet, dense roasted beets; with the mini salad of arugula and lemon underneath it all, and maybe a rye crispbread or two, this salad makes a pretty dynamic lunch.

FOR THE BEETS

- 8 baby beets (about 1 pound 4 ounces/565 g total), trimmed and scrubbed

FOR THE VINAIGRETTE

- 1 tablespoon fresh lemon juice
- 1 tablespoon sherry vinegar
- 1 small shallot, minced
- 1 teaspoon grainy mustard
- Salt and freshly ground black pepper
- 2 tablespoons olive oil
- 2 ounces (57 g) Gorgonzola or other soft blue cheese

FOR THE SALAD

- 5 cups (about 3 ounces/85 g) baby arugula
- 2 teaspoons fresh lemon juice
- 2 teaspoons olive oil
- Salt and freshly ground black pepper

MAKE THE BEETS

Preheat the oven to 400°F (205°C).

Wrap the beets in a large piece of aluminum foil and put the packet on a baking sheet. Roast until a small knife inserted into one (through the foil) slides out easily, 45 to 60 minutes. Let cool for a few minutes, then rub off the skins (or use a vegetable peeler or paring knife to peel them). Cut the beets into ½-inch (12-mm) wedges and set aside to cool completely.

MAKE THE VINAIGRETTE

In a large bowl, whisk together the lemon juice, vinegar, shallot, mustard, ¾ teaspoon salt, and several grindings of pepper. Gradually whisk in the oil until emulsified. Crumble in the cheese and whisk until only small lumps remain and the dressing is creamy.

Add the beets to the bowl with the dressing and toss to coat. (The beets can be roasted, dressed, and refrigerated in an airtight container up to 1 day in advance. They can be served cold or at room temperature.)

MAKE THE SALAD

Put the arugula in a large bowl, sprinkle with the lemon juice, oil, and salt and pepper to taste, and toss well.

Divide the arugula among serving plates and top with the dressed beets. Serve immediately.

Warm Roasted New Potato Salad

SERVES 4 TO 6

VEGAN

Honestly, you can put just about anything on a hot rimmed baking sheet in the oven, go shop online for a while, and then toss those crusted, caramelized vegetables with a dressing of some sort and sit down to a great supper. Roasted celery and cherry or grape tomatoes—in spring, other tomatoes are usually mealy and not worth eating—in a warm new potato salad may seem strange, but they add a refreshing acidity that complements the creamy potatoes.

1 pound (455 g) new potatoes, halved

2 ribs celery, cut into 1-inch (2.5-cm) pieces

4 small shallots, trimmed, peeled, and quartered

5 tablespoons (75 ml) olive oil

Salt and freshly ground black pepper

½ dry pint (about 5 ounces/140 g) small cherry or grape tomatoes

3 tablespoons sherry vinegar

½ teaspoon smoked paprika

1 teaspoon Dijon-style mustard

Preheat the oven to 400°F (205°C). Set a large rimmed baking sheet in the oven while it heats.

In a large bowl, toss the potatoes, celery, and shallots with 2 tablespoons of the oil, several pinches of salt, and several grindings of pepper. Spread them on the hot baking sheet. Roast until tender and nicely browned, turning once or twice with a spatula during the cooking time if you think of it, 25 to 30 minutes. Do not wash the bowl.

Add the tomatoes and another pinch of salt and grinding of pepper to the bowl and toss. Add the tomatoes to the pan with the potatoes during the last 5 minutes of cooking.

In the same bowl, whisk together the vinegar, ½ teaspoon salt, several grindings of pepper, the paprika, and the mustard. Gradually whisk in the remaining 3 tablespoons oil. Taste and add more salt and pepper, if needed—it should be plenty salty.

Scrape the roasted vegetables into the dressing and toss to coat well. Let stand for a few minutes, toss again, taste for seasoning, and serve warm.

Spring Onion Tart with Potato Crust

SERVES 2 TO 4

This is one of those dishes that's so straightforward and adaptable you'll want to make it a regular in your rotation. Naturally sweet, fresh-tasting spring onions—out of season you could most certainly use large, thick scallions, thin wedges of red onion, even slabs of zucchini or peeled eggplant—are seared in a hot skillet and then laid down into an eggy tart with a thin, crisped potato crust. I love the simplicity of just whisking eggs and cheese together for the filling, but by all means feel free to add minced fresh herbs, a dollop of Arugula Pesto (page 256), or spices other than the nutmeg.

2 large eggs

1 cup (150 g) crumbled feta, shredded Gruyère, or other cheese

Salt and freshly ground black pepper

Pinch of freshly grated nutmeg

1 tablespoon olive oil

3 to 4 spring onions, trimmed and halved lengthwise

1 tablespoon unsalted butter

1 medium Yukon Gold or other waxy potato, very thinly sliced

Preheat the oven to 350°F (175°C).

In a medium bowl, whisk together the eggs, cheese, a good pinch of salt, several grindings of black pepper, and the nutmeg. Set aside.

In a 10- to 12-inch (25- to 30-cm) ovenproof skillet or sauté pan, heat the oil over high heat until it shimmers. Add the spring onions, cut sides down, in a single layer and cook, without disturbing them, until the bottoms are nicely seared, about 2 minutes. Using tongs, flip them over and cook on the other side until the onions are just tender, 2 to 3 minutes more. Remove to a plate and set aside.

Return the skillet to medium-high heat and add the butter. As it melts, swirl the skillet to coat the bottom, then quickly arrange the potato slices to cover the bottom of the skillet, overlapping the slices. Sprinkle lightly with salt and pepper and cook without disturbing until the edges of the potato crust are nicely browned, about 5 minutes. Pour the egg mixture over the top, spreading it almost to the edges of the potato, then arrange the spring onions, cut sides up, over the top. Transfer the skillet to the oven and bake until the egg mixture is set, 12 to 15 minutes. Let cool for a few minutes, then use a spatula to slide the tart onto a cutting board or serving platter. Using a chef's knife, cut the tart into wedges or squares and serve warm or at room temperature.

SUMMER

zucchini and yellow squash

You know things are about to get serious when the zucchini and yellow squash start to arrive in farmers' markets—or your garden. And they'll keep on arriving, too, until the very end of the season. There are few vegetables as easy to grow, and luckily these soft-skinned cucurbits (members of the *Cucurbita pepo* species, more specifically) are extremely versatile, and most of the dozens of varieties you'll find are pretty much interchangeable. Because their flavor is so mild, they take well to just about any combination of herbs and spices: In addition to the traditional Italian and French applications, try summer squash with cumin seeds and Mexican oregano and chiles, or with garam masala and lemon in an Indian-style curry.

Summer squash won't keep very long after they are picked from the vines; you can store them in the refrigerator for only a few days before they start to soften.

MORE WAYS TO MAKE THE BEST OF THE SUMMER SQUASH GLUT

- Try them raw, shaved into thin rounds or strips with a mandoline or vegetable peeler, in a tangy vinaigrette; toss in some cooked and cooled grains, too, if you'd like, or some grated or crumbled cheese. Serve thicker slices or spears raw with any quick dip (try the curried feta dip on page 37), setting them out for the kids to nibble on before supper.

- With a mandoline, slice whole zucchini length-wise until you get to the inner seeds; discard the seeds and briefly steam or sauté the slices—leaving them mostly raw—and toss with a light tomato sauce.

- For zucchini chips, thinly slice zucchini or yellow squash, brush them lightly with oil, and dry them in a dehydrator or warm oven until crisp.

- To make a classic ratatouille, cook cubes of yellow squash or zucchini slowly in a deep sauté pan with tomatoes and eggplant, plenty of garlic and olive oil, and fresh herbs.

- Grill ¼-inch-thick (6-mm-thick) slabs, glossed with oil and seasoned with salt and pepper, until they're marked and tender; they're hard to stop eating straight from the grill, but if you can get some back to the kitchen, let them cool, then roll them around an herbed ricotta and goat cheese mixture (or just sprinkle the surface with freshly grated hard cheese and some minced fresh parsley before rolling them up) and serve them as part of an antipasto platter.

- Grill or broil pattypan squash—those scalloped spaceships—cut in half horizontally, then smoosh the flesh in the center with a fork and mash in, well, whatever you like: a dollop of pesto or harissa (page 256 or 252), or salted Greek yogurt and fresh herbs.

- Sauté big chunks of squash in olive oil with chopped onions and garlic, a dusting of cumin, and fresh chiles, fold in some cooked and drained black beans, shower with cilantro, and spoon into warmed corn tortillas—a little feta or cotija cheese and some salsa would be great (there are several salsa recipes starting on page 70), or even a scrambled egg.

Perfectly Sautéed Zucchini
with Cracked Coriander Seeds and Mint

SERVES 2 TO 4

VEGAN

I recently had a zucchini-related epiphany. I know, I know: Happens all the time, right? I was once told that a real Italian would never, ever cook zucchini with something so assertive and coarse as garlic, as the squash's flavor would be overwhelmed, but year after year, zucchini after zucchini, I ignored that rule, which I thought was bunk: Zucchini is bland! You need something at least as strong as garlic to make it the tiniest bit interesting. But then I cooked a seemingly overgrown, knobby, streaky specimen grown by Lisa Lewis, a farmer friend of mine; I just chopped and sautéed it hot and fast, too lazy to add much of anything besides salt. It was the most amazing zucchini I've ever tasted. I annoyed the hell out of my husband because I just couldn't stop exclaiming

over it: such lovely floral undertones, such incredible sweetness. Zucchini, in other words, especially when fresh and well grown, has a flavor!

The recipe below, in which chunks of zucchini are lightly browned and cooked until barely tender, evolved as a way to highlight this. Just a bit of thinly sliced onion becomes sweet in a very hot, uncrowded pan, and will bring out the latent sweetness in the squash. Cracked coriander seeds (try to find pale green Indian ones, which are mild and vegetal rather than spicy; you could even pluck fresh seeds from a patch of late-summer cilantro) give the dish a little texture and depth, and barely wilted, bright green mint keeps the whole thing summery and light.

2 medium or large zucchini

1 tablespoon olive oil

¼ red onion, thinly sliced

Salt

½ teaspoon whole coriander seeds, crushed

2 sprigs fresh mint

Trim the zucchini and quarter them lengthwise, then cut the quarters crosswise into ½-inch (12-mm) chunks.

Heat a 10-inch (25-cm) or larger sauté pan or skillet over high heat for 1 minute. Add the oil, swirl the pan to coat the bottom, then add the zucchini and onion and a generous pinch of salt. Shake the pan so the zucchini are evenly distributed, then cook, undisturbed, for 2 minutes. Toss the zucchini (use a turner or heatproof spatula if you need to) and cook, undisturbed, for 2 minutes more. Toss again and cook for 2 minutes more. Add the coriander and cook for 2 minutes more, tossing frequently. Season with salt to taste. Tear the mint into the pan, toss, and serve hot or at room temperature.

Zucchini Flan with Lemon Cream Sauce

SERVES 4

This creamy zucchini custard is really a cinch to make. The only trick is to extract as much liquid from the cooked zucchini as possible so it doesn't water down the cream-and-egg mixture and keep it from setting. A firm squeeze in your fist does this nicely.

A smooth, egg yolk–thickened lemon sauce serves as a tart counterpoint (and effective concealer of any flaws), but you can serve the flans plain if you'd like, or with a lemon-dressed salad of tender watercress.

Softened butter, for the ramekins

1 pound (455 g) zucchini (about 2 medium), chopped

1 tablespoon chopped fresh basil, plus whole leaves for garnish

Salt and freshly ground black pepper

4 eggs

¾ cup (180 ml) heavy cream

1 tablespoon fresh lemon juice

Preheat the oven to 350°F (175°C). Generously butter 4 ramekins or custard cups and put them in a deep baking pan.

In a saucepan, combine the zucchini and 1 cup (240 ml) water, cover, and bring to a boil over high heat. Cook, stirring occasionally, until the zucchini is very tender, 5 to 7 minutes. Drain in a sieve and rinse under cold running water until cool. Transfer to a double thickness of cheesecloth or good-quality paper towels and squeeze hard over the sink to remove as much water as possible (do this in two batches if necessary).

In a food processor or blender, combine the zucchini, chopped basil, ¾ teaspoon salt, and a couple of grindings of pepper. Puree until smooth. Separate 1 egg and set the yolk aside in a medium heatproof bowl. Add the egg white, remaining 3 whole eggs, and ¼ cup (60 ml) of the cream to the zucchini in the food processor. Blend the zucchini mixture until smooth, then divide evenly among the ramekins. Pour boiling water into the baking pan to come halfway up the sides of the ramekins, cover the pan with aluminum foil, and carefully transfer to the oven. Bake until the custard is firm in the center (it should feel the same in the center as it does at the edge, not softer), 30 to 40 minutes, depending on how deep the custard is in the ramekins.

Meanwhile, put 1 inch (2.5 cm) of water in a saucepan and bring it to a simmer. Add the lemon juice to the egg yolk and set the bowl over the simmering water; whisk constantly for 1 minute. Add the remaining cream and a good pinch of salt and continue whisking until the sauce thickens to the consistency of melted ice cream, 6 to 8 minutes. Taste and season with more salt if needed. If there are little lumps of cooked yolk in the sauce, strain it through a sieve into a glass measuring cup with a spout; you'll have about ⅓ cup (80 ml) sauce. Set the measuring cup in the pan of hot water to keep warm until ready to serve.

To unmold the flans, run a knife around the edges of the flans while they are still warm. Put an individual serving plate face down on top of each ramekin, hold them together firmly, and turn them over together; shake the ramekin to unmold the flan. If part of the flan stays in the ramekin, just gently scrape it out and fit it into place. (You can also certainly serve the flans in the ramekins.) Pour a little sauce over each serving, garnish with basil leaves, and serve warm.

Pan-Fried Zucchini Cakes

SERVES 2 OR 3

These zucchini cakes are held together with ground toasted dal, a common technique in Indian fritters and "cutlets" (see the Note below for substitutions). This is a very basic recipe with which you can make all sorts of variations: Sprinkle in some dried herbs (marjoram and basil are nice) or good curry powder, add a grated clove of garlic, or grate a bit of sweet onion or a carrot into the zucchini before salting it. The tender, pillowy, latkelike cakes are easily adaptable to different meals: great served alongside a simple vegetable curry to soak up some of the sauce, with a chopped tomato salad, or simply adorned with a spoonful of sweet-sour-spicy fruit chutney, or, of course, a dollop of sour cream or Greek yogurt and a side of chunky applesauce.

¼ cup (55 g) *urad dal* (split skinless black gram; see Note)

1 pound (455 g) zucchini (about 2 medium)

Salt and freshly ground black pepper

½ cup (40 g) freshly grated hard cheese, such as Parmesan

1 large egg

2 tablespoons olive or vegetable oil

In a large sauté pan, toast the dal over medium-high heat, tossing frequently, until golden, 3 to 4 minutes. Transfer to a piece of waxed paper and let cool completely.

Meanwhile, coarsely grate the zucchini into a medium bowl and stir in ¾ teaspoon salt. Let stand for 20 to 30 minutes so the salt can draw out some of the water in the zucchini. Put the zucchini in a sieve and press hard to squeeze out as much of the water as possible. Dry the bowl and transfer the squeezed zucchini to the bowl.

In a spice or clean coffee grinder, grind the toasted dal until very fine (it's okay if small bits remain). Add the ground dal to the zucchini along with the cheese, egg, and pepper to taste. Stir well.

Preheat the oven to 200°F (95°C) and put a serving platter in the oven to warm.

In a large sauté pan, heat 1 tablespoon of the oil over medium heat until it shimmers. Scoop ¼-cup (60-g) mounds of the zucchini mixture into the pan, flattening each to about ¼ inch (6 mm) thick. Do not crowd the pan. Cook, undisturbed, for 3 to 4 minutes, until firm and nicely browned on the bottom, then turn and cook the other side for 3 to 4 minutes. Transfer the cooked cakes to the warmed platter and repeat with the remaining zucchini mixture. Serve warm.

Note: *Urad dal*, small black beans that have been skinned (the black part removed to reveal the underlying white) and split in half, are available at any Indian grocery store and in the international section of many supermarkets. They look like ivory-white lentils, and are often misleadingly labeled white or black lentils. (See page 215 for another recipe using these versatile beans.) You can substitute raw rice or rolled oats (check the label if gluten is a concern), following the directions above to toast and grind them, or ¼ cup (30 g) oat or quinoa flour or sifted *besan* (chickpea flour), with no need to toast or grind.

Smoky Yellow Squash

SERVES 4

We'd been living in Lincoln, Nebraska, for almost half a year, and I hadn't yet made supper on one cold, dark-early Friday night. In Lincoln, I'd already had the best Vietnamese food of my life, some excellent tacos, and transcendent shawarma, but I hadn't found any of the kinds of restaurants we'd enjoyed on similar Friday nights in Athens, Georgia, when we were feeling a little celebratory—you know, the ones with the pickled beet stems, the craft cocktails, the house-cured this and that. I was missing the acidic top notes of citrus and the peppery sting of bitter greens in our city of beef.

Then that night Derek, Thalia, and I walked into the wind to the edge of downtown and stepped into Bread & Cup. Jars of pickles and infusions lined the front counter, and the din of happy adults having adult conversations filled the space. I had a dish featuring a smoky cream-and-butter sauce with nubs of bright, tart, juicy tomato. Derek's plate was dark and meaty—this is Nebraska, after all—and fragrant with oregano. The dish that follows, while much simpler and less dramatic than either of our meals, was inspired by those two sauces mingling on my table-wandering fork.

1 tablespoon unsalted butter

½ red onion, diced

Salt

3 yellow squash (about 1¼ pounds/565 g), diced

2 hot fresh red chiles (such as Fresno or jalapeño), seeded and minced

½ teaspoon smoked paprika

½ cup (120 ml) heavy cream

½ pint (5 ounces/170 g) cherry or grape tomatoes, halved, or 1 cup (180 g) diced very ripe tomato

2 teaspoons chopped fresh oregano

In a large sauté pan, melt the butter over medium-high heat. Add the onion and a pinch of salt and cook, stirring frequently, until translucent but not browned, about 5 minutes. Add the squash, chiles, paprika, and ½ teaspoon salt and stir well to distribute the paprika. Add the cream and bring to a boil, then lower the heat and simmer briskly for 10 minutes. Add the tomatoes and continue simmering until the squash is tender and the cream is thick and has been tinted a light pink, 5 minutes more. Taste and season with more salt, if needed. Stir in the oregano and serve hot.

Gingery Zucchini

SERVES 4

My daughter loves these dainty little wedges of zucchini just barely coated in a very fresh-tasting, lightly gingered tomato sauce. Serve with one or two other vegetable dishes, or with brown basmati rice. I like to heat a spoonful of leftovers in the pan alongside a frying egg or corn tortilla for breakfast the next morning.

1 pound (455 g) zucchini (about 2 medium)

1 large tomato, or ½ cup (250 g) canned crushed tomatoes

1 teaspoon sweet paprika

½ teaspoon ground cumin

½ teaspoon turmeric

1 tablespoon olive or vegetable oil

1½ teaspoons minced fresh ginger

1½ teaspoons minced garlic

Salt

Trim the zucchini and quarter them lengthwise, then cut the quarters crosswise into ¼-inch (12-mm) pieces. Halve the tomato horizontally, then grate the flesh from each half into a bowl, discarding the skins; you should have about ½ cup (250 g) tomato puree. Combine the paprika, cumin, and turmeric in a small cup and set aside.

In a large sauté pan, heat the oil over medium-high heat until it shimmers. Add the ginger and garlic and cook, stirring, until fragrant, about 30 seconds. Add the zucchini and cook, stirring occasionally, until most of the pieces are lightly browned, about 5 minutes. Add the spices and cook, tossing, for 30 seconds. Add the tomato and cook for 1 minute. Season with salt to taste. Serve hot.

Yellow Squash Dumplings with Spiced Tomato Sauce

SERVES 2 TO 4

These tender, lightly spiced walnut-size balls are like a cross between *pakora* (batter-fried vegetable fritters) and *vadai* (soft grain- or legume-based dumplings). They're fried and deeply browned, but not crisp-crunchy. The spicing here is fairly mild, and you should feel free to add more chile, some garam masala (page 247), or any other spices you wish. Even if you're wary of frying (as I am—I really dislike cleaning up after a messy frying experience), you should try these: They don't spatter or absorb much oil at all, and the croquettes don't even have to be served right after frying, as they're served with a sauce and aren't meant to be especially crisp or crunchy anyway.

I'd suggest doubling the recipe and freezing the extra fried balls and sauce separately—they reheat nicely for a quick meal. The warmed-up sauce can be used in nearly infinite ways: Simmer some chunks of potato and cauliflower in it until tender, then add a few croquettes to warm through and serve over Spiced Brown Rice (page 219).

continued

With Makeshift Vegetable Biryani (page 218)

FOR THE TOMATO SAUCE

- 2 tablespoons vegetable oil
- 1 to 2 fresh hot green or red chiles, seeded and chopped
- 2 cloves garlic, chopped
- ¾-inch (12-mm) piece fresh ginger, peeled and chopped
- ½ teaspoon freshly ground cardamom
- ¼ teaspoon ground cloves
- 2 bay leaves
- 1 (28-ounce/790-g) can whole peeled tomatoes with their juices
- Salt
- Pinch of sugar

FOR THE SQUASH DUMPLINGS

- 1 pound (455 g) yellow squash (about 3)
- ½ to 1 cup (60 to 120 g) chickpea flour (*besan*), or more if needed
- 1 fresh hot green or red chile, seeded and minced
- 1 tablespoon chopped fresh cilantro
- ½ teaspoon grated fresh ginger
- Salt
- Pinch of freshly grated nutmeg
- Vegetable oil, for deep-frying

Variation

Instead of the spiced tomato sauce, serve the croquettes with a simple *raita*: Rinse off the grater and run a large seeded cucumber (peeled or not) through it. Squeeze out all the excess moisture and put it in a medium bowl. Finely grate 1 clove garlic into the cucumber, add salt, pepper, and chopped fresh cilantro to taste, and stir in about 1 cup (240 ml) plain Greek yogurt.

MAKE THE TOMATO SAUCE

In a medium saucepan, heat the oil over medium-high heat until it shimmers. Add the chiles, garlic, and ginger and cook, stirring, until softened but not browned, about 2 minutes. Add the cardamom, cloves, and bay leaves and stir for 10 seconds, then pour in the tomatoes and their juices. Add a generous pinch of salt and the sugar. Bring to a boil, then lower the heat and simmer, stirring to break up the tomatoes a bit, until the flavors are developed and the liquid is reduced a bit, about 20 minutes.

Remove and discard the bay leaves. Puree the sauce using an immersion blender. Taste and add more salt, if needed. Cover to keep warm and set aside. (The sauce can be made, cooled, and stored in an airtight container in the refrigerator for several days. It also freezes very well.)

MAKE THE SQUASH DUMPLINGS

Coarsely grate the squash into a large bowl. If the squash is quite damp, squeeze handfuls of the shreds over the sink to extract as much liquid as possible. Sift ½ cup (60 g) of the chickpea flour through a sieve into the squash. Add the chile, cilantro, ginger, ½ teaspoon salt, and nutmeg and stir very well. If it's too soft or wet to shape into a very loose, soft ball, add more chickpea flour, a little at a time, until it comes together.

In a large, heavy saucepan, heat 2 inches (5 cm) of oil until it registers about 375°F (190°C) on a candy thermometer. Line a plate with paper towels.

Using your hands, shape some of the squash mixture into a walnut-size ball—it will be soft and will just barely hold its shape, but don't worry, as it'll firm up in the oil. Set it in a slotted spoon and quickly lower it into the oil; repeat to make 2 or 3 more balls. Don't overcrowd the oil. Fry, turning occasionally, until deeply browned and cooked through, about 6 minutes. If the balls start to brown too quickly, lower the heat. Remove to the paper towels to drain. Repeat until you have used all of the squash mixture.

Reheat the sauce, if necessary. Serve the dumplings hot or warm, or even at room temperature, with the sauce ladled over or under them.

snap beans and romano beans

Green beans, pale chartreuse wax beans, purple snap beans, thin and elegant French haricots verts, and flat, wide Romano beans can be used interchangeably in nearly any recipe calling for one or the other—use whichever beans look freshest and most intriguing. Adjust the cooking times as necessary for different varieties; if the beans are thick and have been allowed to mature on the vine or bush they'll also need a little more time in the pan to soften. Leathery yard-long beans will always remain fairly firm and sturdy, which is part of their charm, I think; try them in the dry-fried green beans recipe on page 60.

All snap beans tend to toughen with time, so for best results, use them quickly or blanch, shock, and freeze them soon after you get them into the kitchen. If you come into especially fresh and lovely snap beans, cook them in boiling water just until brightly colored and tender with a bit of snap, then drain and shock them in ice water to cool quickly. Toss with a vinaigrette (see page 260 for some ideas), some toasted nuts, slivered raw radishes or jicama, and/or cooked and drained shell beans (page 226, or use canned or frozen beans) for what I'd consider a perfect light summer meal.

Dry-Fried Green Beans
with Garlic Chips and Peanut Sauce

SERVES 2 TO 4

This cooking method is confusingly called "dry-frying," and I assume it refers to the fact that you're frying (often deep-frying but here I do something more like very-shallow-frying) a bare vegetable, without any batter to protect it from the blistering heat. And blistering it is: The beans wrinkle and pucker in the hot oil and become tender inside their black-spotted skins, a delightful change from both the crunchy-steamed haricots verts that until recently appeared on every plate in every remotely upscale American restaurant, as well as their polar opposite, the soft-cooked (or canned and reheated), olive-drab green bean, sometimes velvety but often sadly mushy. Traditional versions of "dry-fried" green beans or yard-long beans are usually flavored with a bit of ground pork and often Szechuan peppercorns, but here I toss them with a punchy hot-salty peanut sauce and top the dish with crisp garlic chips. It's not a dish for the faint-hearted: strong flavors, interesting textures, and a fun technique. Try this method, changing up the sauce from time to time if you wish, and you very well might think you've discovered an altogether new vegetable.

3 tablespoons crunchy natural peanut butter

2 tablespoons hot water

1 tablespoon tamari

1½ teaspoons shaoxing (Chinese cooking wine), dry sherry, or vermouth

1 teaspoon agave nectar or honey

1 teaspoon grated fresh ginger

Pinch of hot red pepper flakes, or to taste

2 tablespoons vegetable oil

3 cloves garlic, thinly sliced

12 ounces (340 g) green beans, trimmed

2 dried hot red chiles, or to taste

Salt

In a small bowl, stir together the peanut butter, water, tamari, shaoxing, agave nectar, ginger, and red pepper flakes. Set aside.

In a large sauté pan or wok, heat the oil over medium heat until it shimmers. Add the garlic and cook, stirring with a slotted spoon, until golden and crisp, 2 to 3 minutes. Transfer the garlic to a paper towel to drain.

Raise the heat to medium-high heat and add the beans, chiles, and a pinch of salt. Spread the beans out in the pan and cook, without stirring, for 2 minutes. Using tongs, toss the beans a bit and cook for 2 minutes more. Repeat until the beans are evenly blistered and just tender, 8 to 10 minutes total, depending on the size of your pan and the age of the beans. Add the peanut butter mixture and toss or stir until it coats the beans evenly and is heated through, 30 to 60 seconds—be careful not to let the sauce sit in the pan too long, or it will burn. Transfer to a serving platter and top with the fried garlic. Remove and discard the chiles, if you'd like, and serve hot.

Green and White Beans and Small Turnips with Arugula Pesto

SERVES 4 TO 6

VEGAN

Keep a few ⅓-cup (90-g) disks of pesto in your freezer, and basic lunchtime or summer-supper salads like this one come together in minutes. Green beans and potatoes dressed with pesto are classic, but with bitter arugula pesto, why not try using creamy white beans with the green beans and tender Japanese turnips? The bite of the pesto contrasts nicely with the slightly sweet turnips.

1 pound (455 g) small turnips, peeled if necessary and cut into 1-inch (2.5-cm) pieces

1 pound (455 g) green beans, trimmed and cut into 1-inch (2.5-cm) lengths

½ cup (90 g) cooked and cooled white beans (see page 226; canned are also fine)

⅓ cup (90 g) Arugula Pesto (page 256), defrosted if frozen

Salt and freshly ground black pepper

1 teaspoon fresh lemon juice (optional)

Fill a large bowl with ice water.

Bring a large pot of water to a boil and add a few pinches of salt. Add the turnips and cook until almost tender, about 5 minutes. Add the green beans to the turnips and cook until tender, about 5 minutes more. Drain the beans and turnips in a colander, then transfer to the ice water until cool. Pick out any remaining ice and drain the vegetables well in the colander. Return them to the bowl, add the white beans, pesto, ¼ teaspoon salt, and a couple of grindings of pepper. Toss well, taste, and add the lemon juice, if using, and more salt or pepper, if needed. Serve at room temperature or cold.

Sautéed Snap Beans with Caraway and Feta

SERVES 2 OR 3

When I was researching different ways of cooking root vegetables like carrots on the stovetop, I learned that *kinpira*, a word that I thought referred to a common Japanese dish consisting of strips of carrots and daikon sautéed together (see page 136), actually refers to the cooking technique itself. *Kinpira* is what I use for the snap beans here: The vegetables are quickly sautéed, then a little bit of liquid is added and simmered until all the liquid has evaporated. What's left are perfectly cooked vegetables sizzling in the oil. It's what I do anyway if I see that my vegetables need a little more time to become tender, or when I realize I should've blanched my vegetables before sautéing them with other too-quickly-darkening ingredients, and I'm charmed that it's been given a name. And in a typical turn, I have taken this Japanese—or at least Japanese-named—technique, and flavored it with Baltic-tinged ingredients, heady caraway and super-tangy Bulgarian feta.

2 tablespoons olive oil

½ sweet onion, diced

Salt and freshly ground black pepper

1 fresh hot red or green chile, minced, or to taste

1 clove garlic, minced

½ teaspoon caraway seeds

1 pound (455 g) green beans or wax beans, or a combination, trimmed and cut into ½-inch (12-mm) pieces

Juice of ½ lemon

3 ounces (85 g) feta cheese (I like Bulgarian here)

In a large sauté pan, heat the oil over medium-high heat until it shimmers. Add the onion and a pinch of salt and cook, stirring frequently, until it's translucent and golden brown, 5 to 7 minutes. Add the chile, garlic, and caraway and cook, stirring, for 1 to 2 minutes. Add the green beans, about ½ teaspoon salt, pepper to taste, and ¼ cup (60 ml) water. Cover the pan and cook for 2 minutes, then uncover and cook, stirring frequently, until the beans are tender and all the excess liquid has evaporated from the pan, 3 to 5 minutes—the cooking sound will change from simmering-bubbling to a loud sizzling. If the beans aren't tender by the time the liquid is gone, add a little more water and cook for another minute or so. Add the lemon juice and cook, stirring, for 30 seconds more. Remove from the heat and crumble in the cheese. Taste and season with more salt, if necessary. Serve hot.

Healing Stew

SERVES 4 AS A MEAL

VEGAN

I worked at an Italian restaurant in Virginia during college, and my boss there once made me a sauté pan of this spicy and very garlicky tomato-based stew when I was sick (yes, sick and at work, in a restaurant no less—ah, irresponsible youth). It seemed very Old World and grandmotherly, and since then I've actually found myself craving it when I feel run-down.

I went through a tough stretch while working on this book, when all my wacky experiments were failures, nothing I did in the kitchen seemed to be working, nothing tasted right, and even my daughter was starting to dislike the vegetables I'd set, full of hope, in front of her. So I decided to bring back this comforting, warming, and foolproof vegetable stew featuring flat lengths of pale green, meaty Romano beans and bite-size chunks of potatoes. It was just what I needed to remind myself—and Thalia—how amazingly good a meal of vegetables can be. Maybe it'll do the same for you.

It doesn't need much accompaniment, but spooned over some warmed-up goat cheese polenta (see page 206), it is plate-scrapingly good. And if you're eating this for its supposed healing properties, don't skimp on the heat (though you can pass the pepper flakes at the table, if you prefer): The chile heat and marjoram-fragrant steam rising from the bowl will clear any stuffy head, at least for a while.

1 tablespoon olive oil

½ onion, diced

2 to 3 cloves garlic, chopped

Salt and freshly ground black pepper

8 ounces waxy potatoes, cut into ½-inch (12-mm) cubes

6 ounces Romano beans, trimmed and cut into 1-inch (2.5-cm) lengths

Hot red pepper flakes

1 (14-ounce/400-g) can whole peeled tomatoes with their juices, or 2 large ripe tomatoes

2 teaspoons chopped fresh marjoram or oregano, or ¾ teaspoon dried

In a large, deep sauté pan, heat the oil over medium-high heat. Add the onion, garlic, a pinch of salt, and a few grindings of black pepper. Cook, stirring frequently, until the onion is soft and starting to become golden, lowering the heat or adding a splash of water if the garlic or onion starts to brown too quickly, about 8 minutes. Add the potatoes, beans, and a good pinch of red pepper flakes (if using dried marjoram, add it now) and stir for 1 minute. Add 1 cup (240 ml) water and stir up any browned bits, then add the tomatoes and their juices, breaking up the tomatoes with your hand as you add them. (If using fresh tomatoes, you can either just chop them and add them with the peels or, better, cut each in half and coarsely grate the cut sides over the pan, discarding the peels and cores.) Bring to a boil, then lower the heat to low, cover, and simmer, stirring occasionally, until the potatoes and green beans are very tender, about 20 minutes. Stir in the fresh marjoram, if using. Taste and season with additional salt, black pepper, and red pepper flakes, if needed. Serve hot.

tomatoes and cucumbers

In summer, when tomatoes and cucumbers are cheap and amazing, I make simple salads of them just about every day, almost to the point where I can no longer stand the combination—which is fine, because around the time I start to crave tomatoes and cucumbers again it's the following summer and—what do you know?—here they are!

I grew up on homegrown tomatoes, and when a tomato that doesn't taste (or smell) like the ones from the good old days—with a fair acidity, not too sweet, juicy but not watery—happens into my kitchen, it ends up being grated unceremoniously into a cooked sauce. Good farmers'-market tomatoes can be bought at varying stages of ripeness so you can enjoy them throughout the week, letting them ripen sequentially on a sunny windowsill. (Supermarket tomatoes usually won't ripen any more than they already have.) After ripening, they'll decline quickly. Keep them at room temperature, preferably in a container in which air can circulate around them, like a wire basket or colander. If you're only using half of a tomato, set the remainder cut side down on a plate and keep it on the counter—it'll be fine there for a day.

It's probably been twenty years since I've had a bitter cucumber that was not one grown myself with too-sporadic or nonexistent watering. There's really no need to salt cucumbers unless you want to draw out some of the water, and scraping out the seeds is entirely optional. Keep cucumbers in the crisper drawer; wrap the cut end in plastic wrap or a beeswaxed cloth.

A Very Quick Tomato Soup

SERVES 2 OR 3

There are about a hundred and eight ways to make a basic tomato soup, but very often what I want is just tomatoes in a bowl, hot, and I want it on the table *right now*, and I don't want to deal with a lot of post-meal cleanup. This is that tomato soup: light and refreshing, not too thick, just tomatoes in a bowl. It's the soup you'd have with a grilled cheese sandwich, or with some crushed tortilla chips to sprinkle on top. If you want a thicker soup, blend in some torn-up bread or stale corn tortillas. If you feel the urge to make it more elegant or refined, look below and make that tomato soup instead.

4 very ripe large tomatoes (about 2 pounds 4 ounces/1 kg), coarsely chopped

1 sprig fresh basil, tough stem removed

1 tablespoon olive oil

Salt and freshly ground black pepper

1 clove garlic, crushed but left whole

3 tablespoons heavy cream or cream cheese

Pinch of sugar (optional)

Put the tomatoes, basil, oil, 1 teaspoon salt, and a few grindings of pepper in a blender and process until very smooth. Pour into a large saucepan and add the garlic. Bring to a boil over high heat, then lower the heat and simmer for 5 minutes. Remove from the heat, fish out and discard the garlic, and stir in the cream. Taste and season with more salt or pepper, if needed. If it's too tart for you, stir in a little sugar. Serve hot.

Double-Tomato Soup with Curried Nuts

SERVES 2 TO 4

VEGAN

Roast a pan full of summer-fresh tomatoes and sweet peppers to concentrate their flavors, then puree the daylights out of them, along with a few brick-red sun-dried tomatoes, for the most intensely tomato-y soup you've ever tasted. If serving the soup to company or for a special occasion, pass it through a sieve as described below to make it almost unbelievably creamy-smooth; otherwise you can skip that step (more fiber!), or pluck the skins off the tomato and pepper halves before you puree them.

2 tablespoons olive oil, plus more for serving

2 1/2 pounds (1.2 kg) very ripe fresh tomatoes, halved

2 small red bell peppers, halved and seeded

Salt

1/4 cup (155 g) oil-packed sun-dried tomatoes, drained (see Note)

1/4 to 1/2 cup (60 to 120 ml) vegetable stock or water (optional)

1/4 cup (25 g) pecan halves

1/4 teaspoon curry powder

continued

Preheat the oven to 400°F (205°C).

Drizzle 1 tablespoon of the oil over a rimmed baking sheet. Spread the tomato and pepper halves in a single layer on the baking sheet. Drizzle the vegetables with the remaining 1 tablespoon oil and sprinkle with ¾ teaspoon salt. Roast until the vegetables are collapsed and wrinkly and the expelled juices are just beginning to brown, about 45 minutes. Leave the oven on.

Scrape the roasted vegetables and their juices into a blender or food processor and add the sun-dried tomatoes. Pour 2 to 3 tablespoons water onto the baking sheet and scrape up the browned juices; add them to the blender. Puree until very, very smooth—this will take at least 3 minutes. Set a sieve over a medium saucepan and pour in the puree; push it through the sieve with a spatula or wooden spoon and discard the little bits of peel and seeds left in the sieve. Set the saucepan over medium heat and cook the soup, stirring occasionally, until heated through. If the soup is too thick, add vegetable stock or water to thin it out. Taste and season with salt.

Meanwhile, spread the pecans on a baking sheet and toast them in the oven until evenly browned, 3 to 4 minutes; check them often, as they can burn quickly. Transfer them to a small bowl and toss with the curry powder.

Ladle the soup into bowls and top with the hot curried pecans. Drizzle very lightly with additional olive oil and serve immediately.

Note: If using sun-dried tomatoes not packed in oil, soak them in hot water to cover until they're soft, about 30 minutes, then drain well before using.

Crunchy-Topped Broiled Tomatoes

SERVES 2 TO 6

Even if tomatoes are of the highest order, when high-temperature broiled they can turn a bit sour in the heat and become soggy when the excess water hasn't had time to cook off. The simple solution seems obvious to me now: All you have to do is get rid of the juicy seeds and add the merest pinch of sugar to each tomato half before cooking. These are great as they are, warm and upright on a pretty plate with some simply steamed and lemon-dressed vegetables. They're also wonderful served Luisa Weiss–style, turned upside down, peel pinched off, and gently pressed onto a slice of grilled crusty wheat bread—drizzle with some good olive oil and sprinkle with some coarse salt and fresh black pepper, and eat.

6 perfectly ripe round tomatoes

Pinch of sugar

¼ cup (45 g) chopped almonds

6 cloves garlic, chopped

3 tablespoons olive oil, plus more for drizzling

3 large sprigs fresh basil, or 6 sprigs fresh flat-leaf parsley, tough stems removed

Kosher salt and freshly ground black pepper

3 tablespoons finely grated Parmesan cheese

Coarse sea salt

Preheat the broiler and set a rack 6 inches (15 cm) from the heat source. Line a small baking sheet with aluminum foil.

Cut each tomato in half horizontally and gently sweep out the seeds. Set them, cut side up, on the prepared baking sheet. Sprinkle each half with a tiny pinch of sugar.

In a mortar, pound the almonds, garlic, oil, basil, 1¾ teaspoons kosher salt, and a couple of grindings of pepper into a very chunky paste. Stir in the cheese. Use a small spoon to divide the mixture among the tomato halves.

Broil until the topping is nicely browned and the tomatoes are just soft, 5 to 7 minutes. Drizzle with a little more oil, sprinkle very lightly with coarse salt, and serve warm or at room temperature.

With a fried egg and skillet-toasted left-over Goat Cheese Polenta (page 206)

One-Baking-Sheet Tomatoes and Chickpeas

SERVES 2 OR 3 GENEROUSLY

Time for another meal-on-a-baking-sheet! This one is perfectly appropriate for the colder months, when cranking up the oven is appealing for reasons beyond the prospect of an imminent meal. Cherry and grape tomatoes from the grocery store can be just as fine as regular tomatoes in summertime, and of course chickpeas and greens are always around. This kind of meal is incredibly versatile, and I encourage you to grunge up your baking sheet—a large stainless-steel one with a rim is best (look for inexpensive ones at a restaurant-supply store)—with seasonal experimentation. Preheat it in the oven to ensure a quick and generous sear, toss together a selection of vegetables with similar roasting times (try chopped root vegetables and winter squash, zucchini and eggplant, radishes and young carrots, or broccoli rabe and finely chopped cauliflower), and think about throwing in some interesting spice and herb combinations. At the last minute, pile on some greens—not just arugula or spinach, but kale, mustard greens, shredded collards—and toss them together with the hot vegetables; for sturdier greens, put the baking sheet back in the oven for a few minutes to wilt them further.

1½ cups (245 g) cooked and drained chickpeas (see page 226), or 1 (15-ounce/425-g) can, drained

1 dry pint (about 10 ounces/280 g) small cherry or grape tomatoes

2 tablespoons olive oil

Salt and freshly ground black pepper

Pinch of hot red pepper flakes

1 clove garlic, minced

2 ounces (55 g) fresh mozzarella, torn into shreds

Juice of ½ lemon

1½ cups (45 g) packed arugula or baby spinach (optional)

Put a large rimmed baking sheet in the oven and preheat to 400°F (205°C).

In a large bowl, toss together the chickpeas, tomatoes, oil, ¾ teaspoon salt, several grindings of black pepper, and the red pepper flakes. Taste and add more salt and pepper, if needed. Spread the mixture out in a single layer on the hot baking sheet and roast, shaking the pan once or twice, until the tomatoes have partially collapsed, the juices are sizzling, and the chickpeas are golden, about 30 minutes.

Remove the baking sheet from the oven and add the garlic, cheese, lemon juice, and arugula, if using. Toss with a metal spatula. Taste and add more salt, if needed, then scoop into a serving bowl and serve warm.

Classic Fresh Chopped Tomato Salsa

MAKES ABOUT 3 CUPS (565 G)

VEGAN

I have been making fresh tomato salsa since I was in high school. The salsa I made back then, I now realize, suffered greatly from the fact that I couldn't stand the taste of cilantro. I thought it was like licking a stainless-steel bowl: awful. Then I grew up and decided quite suddenly, probably over a bowl of *pho*, that cilantro is in fact the best herb in the world (and that tarragon, on the contrary, has no place in any salsa), and my salsas gradually became simpler and simpler, until finally what I was making was actually a pretty standard *pico de gallo*. There's nothing groundbreaking in the following recipe unless, like me in my twenties, you need a reminder that this is how it's supposed to be. I use two serrano chiles here, but feel free to use more or less, or a milder variety like jalapeños, to taste.

1 pound (455 g) ripe plum tomatoes (about 4), diced

Salt and freshly ground black pepper

2 fresh hot chiles, stemmed, seeded, and minced

4 scallions, thinly sliced

½ bunch fresh cilantro, finely chopped (including the stems)

3 tablespoons fresh lime juice

Put the tomatoes in a colander set over a bowl. Toss with ½ teaspoon salt and let drain for 10 to 20 minutes, tossing the tomatoes with your hands every now and then to remove excess liquid.

Put the chiles, scallions, cilantro, lime juice and a few grindings of black pepper into a large bowl. Dump the drained tomatoes from the colander into the bowl (discard their liquid) and sprinkle in ½ teaspoon more salt. Toss well, then set aside for at least 1 hour to let the flavors come together and the salt dissolve.

Taste and add more salt, if needed. Serve at room temperature, or refrigerate in an airtight container for up to 4 hours before serving.

Thick Roasted Tomato Salsa

MAKES ABOUT 2 CUPS (360 G)

VEGAN

This is a hearty, warm, easily scoopable cooked tomato salsa, with little bits of charred vegetables. If you'd like, chop half a bunch of fresh cilantro and fold it in just before serving.

1 pound (455 g) ripe plum tomatoes (about 4)

½ onion, peeled and cut into wedges

1 or 2 fresh hot chiles, stemmed

4 cloves garlic, unpeeled

2 tablespoons tomato paste (optional)

2 tablespoons fresh lime juice

¼ teaspoon ground cumin

Salt and freshly ground black pepper

Preheat the broiler and set a rack 6 inches (15 cm) from the heat source. Line a rimmed baking sheet with aluminum foil.

Put the tomatoes, onion, chiles, and garlic on the lined baking sheet and broil them, turning occasionally with tongs, until the tomato and chile peels are blistered, the garlic is very soft, and the onion has black spots, about 30 minutes—if the garlic starts to brown more quickly than the rest of the vegetables, remove it from the oven with tongs.

Using tongs, pull off the tomato and garlic peels (alternatively, let the vegetables cool for a few minutes and then peel them with your fingers); save a few of the charred parts of the tomato peels for flavor and discard the rest. Transfer all the vegetables, along with any juices from the pan, to a food processor or blender. Add the tomato paste, if using, the lime juice, cumin, ¾ teaspoon salt, and several grindings of black pepper and pulse to make a chunky puree. Taste and add more salt, if needed. Serve warm or at room temperature, or cover and refrigerate in an airtight container for up to 3 days before reheating and serving.

Last-Minute Blended Salsa

MAKES ABOUT 3½ CUPS (630 G)

VEGAN

There's one, and only one, problem with eating fresh salsa every day, a fantasy I have entertained since I was about sixteen: the chopping. So much chopping. Enter the blended salsa, easy to make and easy to scoop up! This makes a large-ish batch that you can keep in your refrigerator for several days to spoon onto omelets or scrambled eggs, over quesadillas or tostadas alongside a big plate of runny black beans (page 226) and rice, or into some cooked lentils with crumbled feta or shredded cheddar.

I know a lot of people will blanch at the mere mention of granulated garlic, but I actually prefer it to fresh in this case: It has a slightly musky, slightly metallic flavor, and is mellower and less intrusive than fresh raw garlic.

1 ½ pounds (685 g) ripe tomatoes (about 5 medium), seeded and roughly chopped

½ onion, roughly chopped

2 to 3 fresh hot chiles, such as serrano or jalapeño, seeded, if desired, and roughly chopped

3 mini sweet peppers, seeded and roughly chopped (optional)

½ bunch fresh cilantro, (including the stems), chopped

4 to 5 tablespoons fresh lime juice, or more to taste

½ teaspoon granulated garlic, or 1 clove garlic, chopped

Salt and freshly ground black pepper

In a blender, combine the tomatoes, onion, chiles, sweet peppers, cilantro, lime juice, garlic, 1 teaspoon salt, and a couple of grindings of black pepper. Pulse until everything is evenly and quite finely chopped, but not yet a smooth puree. Taste and season with more salt or lime juice, if needed. Serve at room temperature, or refrigerate in an airtight container for up to 4 hours before serving.

Fresh Tomatillo and Avocado Salsa

MAKES ABOUT 2½ CUPS (430 G)

VEGAN

Crisp, crunchy raw tomatillos, diced finely, mingle here with chunks of creamy avocado that break down a bit as you stir. The lime juice keeps the avocado from darkening, so the salsa will keep nicely in the fridge for a couple hours.

6 ounces (170 g) firm tomatillos (about 5 small), husked, rinsed, and very finely diced

1 large Hass avocado, pitted, peeled, and diced

¼ sweet onion, very finely diced

1 to 2 fresh hot green chiles, seeded and minced

⅓ cup (20 g) chopped fresh cilantro

2 tablespoons fresh lime juice

Salt and freshly ground black pepper

In a medium bowl, combine the tomatillos, avocado, onion, chile, cilantro, lime juice, ½ teaspoon salt, and a couple of grindings of black pepper. Toss well with a fork, mashing the salsa a little bit as you do. Taste and season with more salt, black pepper, and fresh chile, if needed. Serve immediately at room temperature, or refrigerate in an airtight container for up to 2 hours before serving.

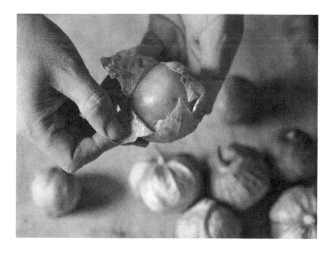

Pepper Water

SERVES 4

VEGAN

My good friend Leda Scheintaub was introduced to pepper water by her husband, Nash, who is Anglo-Indian, and Leda's recipe for the real thing appears in a book she wrote with Rebecca Wood, *The Sage and the Cook: Two Generations of Gluten and Dairy Free Recipes*. Pepper water is an aggressively spiced (though not always terribly spicy-hot—unless that's how you want it), sour, thin soup with a fresh tomato base that's sometimes sipped as a digestif following a meal. Leda's pepper water is very different from the one that follows, and is very much worth seeking out. My version is simplified from the traditional method, making it easy to throw together for a quick lunch or as the opening or closing course in a more elaborate meal. If you'd like to make the soup itself more substantial, do as Leda and Nash suggest and put a big scoop of steamed basmati rice in the center of a shallow bowl and ladle the pepper water over it.

Be sure you have everything you need, prepared and at hand, before you turn on the burner: vegetables chopped, spices located and measured, limes squeezed, large saucepan and small sauté pan cleaned and ready to go. After that, the soup comes together in just a few minutes. Serve with shards of pappadum that have been crisped in a dry or oiled skillet or in a microwave.

2 tablespoons vegetable oil

4 cloves garlic, thinly sliced

2 coins peeled fresh ginger, cut into thin slivers

Salt and freshly ground black pepper

1 teaspoon tamarind concentrate (see page 80)

½ teaspoon garam masala

¼ teaspoon ground cayenne or hot paprika

2 large ripe tomatoes (about 1 pound/455 g total), diced, juices reserved

1 to 2 fresh hot green or red chiles, thinly sliced (keep the seeds in for more heat)

¼ cup (60 ml) fresh lime juice, or to taste

10 fresh curry leaves (optional)

1 teaspoon cumin seeds

¾ teaspoon black or brown mustard seeds

½ teaspoon *kalonji* (nigella seeds; optional)

In a large saucepan or pot, heat 1 tablespoon of the oil over medium heat until it shimmers. Add the garlic, ginger, and a pinch of salt. Cook, stirring, until the garlic is golden and softened, 2 to 3 minutes. Add 4 cups (1 L) water, the tamarind, garam masala, cayenne, a few grindings of black pepper, and 1 teaspoon salt. Increase the heat and bring the mixture to a boil, stirring to dissolve the tamarind.

When the liquid comes to a boil, add the tomatoes and their juices, the chile, and lime juice. Return the mixture to a boil.

Meanwhile, before the soup in the saucepan returns to a boil, in a cup, combine the curry leaves, if using, cumin, mustard seeds, and *kalonji*, if using. In a small sauté pan, heat the remaining 1 tablespoon oil over medium heat until it shimmers. Add the whole spices and curry-leaf mixture to the oil. Cook, stirring with a heatproof spatula, until the mustard seeds just begin to pop, the curry leaves look bruised, and the cumin has darkened a shade, about 2 minutes. Just as the soup comes to a boil, scrape the hot oil and spices into the soup, cover, and remove from the heat. Let stand for a few minutes. Stir. Taste and add more salt and/or lime juice, if needed—it should be salty and sour—then ladle into bowls and serve hot.

Amy's Breakfast Poha

SERVES 1 OR 2 AS A MEAL

My friend Amy Trauger is a social geographer at the University of Georgia who studies food systems around the world. A sabbatical a couple of years ago took her to commercial farms, small-scale farms, markets, home kitchens, and restaurants in Belgium and Portugal, the Caribbean, India, and the White Earth Nation in Minnesota (take an afternoon to read the online journal she kept during her travels: growcookandeat.blogspot.com). Now back to her own kitchen in Athens, Georgia, she makes the Indian flattened rice called *poha* for breakfast, one of the best ways to get a ton of vegetables into your first meal. Savory, as spicy as you like it (a mint and cucumber smoothie would make a cooling accompaniment), and completely satisfying, *poha* comes together quickly in the pan and is easy to adapt to whatever you have on hand. True, there's some chopping involved, and I try to avoid chopping anything before six in the morning, but if you're the plan-ahead type you can get much of the dish ready the night before by preparing all the vegetables and refrigerating them overnight in a sealable container, measuring the *poha* into a sieve, and even putting the spices by the stove, ready to go.

1 cup (65 g) thick *poha* (flattened rice; see page 76)

3 teaspoons vegetable oil

½ teaspoon cumin seeds

½ teaspoon brown mustard seeds

½ sweet onion, diced

1 coin peeled fresh ginger, minced

Salt and freshly ground black pepper

1 to 2 large eggs, beaten

6 grape or cherry tomatoes, halved or quartered

1 to 2 fresh hot red or green chiles, seeded and minced

½ teaspoon turmeric (optional)

Pinch of sugar

Handful of fresh tender greens, such as spinach or mixed lettuce greens

¼ cup (10 g) chopped fresh cilantro

Handful of *sev* or *boondi* (see page 76; optional)

Variation

To make this a whole-grain dish, use rolled oats instead of the *poha*, and soak them in cold water until soft, about 5 minutes, then drain them in a sieve. The dish won't be as fluffy and light, but the flavors will be there and it'll be just as satisfying.

Put the *poha* in a sieve and rinse it under cold running water until evenly wet. Set aside to drain in the sieve.

In a large sauté pan, heat 1 teaspoon of the oil over medium-high heat until it shimmers. Add the cumin and mustard seeds; stir for 1 to 2 minutes, until the seeds begin to pop. Add the onion, ginger, a pinch of salt, and a grinding of pepper and cook, stirring frequently, until the onion is translucent and starting to brown a bit, 5 to 7 minutes.

Scoot the onion mixture to one side of the pan and pour 1 teaspoon of the oil into the empty part of the pan. Wait a few seconds for the oil to heat up and spread out, then pour the egg into the oil. Let it cook undisturbed for 30 seconds, then add the tomatoes, chile, turmeric, and sugar and cook for about 2 minutes, stirring to break up the egg and mix everything together.

Scoot it all to one side again and add the remaining 1 teaspoon oil. When it's hot, add the drained *poha*, the greens, half of the cilantro, and salt to taste. Cook, stirring and turning with a heatproof or metal spatula, until the *poha* is heated through and the greens are wilted, 1 to 2 minutes. Spoon onto a serving plate (or two), top with the remaining cilantro and the *sev*, if using, and serve hot.

SHOPPING THE INDIAN GROCERY STORE

There's an Indian grocery store near you, I just know it. (There are even Indian grocery store locators online, though they're not always up to date.) You may have to seek it out, and it may be in the next town over, but it's worth finding: It's one of the best places to stock up on everyday spices, but also a rich source of interesting ingredients that might be unfamiliar to you—take something new home and figure out what to do with it. Here's a shopping list of items you'll find there, to get you started:

- A bag of *poha*, which is just flattened rice. It comes in thick and thin varieties. Get the thick kind; it has a fluffier consistency when it's mixed up and cooked. It's not whole grain, but it's fun.

- **Spices.** The basics: ground and whole cumin, mustard seeds, coriander, green cardamom pods, cinnamon sticks, and black peppercorns (cheaper and fresher here than at the supermarket). When you're ready to expand your options: *kalonji* (aka nigella; see page 247 for a very good use for it), black salt (which is actually pinkish-purple and smells terrible until it's mixed with other spices; double-bag it when you get home and then use it in the chaat masala on page 109), citric acid (you might also find this in the bulk spice section of a good co-op or natural foods store; it's for the chaat masala on page 109), and *amchur*, a sour powder made from dried green mangoes (also for chaat masala, and you can use it instead of lemon in dishes like Regan's amazing okra on page 92).

- Look for Tamicon-brand **tamarind concentrate**— the very dark, thick, smooth paste. See page 80. This is also a good place to search for pomegranate molasses.

- Some **beans and lentils**, especially *urad dal*, which are split and peeled black gram (see page 215), and yellow split peas. Also, chickpea flour (aka *besan*): Use it in the *pakora* on page

156, the dumplings on page 56, the crêpes on page 200, the hash browns on page 179, and in pretty much any situation in which you need a little neutral, gluten-free flour to hold a mixture together. (If you need more ways to finish off the bag, check out Naomi Duguid's fascinating book *Burma: Rivers of Flavor*, in which pan-toasted chickpea flour is used extensively as a seasoning and thickener.)

- **Crisp chaat toppings** made from chickpea flour, like *sev* (thin strands) and *boondi* (balls). These are in the snacks section. If you're not staying gluten free, wheat-flour puris, flat white disks like crackers, are great mixed into the base vegetables in a chaat.

- **Fresh curry leaves**, or *neem*. Look in the refrigerator. Even if there isn't a lot of produce in the store, often there will be a few bags of curry leaves stashed in a refrigerated drinks case. If you find some, add a handful to your *poha*, with the spices. Keep curry leaves tightly wrapped and store them in your crisper drawer; they'll keep for at least a month. You can freeze them, but I've found they get a bit tough after freezing.

- If there is **produce**, even if it's a little subpar, pick out a vegetable and ask the cashier how to prepare it. The advice you get may well be worth the cost of one wrinkly eggplant.

Online, an excellent source for nonperishables is Kalustyan's (kalustyans.com), and for spices, Penzeys (penzeys.com).

Cucumber and Olive Salad

SERVES 3 OR 4

This is a great salad to toss into the fridge at the beginning of the week and nibble on over the course of a few days. Pack it into a bento-type lunch box with some thick hummus or crunchy roasted chickpeas, and maybe a toasted whole wheat pita wrapped in waxed paper.

2 tablespoons red wine vinegar

Salt and freshly ground black pepper

Pinch of hot red pepper flakes

A few drops of honey or agave nectar

2 tablespoons olive oil

1 shallot, thinly sliced

1 large English cucumber, or 6 Persian cucumbers, cut into ½-inch (12-mm) chunks

¼ cup (35 g) pitted kalamata olives, torn into pieces

2 ounces (55 g) feta cheese, crumbled

3 tablespoons sunflower seeds, toasted

In a large bowl, combine the vinegar, ¾ teaspoon salt, several grindings of black pepper, the red pepper flakes, and the honey and whisk to dissolve the salt. Gradually whisk in the oil.

Add the shallot, cucumber, olives, and cheese. Toss well. Serve, or cover and refrigerate in an airtight container for up to 3 days. Top with the sunflower seeds just before serving.

Lemon-Pepper Sautéed Cucumber

SERVES 2 TO 4

VEGAN

Simply cooked cucumber makes a lovely addition to a plate of vegetables. This version, with a splash of lemon juice and plenty of black pepper, was inspired by a dish I had at the Five and Ten restaurant in Athens, Georgia, years ago; there, the cucumber was cooked in butter (the first time I'd ever seen that vegetable in a cooked state!) and served alongside salmon and grits with a creamy lemon sauce.

1 tablespoon olive oil

1 clove garlic, minced

2 medium cucumbers, peeled if desired, halved, seeded, and cut on an angle into ¼-inch-thick (6-mm-thick) slices

6 small sweet peppers (about 6 ounces/170 g), or 1 red bell pepper, seeded and thinly sliced

Salt and freshly ground black pepper

Pinch of sugar

1 tablespoon fresh lemon juice

1 large sprig fresh basil

In a large sauté pan, heat the oil over medium-high heat until it shimmers. Add the garlic and stir until golden, about 1 minute. Add the cucumber, sweet peppers, ½ teaspoon salt, and several grindings of black pepper. Cook, stirring and tossing frequently, until the vegetables are just tender and beginning to turn golden in spots, about 7 minutes. Add the sugar and lemon juice and toss over the heat for 1 minute. Tear the basil into the pan and toss. Taste and add more salt and black pepper, if needed—it should be quite peppery. Serve hot.

Cucumber and Asian Pear with Carrot-Ginger Dressing

SERVES 4 TO 6

This dressing comes together very quickly in a mini food processor, and is very versatile. Try it with chopped crisp greens like romaine, a pita sandwich with a slab of deeply browned pan-fried firm tofu, a Seedy Quinoa Cake (page 222), or Herby Falafel (page 106), or use it to dress a soba- or rice noodle–based salad.

FOR THE DRESSING

2 carrots, chopped

½ Granny Smith apple, cored and chopped

1 fresh red serrano, jalapeño, or Fresno chile, seeded and chopped

2 coins peeled fresh ginger, chopped

Juice of ½ lemon

2 tablespoons rice vinegar

1 tablespoon miso paste (any kind)

Salt

⅓ cup (80 ml) neutral vegetable oil

FOR THE SALAD

1 large English (seedless) cucumber, or 2 regular cucumbers, halved, seeded, cut into ¾-inch (2-cm) pieces

1 large Asian pear, or 2 Ya pears, cored and cut into ¾-inch (2-cm) pieces

1 fresh red serrano, jalapeño, or Fresno chile, thinly sliced, with or without seeds

MAKE THE DRESSING

In a blender or mini food processor, combine the carrots, apple, chile, ginger, lemon juice, vinegar, miso paste, a pinch of salt, and 3 tablespoons water and puree until very finely chopped. With the motor running, add the oil in a thin stream through the lid. Taste and season with more salt, if needed. (The dressing will keep in a clean glass jar in the refrigerator for at least 4 days.)

MAKE THE SALAD

In a large bowl, combine the cucumber and pear. Add most of the carrot dressing and toss well. Scatter the chile over the salad. Serve at room temperature, or refrigerate for up to 4 hours and serve cold.

Simple, Spicy Cucumber Soup

SERVES 2

This was so much a go-to meal for me when I lived alone, and I ate it so often for such a long period of time, that until recently I couldn't even bear to think of making it again. What I'm saying is that you should be wary of relying so heavily on this easy, surprisingly satisfying, light, and healthful soup. Learn from my mistake and pace yourself.

2 medium cucumbers, chilled, peeled seeded if desired, and chopped

2 jalapeño chiles, stemmed, seeded if desired, and chopped

2½ cups (600 ml) cold plain yogurt or buttermilk, or half of each

2 tablespoons fresh lemon juice

2 tablespoons olive oil

1 tablespoon chopped fresh dill

Salt and freshly ground black pepper

In a high-speed blender, combine the cucumbers, chiles, yogurt, lemon juice, olive oil, dill, ¾ teaspoon salt, and a couple of grindings of black pepper. Blend until very smooth, scraping down the sides of the blender jar a few times, if necessary. Serve in small bowls, or chill in the refrigerator for up to 4 hours and serve cold.

corn, peppers, and chiles

In mid- to late summer, I'll swerve to the side of the road and let Thalia pick out a half-dozen or so ears of corn from the farmstand while I finger the odd-size tomatoes and deformed chiles. If I can manage to satisfy Thalia's demand for plain corn on the cob and still have a few ears left, I'll cut the kernels off and cook them quickly in a succotash with peppers, fresh shell peas or flat Romano beans if we got lucky, okra, tomatoes, and basil. Or I'll make a light corn chowder with sweet potatoes and red peppers and smoked paprika. I never get tired of good sweet corn, and if I can, before the season's over I'll blanch as many ears as possible and freeze the kernels for wintertime.

While you're thinking ahead, you should also try to put up some sweet peppers and chiles. A freezer-bag-ful of diced roasted chiles (or even raw chopped peppers) will really come in handy as you turn on the slow cooker on a cold winter morning and wonder what to put in it (roasted milder peppers like poblanos or Hatch chiles, plus some vegetable stock and dried beans is a fine start). Blacken fresh chiles, any kind, on the grill, under the broiler, or directly over a gas stove's flame (why not use all of your burners at once and get it done quickly?). After you roast, simply peel, seed, and freeze.

SHOPPING THE ASIAN GROCERY STORE

Lincoln, Nebraska, like many small- to midsize North American cities these days, is blessed with an abundance of Asian grocery stores. Most of them are conveniently clustered along a several-block stretch of 27th Street among an array of other ethnic markets, so naturally that's where I do most of my shopping. I encourage you to find an Asian grocery near you, and to take a shopping list that includes some of these items:

- **Condiments:** tamari; Chinese light soy sauce (not "lite" or low-sodium, just look for "light" on the label; if you're not strictly gluten free, this is the best all-purpose soy sauce); rice vinegar; and *sambal oelek* (the red chile paste that comes in a cylindrical plastic jar with a green lid). Also look for a small plastic tub of very dark, almost black, Indian tamarind concentrate with a brick-red lid (yellow-red-and-green-labeled Tamicon brand is what you're looking for).

- **Noodles and rice products:** rice stick noodles (the flat ones about 1/4 inch/6 mm thick); mung-bean noodles (thin strands made of mung beans), glass or cellophane noodles (little bundles of noodles, often individually wrapped and packaged in pink or red mesh bags); and Vietnamese rice paper wrappers. For kicks, bring home a package of the slightly sweetened and gingered, caramel-colored rice paper disks studded with sesame seeds. Put one in the microwave for a minute or so and watch what happens. It makes a fun after-school "snack-treat" (as my daughter and I call sweet but not *too* sweet snacks).

- **Dried seaweed, mushrooms, and beans:** sheets of toasted nori for sushi or for crumbling over scrambled eggs and rice for breakfast, strands of wakame, rectangles of kombu; dried shiitake mushrooms; dried fermented black beans (see page 81).

- **Sesame seeds, poppyseeds, and Szechuan peppercorns** (dried prickly ash berries, not related to peppercorns).

- **Limes:** They're much, much cheaper here than at the regular supermarket, and worth stocking up on because they keep so well. In winter I keep a big bowl of limes and lemons in the chilly mudroom just off our kitchen.

- **Shallots:** Again, much cheaper in Asian groceries, though they might be smaller and require some picking over to find good firm ones. Take a look at the Roasted Shallot Salad on page 145 and decide if you need a second bagful.

- **Greens galore:** *gai lan* (Chinese broccoli), baby bok choy, baby *choy sum*, and pea shoots. Maybe some Napa cabbage, too.

- **Special vegetables:** good firm daikon and long, slender Chinese or Japanese eggplants, or tiny spherical green Thai or Indian ones.

- **Fresh chiles:** Get a lot, and put most of them straight into a bag to freeze when you get home. To use in cooked dishes, just pull one out of the bag, rinse it, and use it whole or mince/chop it while still frozen.

- **Ginger and garlic:** Again, go ahead and get lots: a big hand of ginger and a half-dozen or so heads of garlic. The ginger will keep for weeks in the crisper drawer, or you can freeze it: Peel and chop it all and then mince it in a mini food processor with a little water (and some garlic, too, if you'd like); dollop tablespoon-size mounds of the chunky paste onto a sheet of waxed paper on a plate, freeze until firm, then peel off the mounds and put them in a freezer bag.

- **Herbs:** Mint, cilantro and/or *culantro* (sawtooth cilantro), Thai basil, and lemongrass. Check the freezer for Kaffir lime leaves and pandan leaves. Just for the heck of it, look for small single-serving packages of Burmese green tea leaf salad (*laphet thoke*) fixings so you can try fermented tea leaves—they're so unusual and tasty. See page 189 for a recipe inspired by this ingredient using plain green tea.

- **Seasonal or new-to-you fruit:** Asian grocers often have inexpensive mangoes and unusual melons in the summer; good persimmons (choose ones that are as soft as a very ripe tomato, or let them soften on your counter), fresh rambutan and lychees, and big, crisp, tan Asian pears in late summer and fall; pomelos and custard apples in winter.

Sweet Corn and Bok Choy
with Glass Noodles and Something Fermented

SERVES 2 OR 3 AS A MEAL

> VEGAN

This started out as a version of the quirkily named Szechuan dish Ants Climbing Trees, in which bits of ground pork appear to be clinging to (very thin, glass-like) noodle tree trunks or twigs. I suppose the bits of fermented black beans or black garlic I use here might resemble ants as well as the noodles do trees. In any case, this is one of those satisfying one-dish meals you can throw together quite easily at the last minute; it's a little bit sweet, salty, and hearty, with fun slippery noodles and greens and little hits of darkly fermented tang in every other bite or so.

2 tablespoons fermented black beans, or 2 to 3 cloves black garlic, minced (see Note)

2 (2-ounce/55-g) bundles mung-bean noodles (also called glass or cellophane noodles)

1 large head bok choy, or several heads baby bok choy

6 scallions

2 tablespoons tamari

2 tablespoons shaoxing (Chinese cooking wine), or dry sherry or vermouth

2 teaspoons sugar

2 tablespoons vegetable oil or virgin coconut oil

2 coins peeled fresh ginger, minced

2 cloves garlic, minced

1 cup (165 g) fresh sweet corn kernels (from about 2 ears)

Salt

1 teaspoon sesame seeds, toasted in a skillet (optional)

If using fermented black beans, soak them in cold water to cover for 20 minutes. Drain and set aside.

Put the noodles in a heatproof bowl and pour hot water over them to cover. Soak for 15 minutes. Using kitchen shears, stab down into the mass of noodles and cut them into shorter pieces—make 5 or 6 cuts. Drain and set aside.

Cut the bok choy head in half lengthwise, then cut the white stems crosswise into ½-inch (12-mm) pieces and the green leafy parts into 1-inch (2.5-cm) pieces; set aside separately. Thinly slice the white parts of the scallions and put them with the bok choy stems; cut the green parts into 1-inch (2.5-cm) pieces and put them with the bok choy greens.

In a cup, combine the tamari, shaoxing, and sugar and stir to dissolve the sugar. Set the sauce aside.

In a large, deep sauté pan, heat the oil over high heat until it shimmers. Add the ginger, garlic, bok choy stems, and the whites of the scallions. Cook, stirring constantly, until the stems are just tender, about 5 minutes. Scoot the vegetables to the edge of the pan and add the drained beans or the black garlic, if using, to the center. Smoosh the beans a bit with a metal spatula (no need to do this with black garlic), then stir them into the vegetables. Add the greens of the bok choy and scallions and the corn and cook, stirring frequently, until the bok choy is wilted and tender, about 3 minutes. Add the soaked noodles and stir well, then drizzle in the sauce. Cook, stirring, until heated through and the sauce is well incorporated, about 1 minute. Taste and add a pinch or two of salt, if necessary. Sprinkle with sesame seeds, if you'd like, and serve hot.

Note: Fermented black beans are actually soybeans that have been salted and left to ferment and turn black. They can be found in canisters or vacuum-packed bags in Asian grocery stores, usually not refrigerated. They'll keep nearly forever if stored in a cool, dry spot. In this dish, they add an earthy, funky flavor that goes nicely with the sweet corn.

Black garlic is simply fermented garlic. It's sold in cellophane bags by the whole head (they look like dark, papery heads of roasted garlic), and can be found in the specialty produce area of better supermarkets. The cloves take on an unusual dense, sticky texture, almost like a gumdrop. It's weird, slightly sweet and sour, and delicious.

Harissa-Aioli Grilled Sweet Corn

SERVES 4

If you're going to adulterate corn on the cob, this is the way to do it: Grill, slather with garlicky, harissa-streaked homemade aioli, and throw it back over the coals for a bit to sizzle.

> 8 ears sweet corn
>
> ½ cup (120 ml) Classic Aioli (page 000), or ½ cup (120 ml) mayonnaise plus 1 grated clove garlic and 1 teaspoon fresh lemon juice
>
> ¼ cup (60 ml) mild harissa
>
> Salt
>
> Fresh lemon juice, if needed

Prepare a charcoal fire.

Shuck the corn and remove as much of the silk as possible; rinse and drain. Place the corn on the grill over medium to high heat and cook, turning occasionally, until the kernels on all sides are bright yellow (if you're using a yellow variety) and speckled brown, about 8 minutes total.

Meanwhile, in a small bowl, stir together the aioli and harissa; taste and add salt and lemon juice, if needed.

Brush the ears all over with the aioli mixture and return them to the grill. Grill until sizzling, about 2 minutes more. Serve hot.

How to Eat Corn on the Cob

VEGAN

I feel a tiny pang of regret every time I cut corn kernels off an ear of corn to use in some dish that contains, well, something besides corn. An ear of corn is just so perfect and complete on its own, as simply prepared as possible. I think my daughter feels this even more acutely: Once, recently, she begged me not to grill the corn. "Please, please, Mom, just boil it!"

> The best sweet corn, from the garden or a farmer, never refrigerated
>
> Lots of fresh basil sprigs
>
> Salt

I've tarted up butter with all manner of minced herbs to slather on it; I've rolled the corn cob in this or that spice or even mayonnaise and crumbled cotija cheese, street food–style. I've sautéed it and roasted it. But one evening, toward the end of my first summer living in Cornhusker Nation (i.e., Nebraska), I hit upon this, perhaps the only way one can truly improve a great ear of corn. No butter required.

Bring a pot of water to a boil. Shuck the corn and cook it in the boiling water until it is just a bit more tender than raw, no longer than 5 minutes. Drain. Serve with piles of basil and some salt on the side. To eat, take a couple sprigs of basil and rub them all over the hot corn cobs; set the basil aside (eat it later, if you'd like, maybe with that beautiful, warm, tart tomato you also got from the farmer). Sprinkle salt all over the basil-scented corn and enjoy. Or smush the basil into a little pile of coarse salt and use the basil to distribute the salt, rubbing it gently in between the rows of kernels. Yes, it's true: I'm a little obsessed with corn on the cob.

Grilled Sweet Corn and Feta Salad

SERVES 4

This salad works equally well as a salsa or a side dish, and it'll go with just about any summer meal you can dream up. If you're serving it as a side dish, use a creamy, mild, French-style feta; if it's to play a salsa or a relish role, where a bigger flavor punch is expected, sour Bulgarian feta works best.

6 small ears grilled sweet corn, kernels removed, cobs discarded (about 3 cups/435 g kernels)

½ small red onion, finely diced

½ cup (20 g) chopped fresh cilantro

1½ ounces (40 g) feta cheese, crumbled

2 tablespoons olive oil

1 tablespoon minced fresh chives

2 to 3 tablespoons fresh lemon juice

1 to 2 fresh hot red chiles, seeded and minced

Salt and freshly ground black pepper

In a medium bowl, combine the corn, onion, cilantro, feta, oil, and chives. Add lemon juice, chiles, salt, and pepper to taste. Let stand at room temperature for 1 hour before serving, or refrigerate in an airtight container for up to 4 hours. Serve at room temperature or cold.

Padrón Peppers

SERVES 4

VEGAN

Padrón peppers, named for the Spanish city where they're grown most extensively, are hard to find outside very good farmers' markets, as they are apparently a difficult variety to grow. But I intend to try this summer because they are extraordinary, cooked in a hot pan with nothing more than olive oil and salt. I first tasted them this way at the National in Athens, Georgia, and now I snap them up by the bagful whenever I happen to see them for sale. Pick one up by the stem and eat the rest, tender seedpods and all. The thing about these chiles, though, is that while most of them are mild—not sweet, but not hot either—every fourth or fifth one will be unbelievably spicy. Keep a cold beer or chilled wine (or, if you're really worried, some bread or even cold milk) on hand just in case you get lucky. You can also cook dark green, ridged Italian peperoncini this way, though they're more reliably mild.

10 ounces (285 g) Padrón peppers

1 tablespoon olive oil

Coarse salt

Rinse the peppers, leaving the stems on. Drain them well and pat dry with a clean towel.

In a large sauté pan, heat the oil over high heat until it's almost smoking. Add the peppers and a generous pinch of salt. Cook, tossing frequently, until the peppers have blistered in spots and softened, about 5 minutes. Sprinkle with a little more salt (they should be pretty salty) and serve hot or at room temperature.

Sweet Peppers with Dates, Cumin, and Cinnamon

SERVES 4 TO 6

VEGAN

This spiced *agrodolce*—a sweet-and-sour dish, similar to a relish—would be just as great with a few fresh hot chiles thrown into the mix. It's nice to have a container of these peppers in the fridge, where they'll keep for several days, ready to spoon alongside brown or green lentils and grilled summer squash, zucchini, and eggplant to make a sophisticated vegetable plate.

1 tablespoon olive oil

1 pound (455 g) sweet bell peppers, stemmed, seeded, and cut into ¾-inch (2-cm) pieces

½ red onion, cut into ¾-inch (2-cm) pieces

½ teaspoon cumin seeds

1 cinnamon stick

Salt and freshly ground black pepper

½ cup (120 ml) red wine vinegar

⅓ cup (45 g) pitted dates (about 6 small), diced

1 tablespoon fresh oregano leaves

In a large sauté pan, heat the oil over medium heat until it shimmers. Add the peppers, onion, cumin, cinnamon stick, a generous pinch of salt, and a grinding of black pepper. Cook, stirring occasionally and lowering the heat if the vegetables start to brown too quickly, until the peppers are just tender and the onion is beginning to turn translucent and brown slightly at the edges, about 15 minutes.

Add the vinegar, dates, 2 tablespoons water, and several more pinches of salt, to taste. Cook, stirring frequently, until the liquid has reduced to a syrupy consistency and has taken up some of the sweetness from the dates, about 5 minutes. Scatter in the oregano and serve hot, warm, or at room temperature.

Poblano Casserole

Yes, it's a chiles relleños casserole, and yes, it's pretty trashy. But it's pure comfort food, and that's an important culinary category for vegetarians and omnivores alike. With plenty of the tangy, smooth, clove-spiced tomato sauce, be sure to serve brown rice, Green Riced Cauliflower (page 127), or warmed corn tortillas for soaking it up.

Vegetable oil, for the baking dish

4 large eggs, separated

Salt

3 tablespoons masa harina

2 tablespoons milk or half-and-half

2¼ cups (540 ml) The Correct Chile Relleño Sauce (page 250)

6 large poblano chiles, roasted, peeled, seeded (see Note), and torn in half

8 ounces (255 g) Monterey Jack cheese, sliced or shredded

Preheat the oven to 350°F (175°C). Lightly oil a 7-by-10-inch (17.5-by-25-cm) baking dish.

Put the egg whites in a large bowl with a pinch of salt, then whisk until soft peaks form.

Put the egg yolks in a large bowl and whisk in the masa harina, milk, and ½ teaspoon salt. Using a rubber spatula, stir in about one-third of the whisked egg whites, then gently fold in the remaining whites.

Spoon 1 cup (240 ml) of the chile relleño sauce into the bottom of the prepared baking dish. Arrange roasted chiles in a single layer over the sauce. Top with half of the cheese, then another layer of chiles, then the remaining cheese, and a final layer of chiles. Spoon the egg mixture evenly over the top, taking care not to let it deflate too much. Bake until the top is nicely browned and no eggy liquid rises when you press gently on the surface, 50 to 60 minutes. Let stand for 10 minutes.

Reheat the remaining 1¼ cups (300 ml) chile relleño sauce in a small saucepan. Scoop out servings of the casserole and serve with the warm sauce on the side.

Note: To roast poblano or other chiles (like green Hatch chiles), preheat the broiler and set a rack about 4 inches (10 cm) from the heat source. Line a rimmed baking sheet with aluminum foil first, if you'll like, for easy cleanup (if you've seen my baking sheets you'll know I never do this). Put the chiles on the baking sheet and broil them for about 15 minutes, until the skin is blackened and blistered. Turn the chiles over and broil the other side. (Roasting the chiles on a charcoal grill is another great option—and it's the norm with Hatch chiles.)

Transfer the hot chiles to a bowl, cover it with plastic wrap, and let the chiles steam for a few minutes, which helps loosen the skin. Rub the charred skin off and pull out the stem and seeds—do not rinse the peppers, or you'll lose some of the flavorful juices. Don't worry about stubborn areas of skin that didn't blister and are hard to peel off. You won't notice them in the finished dish.

Scotch Bonnet Chile and Mango Salsa

MAKES ABOUT 2¾ CUPS (500 G)

VEGAN

Here the classic flavors of a Caribbean jerk marinade—allspice, thyme, and Scotch bonnet (or habanero) chile—are combined with sweet mango and crisp apple (you could also use jicama). If your thyme is tender, thin-stemmed, and mild, use a full tablespoon, and chop the stems along with the leaves; if it's woody and very strong, strip the leaves and chop about 2 teaspoons of them to start, adding more to taste.

1 large ripe mango, peeled and diced

1 to 2 Scotch bonnet or habanero chiles, seeded and very finely minced (use gloves!)

½ Granny Smith apple, finely diced, or ¼ jicama, peeled and finely diced

¼ red bell pepper, seeded and finely diced

3 scallions, thinly sliced

2 tablespoons fresh lime juice, or to taste

1 tablespoon chopped fresh thyme

¼ teaspoon ground allspice

Salt and freshly ground black pepper

In a medium bowl, combine the mango, chile, apple, bell pepper, scallions, lime juice, thyme, allspice, ½ teaspoon salt, and a few grindings of black pepper. Let stand for about 30 minutes, then taste and add more lime juice, chile, salt, and black pepper, if needed. Serve immediately at room temperature, or refrigerate in an airtight container for up to 2 hours before serving.

Coin Purse Egg with Fresh Chiles and Spinach

SERVES 1 AS A MEAL

I'm always looking for more ways to cook a high-protein, vegetable-heavy breakfast quickly, in one pan, and only recently read about "coin purse" eggs, which are simply fried eggs that are folded in half to enclose the soft yolks soon after being cracked into the pan. This leaves half the pan free! I like to load it up with slivers of onion and fresh chiles, then pile in some spinach or kale to just wilt as the egg finishes up.

2 teaspoons unsalted butter

1 large egg

Salt and freshly ground black pepper

¼ small onion, thinly sliced

½ to 1 fresh hot red or green chile, thinly sliced

Handful of spinach leaves

Splash of tamari

In a sauté pan, melt the butter over medium-high heat. When the foam subsides, crack in the egg. Season with salt and pepper and cook, undisturbed, until just the edges of the whites are set, about 1 minute. Use a metal spatula to gently fold half of the egg over the other half to make a half-moon (or coin purse) shape. Lower the heat to medium.

In the now-empty side of the pan, put the onion and chile. Without disturbing the egg, sauté the vegetables until golden, about 3 minutes. Add the spinach and tamari to the onion and sauté until wilted. By this time the egg yolk will be thickened but still runny. Transfer the egg to a plate and top it with the spinach mixture, or if you prefer a firmer yolk, transfer the vegetables to a plate and let the egg cook a little longer, then set it atop the vegetables and serve. (If you'd like, you can turn the egg purse over to brown the other side a bit.)

ON THE TO-TRY LIST: CHILES PRESERVED IN OIL

As much as we're anticipating the roasting of Hatch chiles here in our first full summer living west of the Mississippi, we're also looking forward to trying the method for preserving peppers Eugenia Bone describes in her wonderfully inspiring half-memoir, half-cookbook, *At Mesa's Edge: Cooking and Ranching in Colorado's North Fork Valley.* Bone learned the technique from a friend, and it's apparently how everyone in the valley deals with the late-summer glut of chiles. Seeded and thinly sliced chiles are layered in a crock with lots of salt and then weighted down. The liquid released by the chiles is poured off and more weight is added. Finally, the much-reduced chiles are preserved in oil and kept in the refrigerator (indefinitely, Bone says). It sounds pretty brilliant to me.

okra and eggplant

Okra: You love it or you hate it, right? And nothing will change your mind if you're in the latter camp? This is why I open this section with my friend Regan's method of shallow-frying these strange pods, very thinly sliced: It very well might encourage you to think differently about them. Relatively dry cooking is the key, I think, to okra—in a gumbo or anything saucy they tend to live up to their stereotype. Also important is to choose small, young, firm okra pods with a bright color and as few brown spots as possible; these will be tender and pleasant.

If you're going to be eating a lot of vegetarian meals, and you want them to be focused primarily on fresh vegetables, it's my feeling that you should probably come to terms with the eggplant. Let me rephrase that: *Embrace the eggplant!* I hate to describe it as "meaty," because I'm loath to offer vegetables or anything else as a substitute for meat, but no other word quite captures the role eggplant can play in your meals, which is why there are more recipes for eggplant in this book than for most of the other categories of vegetable. You can do nearly anything with eggplants, and there are dozens of different varieties to try, from fat dark purple lobes to tiny green-striped golf balls. Grill it, broil it, stuff it . . .

Reputable sources will tell you that the trick to choosing an eggplant that is not excessively seedy—the seeds in older specimens can be bitter and tough—is to find one with an oval dimple on the bottom as opposed to a round dimple (an oval indicates a male fruit), and to choose eggplants that are lightweight for their size (as seeds are heavier than the spongy flesh). I've never found either to be a 100-percent reliable indicator, but you might increase your odds if you keep these criteria in mind. In any case, if an eggplant is soft in spots, or moldy at the stem, leave it.

FIVE WAYS TO LOVE YOUR EGGPLANT

- Grill thick slabs of eggplant over a hot charcoal fire, or skewer cubes of it and baste with a marinade as it grills or broils. Any marinade you'd use on meat would work well, but you could concoct your own by whisking together oil, vinegar or citrus juice, any sort of minced fresh herbs, and a little agave nectar.

- Slit and stuff small eggplants with a flavorful paste of spices, nuts or seeds, and sautéed onion and roast them on a baking sheet until they collapse and ooze.

- Broil rounds of large eggplant, top them with sliced fresh tomatoes and cheese, and broil to melt.

- Dip slices of eggplant in beaten egg, press grated hard cheese into each side, and roast them on a parchment paper–lined baking sheet.

- Gently steam finger-size spears of peeled eggplant (with some white vinegar in the steaming water), then toss the silky, soft pieces in a minty vinaigrette.

Regan's Amazing Madhur Jaffrey Okra

SERVES 2 TO 4

VEGAN

You know how one person can cook from a recipe, and another person can follow the same recipe to the letter and come up with something completely different? (As a writer of recipes, this is one phenomenon that keeps me up at night.) My good friend Regan made okra for me once, and she told me it was from a Madhur Jaffrey recipe. Of course it was the best okra I've ever had, and I wanted to make it again myself. I looked up the recipe and saw that there was no way I would have come up with even remotely the same bowl of okra as Regan had. Curious, I searched online for evidence that other people had cooked from that recipe, and sure enough none of the pictures I saw looked even vaguely familiar. I've fantasized about someday asking Jaffrey herself to make her okra for me, just to confirm my suspicion that it'd be nothing like Regan's.

There are a few things to keep in mind: First, you must slice the okra very thinly, and this is not how okra is generally treated, so that might seem strange as you do it. There will be slime. But because of how you cook it—for a long time, in plenty of oil, until it withers and browns and starts to resemble feathery, holey wheels—the sliminess will not be a factor in the finished dish. Second, don't leave out the lemon juice: The dish needs to be very tart and very browned-tasting; otherwise it'll be insipid. (Jaffrey's recipe, incidentally, calls on *amchur* powder, ground dried green mango, to hit the sour note. That works well too, of course, if you happen to have some in the spice cupboard.)

½ small red onion

12 ounces (340 g) okra

6 tablespoons (90 ml) vegetable oil

Salt

½ teaspoon cumin seeds

¼ teaspoon hot red pepper flakes, or to taste

Juice of ½ small lemon

Cut the onion into very thin slivers. Set aside.

Thinly slice the okra on a sharp angle—⅛ inch (3 mm) or thinner! Discard the stem ends as you go. Your knife and cutting board will get slimy, which is why you did the onion first.

Line a plate with paper towels. In a large sauté pan, heat the oil over medium-high heat until it shimmers. Add the okra and a generous pinch of salt. Cook, turning and stirring occasionally with a metal spatula, until the okra is deeply browned, decreased substantially in volume, and no longer slimy looking, about 15 minutes. Don't rush the cooking; lower the heat to medium if you're uncomfortable with the speed of browning. Using a slotted spoon, remove the okra slices and as many of its little seeds as possible to the paper towel–lined plate and spread them out.

Return the pan to medium heat and add the onion and a generous pinch of salt. Cook, stirring frequently, until it, too, is deeply browned, about 5 minutes. If there's still a lot of oil in the pan, remove the pan from the heat and ball up a paper towel, hold it with tongs, and use it to blot the pan dry.

Off the heat, add the cumin and red pepper flakes to the pan and stir for 30 seconds. Squeeze in the lemon juice, add the okra back in, season with salt, and toss well. Serve hot, in small quantities.

Seared Okra with Basil and Tamari

SERVES 4

VEGAN

Cooking halved okra pods quickly over high heat helps to minimize the sliminess factor. Torn fresh basil leaves (Thai basil is excellent, if you can acquire it) and a splash of tamari make the dish deeply comforting. It'd easily make a full meal with some lentils and rice.

3 tablespoons vegetable oil

3 shallots, thinly sliced (about ½ cup/70 g)

1 pound (455 g) young okra, tops trimmed, halved lengthwise

Pinch of hot red pepper flakes

2 to 3 teaspoons tamari

6 sprigs fresh basil

In a large sauté pan, heat 1 tablespoon of the oil over high heat until it shimmers. Add the shallots and cook, stirring, until lightly browned, 2 to 3 minutes. Add another tablespoon of the oil and half of the okra; spread the okra out in the pan so as many pieces as possible are in contact with the hot surface. Cook, tossing occasionally, until all of the pieces have some dark brown spots, about 4 minutes. Scrape everything into a bowl. Heat the remaining 1 tablespoon oil and cook the remaining okra as before.

Return the first batch of okra and shallots to the pan, sprinkle in the red pepper flakes and 2 teaspoons of the tamari, and tear the basil into the pan. Toss to combine, then cook to heat through, about 2 minutes. Taste and season with more tamari, if needed. Serve hot.

Miso-Crusted Chinese Eggplant

SERVES 4

VEGAN

Spectacularly simple to prepare, these miso-topped broiled eggplant halves are as dramatic looking as any T-bone, and are just as deep and complex tasting. Serve them with sautéed greens and Buttermilk–Celery Root Puree (page 178) and set the table with steak knives.

2 long Chinese eggplants (about 8 ounces/255 g each), halved lengthwise

1 tablespoon olive oil

¼ cup (60 ml) miso paste (any kind)

1 tablespoon agave nectar or honey

Variation

To make balsamic vinegar–glazed eggplant, replace the miso-agave mixture with a dressing of 1 tablespoon balsamic vinegar, 2 teaspoons agave nectar or honey, 1 teaspoon grainy mustard, 1 teaspoon salt, and a few grindings of black pepper. Brush the dressing generously over the cut sides of the broiled eggplants (you may not use all of it) and broil until bubbly, about 4 minutes.

Preheat the broiler and set a rack 6 inches (15 cm) from the heating element. Lightly oil a rimmed baking sheet.

With the tip of the knife, carefully score the flesh on the cut side of each eggplant half a few times, almost down to but not through the skin. Arrange them, cut side up, on the baking sheet and brush with oil. Broil until the flesh is nicely browned and quite soft, about 15 minutes.

Meanwhile, in a small bowl, whisk together the miso paste, agave nectar, and 1 tablespoon water until smooth.

Spread the miso mixture evenly on the cut sides of the eggplant and broil until the miso mixture is bubbling and beginning to blacken in spots, 4 to 5 minutes. Serve hot.

Persian-Style Eggplant Dip

MAKES ABOUT 1½ CUPS (360 ML); SERVES 4

Kansas City is only a few hours away from Lincoln, so one weekend we hopped in the car and drove, thinking about dinner. Derek casually told me that one of his coworkers had said there was a Persian restaurant in the city that was worth trying. Hours later, having driven to several far corners of town on both the Kansas and the Missouri sides in search of this mythical place (smart phones are wonderful, but they emphatically do not know everything), Derek was starting to regret his off-hand comment. I refused to let it go. Persian (Iranian) restaurants have always been so rare in the places I've lived that I'd only ever been to one in my life and I was not willing to give up searching for this one until—well, until we found it, whether it was still extant or not. We found it. It was everything I'd hoped it would be, lively and full of large families celebrating birthdays and who knows what else.

One of the best things we ate that night was *kashk badenjan*, an eggplant puree similar to baba ghanoush except that it has sour, nutty, creamy *kashk* (a soured, sun-dried yogurt paste) swirled into it and drizzled on top. I have not been able to score any *kashk* yet, even though the guy at the Middle Eastern market made some calls on my behalf, but I've found that sour, very thick labneh whisked with tahini is a fine substitute. Serve with thick diagonal slices of cold cucumber, red bell peppers, and endive leaves for scooping up the dip, and perhaps potato wedges roasted with olive oil and thinly sliced lemons, or a mound of tangy potato salad with yogurt.

> 1 large eggplant (about 14 ounces/400 g)
>
> 4 tablespoons (60 ml) olive oil
>
> 1 small sweet onion, diced
>
> 1 clove garlic, minced
>
> Salt and freshly ground black pepper
>
> 1½ teaspoons dried mint
>
> Pinch of saffron
>
> 5 tablespoons labneh or very thick plain Greek yogurt
>
> 1½ tablespoons tahini

Preheat the oven to 400°F (205°C).

Prick the eggplant in a few places with a knife or fork and put it on a baking sheet. Roast, turning it once with tongs halfway through cooking, until it is very soft, collapsed, and leaking, about 1 hour 15 minutes. Let cool completely.

In a large sauté pan, heat 2 tablespoons of the oil over medium heat until it shimmers. Add the onion and garlic and a pinch of salt and pepper. Cook, stirring frequently, until the onion is very soft, deep golden brown, sweet, and caramelized, at least 20 minutes; if it's browning too quickly, lower the heat and add 1 tablespoon water. Scrape the onion into a small bowl and set aside.

Return the pan to medium-high heat and add 1 tablespoon of the remaining oil. Add the mint and stir until it darkens a shade, 30 to 60 seconds, then scrape it into another small bowl.

In a small cup, steep the saffron in 1 tablespoon warm water.

In another small bowl, whisk together 1 tablespoon of the labneh, ½ tablespoon of the tahini, a pinch of salt, and just enough water to yield a drizzle-able consistency.

Cut off the stem and remove the peel of the eggplant. In a mini food processor (or in a deep bowl with an immersion blender or potato masher), puree the eggplant with the remaining 4 tablespoons labneh and 1 tablespoon tahini, the remaining 1 tablespoon oil, ½ teaspoon salt, a grinding of pepper, half of the onion mixture, and half of the mint. Taste and season with more salt, if needed. (The eggplant mixture, saffron water, remaining onion and mint, and the labneh-tahini mixture can all be stored separately in airtight containers in the refrigerator for up to 1 day before assembling; bring to room temperature before serving.) Spread the eggplant mixture in a shallow serving bowl and top with the remaining onion and mint. Sprinkle it with the saffron water and drizzle it with the labneh-tahini mixture. Serve.

Spice-Stuffed Baby Eggplant

SERVES 4

VEGAN

This is one of my favorite dishes in the book; it's centerpiece-worthy, and needs only a big green salad or sautéed greens to accompany it. Baby eggplants are split into quarters from the bottom and stuffed with a sweet-sour paste featuring toasted sesame seeds, spices, coconut, and onion, then roasted until the flesh is very soft and the paste begins to ooze and caramelize on the baking sheet.

1 teaspoon tamarind concentrate (see page 80)

2 tablespoons brown sugar

Salt

1 tablespoon sesame seeds

1½ teaspoons cumin seeds

2 tablespoons unsweetened shredded coconut

3 tablespoons olive oil

1 onion, diced

1 clove garlic, minced

Seeds from 5 green cardamom pods, crushed with the side of a chef's knife or in a mortar

4 single-serving-size eggplants, or more smaller ones (about 1 pound total)

A few shreds of orange zest (optional)

Preheat the oven to 350°F (175°C).

In a small cup, stir together the tamarind concentrate, brown sugar, 1 teaspoon salt, and ½ cup (120 ml) water and set aside.

Heat a large sauté pan over medium heat. Add the sesame seeds and toast, stirring with a heatproof spatula, until golden and shiny, 2 to 3 minutes. Scrape onto a piece of waxed paper and return the pan to the heat. Toast the cumin and then the coconut (separately), adding them to the sesame seeds as they turn golden—each will take no more than 2 minutes, and you should watch them constantly so they don't burn.

Return the pan to medium-high heat and add 1 tablespoon of the oil, the onion, and the garlic. Cook, stirring frequently, until the onion is nicely browned, about 8 minutes. Add the cardamom and stir for 30 seconds. Add the tamarind mixture and cook, stirring, until the liquid is reduced to just a few tablespoons, about 3 minutes. Scrape the onion mixture into a mini food processor and add the sesame seed mixture. Grind to a chunky paste. Taste it: It should be very flavorful, sweet-tart, and quite salty.

Leaving the stem caps on, peel the eggplants—either totally or leaving some strips for looks. (You can also leave them unpeeled, which is prettier but a little more difficult to eat.) Leaving the stem end intact, cut the bottom of each eggplant into quarters; the slits should reach up to the stem end, but remain connected. Gently hold an eggplant open and stuff as much of the onion paste inside the cuts as you can, then close it up again and place it in a baking dish or on a rimmed baking sheet. Repeat with the remaining eggplants and filling, then drizzle the remaining 2 tablespoons oil over them, turning to coat them on all sides. Sprinkle them with a little salt. Roast, turning the eggplants over once or twice with tongs or a metal spatula, until nicely browned and collapsed, 50 to 60 minutes. Grate a bit of orange zest over them if you'd like, and serve hot or at room temperature.

With Chinese Broccoli (Gai Lan) with
Garlic-Miso Sauce (page 124)

Twice-Roasted Eggplant and Red Pepper

SERVES 2 TO 4

One day a while back, I was stocking up on spices or something at the Indian grocery store, and for some reason I felt like I needed to buy an eggplant, even though the pickings were slim. I brought the least-far-gone one I could find to the counter with all my other purchases, and the cashier, after some other small talk, asked me pointedly, in a lilting and precise accent, "You know how to prepare this eggplant?"

The four or five eggplant dishes I'd cooked with varying degrees of success in the last few days flashed before my eyes, and I said, "Well . . . what would you suggest I do with it?"

"It's easy!" he said. "You just boil it, take out all the bark . . . and mix in whatever you like!"

Except for the boiling, that's exactly what I did with that eggplant: added things I like to it—garlic, roasted pepper, goat cheese, fresh herbs, and plenty of olive oil.

1 large eggplant

1 large red bell pepper

1 clove garlic, minced

2 tablespoons olive oil

½ teaspoon salt

Freshly ground black pepper

2 ounces soft goat cheese

Fresh basil or tender oregano or flat-leaf parsley sprigs

Preheat the oven to 400°F (205°C). Set a small rimmed baking sheet in the oven while it heats.

Prick the eggplant skin in a few places and put it and the bell pepper on the baking sheet. Bake until the eggplant is very soft and the skin of both the eggplant and the pepper are blackened and charred in spots, about 1 hour 15 minutes (turn the eggplant and pepper over with tongs about halfway through). Remove the baking sheet from the oven and let the vegetables cool for a few minutes; leave the oven on.

Carefully slit the eggplant skin open along its length and use a metal spatula or a knife to score the flesh through to the skin. Scoop the flesh from the skin in large chunks and transfer them to a pie plate or similar-size baking dish, spreading them out evenly; discard the skin and stem. Remove the charred skin from the pepper and pull out and discard the stem and seeds. Tear the flesh into pieces and scatter them over the eggplant in the baking dish. Tip the baking sheet over the baking dish to pour any pepper and eggplant juices over them.

Scatter the garlic over the roasted vegetables, drizzle with the oil, and sprinkle with salt and several grindings of black pepper. Arrange bits of the cheese on the top. Bake until the juices are bubbling and the cheese is very soft, about 20 minutes. Tear the basil and scatter it over the vegetables. Serve hot, warm, or at room temperature.

The Perfect Caponata

SERVES 6 TO 8

VEGAN

I have no dog in this fight, but for some reason I cringe whenever I encounter a caponata that isn't made just like this, one that doesn't have the necessary sweet-tart edge that makes it less a soupy sauce and more a concentrated condiment. It should be celery crunchy, green-olive-and-caper salty, pine-nut toasty, and intense enough to be consumed mostly in small quantities. Spread a spoonful on grilled bread, or mound it alongside grilled summer vegetables or Seedy Quinoa Cakes (page 222) or sliced and griddle-cooked leftover polenta.

3 tablespoons olive oil

1 sweet onion, diced

2 cloves garlic, minced

Salt and freshly ground black pepper

1 pound (455 g) eggplant (about 1 large), peeled and cut into ½-inch (12-mm) cubes

2 stalks celery, diced

1 (28-ounce/795-g) can whole tomatoes with their juices, pureed

¼ cup (60 ml) red wine vinegar

2 to 3 tablespoons brown sugar

1 heaping tablespoon drained capers

¼ cup (20 g) halved and pitted green (Sicilian-style) olives

3 tablespoons pine nuts, toasted in a skillet

In a large, deep sauté pan or Dutch oven, heat 1 tablespoon of the oil over medium-high heat until it shimmers. Add the onion and garlic and a pinch of salt and cook, stirring frequently, until the onion is translucent, about 5 minutes. Scoot the vegetables to the edge of the pan and pour the remaining 2 tablespoons oil into the center. Add the eggplant, celery, a pinch of salt, and a few grindings of pepper and cook, stirring frequently, until most pieces are a little brown, about 3 minutes. Add most of the tomatoes, the vinegar, and 2 tablespoons of the brown sugar; stir well and bring to a boil, then lower the heat and simmer, stirring occasionally, until the eggplant is tender, the celery still has a bit of crunch, and the sauce has reduced to a thick, jammy consistency, 10 to 15 minutes. If it seems too thick or dry, add more of the remaining tomatoes.

Add the capers, olives, and pine nuts. Season with salt, pepper, and more brown sugar, if needed. Serve hot, warm, or at room temperature. Store leftovers in an airtight container in the refrigerator for up to 3 days.

Grilled Orange-Glazed Eggplant Kabobs

SERVES 4

VEGAN

As much as I like thin slabs of simply grilled eggplant, I find it hard to justify using so much grill surface area for it. These skewers of thick cubes of eggplant, basted with a warm, fragrant, sweet-tart and slightly spicy glaze, allow you to get more on the grate. If you'd like, slip squares of sweet onion, or chunks of leeks, or even quartered apricots or cubes of pineapple onto the skewers between eggplant pieces. Serve the skewers with a platter piled high with grilled corn on the cob and a big bowl of spicy slow-braised collards or other hearty greens.

1 large eggplant

Salt

¾ cup (180 ml) fresh orange juice

2 tablespoons fresh lemon juice

3 tablespoons agave nectar, honey, or sugar, or more if needed

1 tablespoon tamari

¼ teaspoon hot red pepper flakes

Freshly ground black pepper

2 teaspoons coarsely grated orange zest

2 teaspoons sesame seeds, toasted (optional)

Prepare a charcoal fire. Soak 8 bamboo skewers in water for 30 minutes.

Cut off the stem end of the eggplant, peel the eggplant, and cut it into 1-inch (2.5-cm) chunks. Put the eggplant pieces in a colander set over a bowl and toss with ½ teaspoon salt, then set aside to drain while you make the glaze.

In a small saucepan, combine the orange juice, lemon juice, agave nectar, tamari, red pepper flakes, and a few grindings of black pepper. Bring to a boil over high heat, then lower the heat and simmer for 10 minutes. Stir in the orange zest and remove the pan from the heat. Taste and season with salt, if needed—it should be quite salty, sweet, and tart.

Rinse the eggplant, drain it well, and thread the pieces onto the skewers (discard any liquid in the bowl). Brush them generously with the glaze, then put them on the grill. Cook, turning frequently and brushing them occasionally with more glaze, until nicely browned and tender throughout, 8 to 10 minutes. Transfer the skewers to a platter, drizzle with some of the remaining glaze, and sprinkle with sesame seeds, if using. Serve hot.

herbs

In the colder months, herbs can be ridiculously expensive if you don't have a plot of them that will survive the winter or a windowsill planter, so it makes sense to take advantage of their abundance in summer. Fill up falafel and dumplings with greens, make loads of pesto and cilantro-mint chutney (freezing some for later), put herbs in everything from drinks to salsas to egg dishes, from marinades to sauces to dressings. And don't forget that you can use tender sprigs of herbs like parsley, mint, basil, chervil, and tarragon as salad greens (see the Warm Roasted Kabocha Squash Salad on page 170, for example).

There are many effective ways to keep herbs fresher longer:

- Woody herbs like rosemary and thyme should be bagged (unwashed) and stashed in the refrigerator; they should keep for a couple weeks.
- For tender fresh herbs like basil, parsley, and tarragon, unbundle the sprigs and gently rinse them in cold water. Spin them dry in a salad spinner, then wrap them in a paper towel and slide the bundle into a sealable plastic bag. Keep the bag in the crisper drawer.
- Alternatively, for tender herbs, hold the bunch together and rinse it under cold running water, then shake off excess water. Trim the stems and put the sprigs in a jar of cold water. Cover the leaves with a plastic bag, securing the bag around the rim of the jar with a rubber band. Keep the bagged bouquet in the refrigerator.

Herby Falafel

MAKES ABOUT 20 FALAFEL; SERVES 4 TO 6

VEGAN

These are very green, fresh-tasting falafel, made with a combination of soaked and ground dried chickpeas and lima beans. They have much more texture and character than any falafel made from a boxed mix (not to say that the mixes aren't pretty good too). They're wonderful freshly fried, on top of a spear of romaine, drizzled with creamy tahini sauce (see page 250), and topped with cucumber, tomato, and perhaps a cold pickle, but are also delicious at room temperature—a great addition to a bento-type lunch box.

Note that here the dried chickpeas and lima beans are simply soaked overnight before being ground to make the falafel mixture; they are not cooked first. This is an easy recipe to double, if you have a very large mixing bowl. Scoop the extra falafel mixture into a freezer bag, flatten it out, and freeze the mixture for up to 3 months. You can break off half or so at a time, thaw it overnight in the fridge, then shape and fry a few falafel at a time as needed.

8 ounces (225 g) dried chickpeas

8 ounces (225 g) dried baby lima beans

1 cup (40 g) chopped fresh flat-leaf parsley

½ cup (20 g) chopped fresh cilantro

½ sweet onion, coarsely chopped

1 large clove garlic, chopped

¼ cup (30 g) oat flour, or more if needed (see Note)

¾ teaspoon ground cumin

½ teaspoon ground coriander

½ teaspoon baking powder

¼ teaspoon ground Aleppo pepper (or cayenne, if you prefer more heat)

Salt and freshly ground black pepper

Vegetable oil, for shallow frying

Rinse the chickpeas and lima beans, put them in a large bowl or pot, and add cold water to cover the beans by 3 inches (7.5 cm). Soak for 8 hours or overnight. Drain well.

Working in batches as necessary, in a food processor, grind the chickpeas and lima beans until very fine—almost a paste—and transfer the ground beans to a large bowl. In the last batch or two, grind the parsley, cilantro, onion, garlic, flour, cumin, coriander, baking powder, Aleppo pepper, 1¾ teaspoons salt, and a few grindings of black pepper along with the beans and transfer the mixture to the bowl. Thoroughly mix the ingredients in the bowl. Taste the mixture and add more salt or pepper, if necessary. Cover the bowl with plastic wrap and set aside in the refrigerator for at least 1 hour or up to 1 day. (This will allow the flour to absorb some of the moisture so the dough holds together better; after chilling, if the dough is still very loose when squeezed tightly in your hand, stir in a little more flour. The dough should just barely hold together.)

Preheat the oven to 250°F (120°C). Line a baking sheet with a paper bag or paper towels. Line a plate with waxed paper.

Scoop out well-packed ¼-cupfuls (about 60 g) of the falafel dough and squeeze the mixture between your hands into thick, compact patties about 1½ inches (4 cm) in diameter, putting them on the waxed paper–lined plate as you finish. (At this point you can delay the cooking step for up to 1 day: Wrap the plate and refrigerate the patties until ready to cook.)

continued

Clockwise from top left: Tahini-Pomegranate Sauce, sliced tomatoes, Herby Falafel, Roasted Shallot Salad (page 145), Grilled Sweet Corn and Feta Salad (page 84), and cucumbers with yogurt and herbs.

In a large sauté pan, heat ¼ inch (6 mm) of oil over medium-high heat until it shimmers. Carefully add a few patties to the oil (don't overcrowd the pan) and cook them, undisturbed, until nicely browned on one side, about 3 minutes; using a metal spatula, turn each falafel and cook until the other side is well browned. As you cook the first side, the surface may crack a bit, but don't worry: It'll firm up as it browns. Transfer the cooked patties to the lined baking sheet to drain, and keep them warm in the oven while you cook the remainder. If you're cooking a lot, you might need to strain the oil after cooking a batch or two to remove blackened bits, or scoop out the bits with a small sieve.

(Alternatively, bake rather than shallow-fry the falafel: Preheat the oven to 450°F (230°C) and generously oil a baking sheet. Shape the patties a little thinner than usual—about ¾ inch (2 cm) thick—and arrange them on the baking sheet. Bake until the bottom is nicely browned, about 10 minutes, then flip them over and bake for another 10 minutes.)

Serve the falafel warm.

Note: You can use any kind of neutral flour here, but oat will keep it gluten free.

Spinach, Herb, and Ricotta Dumplings

MAKES 12 TO 14 WALNUT-SIZE DUMPLINGS; SERVES 2 TO 4

Similar to *malfatti*, which means "malformed," referring to the rustic appearance of those misshapen dumplings, these tender, green-flecked little balls are simmered in water, then broiled to crisp up the tops a bit and help them firm up. Serve them on their own, with a shower of Parmesan shavings and a lemon wedge—or drop the broiled dumplings into a simmering marinara sauce and serve with pasta or polenta as a main course.

10 ounces (285 g) spinach

½ cup (20 g) fresh flat-leaf parsley, or half parsley and half basil

1 cup (8 ounces/225 g) ricotta

1 large egg

½ cup (50 g) oat flour, or more if needed

3 tablespoons grated Parmesan cheese

½ teaspoon finely grated lemon zest

Salt and freshly ground black pepper

1 tablespoon unsalted butter, softened

Bring a large pot of water to a boil. Add the spinach and parsley and cook for 2 minutes. Drain in a sieve and rinse under cold running water to cool completely. Squeeze all the excess water out of the greens—and I mean all of it: Squeeze clumps of it in your fist until it's practically crumbly. Transfer the greens to a cutting board and finely chop them, then scrape them into a large bowl. Add the ricotta, egg, oat flour, 2 tablespoons of the Parmesan, the lemon zest, ¾ teaspoon salt, and pepper to taste. Stir well, then cover and set aside in the refrigerator for at least 30 minutes or up to overnight.

Lightly oil a small rimmed baking sheet.

Bring a large pot of water to a boil. Shape a generous pinch of the dumpling dough into a small test ball and drop it into the water. Some bits of green will fly off in the water, but the ball should stay intact—if it disintegrates, stir a bit more oat flour into the dumpling mixture.

Shape the dough into 1 ½-inch (4-cm) balls. Roll them in a dusting of oat flour and roll them again between your palms to shape them into neat, compact spheres. Gently lower them into the boiling water and cook until they rise to the surface, 2 to 3 minutes, removing them with a slotted spoon as they're done and placing them on the prepared baking sheet. (At this point you can cover and refrigerate the dumplings for up to 1 day. Bring them to room temperature before broiling.)

Preheat the broiler and set a rack about 6 inches (15 cm) below the heating element.

Dot the dumplings with the butter and sprinkle them with the remaining 1 tablespoon Parmesan. Broil until heated through and lightly browned on top, 8 to 10 minutes. Serve hot.

Chaat Party

CAN BE VEGAN

I know I included a chaat—a fresh and delightful Indian street-food snack consisting of vegetables swirled with yogurt, tangy chutneys, and spice mixes—in *Whole Grains for a New Generation*, and therefore it might seem like I'm pushing the stuff too hard. But I suppose I'm on a mission: There needs to be more chaat in the world. And since I'm not about to open up a food truck operation and send chaat vendors out onto the streets of Lincoln, Nebraska, any time soon, here I am, sharing another recipe. This one is an especially easy-to-pull-together offering featuring the best and brightest summer vegetables and a chutney loaded with cooling mint and cilantro.

Making chaat at home can seem daunting at first because there are so many elements, but there are a few parts that can be prepared ahead of time—and surpris-

ingly, it isn't hard to throw a chaat together when you have a few of the pieces of the puzzle ready in advance. Make the wonderfully sour chaat masala (the tangy spice mix) and apricot-tamarind chutney a week before, prepare the potatoes the day before, and make the mint-cilantro chutney the morning you plan to serve it so it keeps its vibrant green color. Chop the rest of the ingredients before dinner and put everything in some pretty dishes. No assembly required.

A chaat-themed dinner party (or luncheon) is a great way to serve this, as it's such a colorful and interactive dish—everyone gets to create their own with just the right amount of heat, sourness, freshness, and crunch. Think about a dessert to serve, too: The little cheesecakes on page 235 would be nice, and they can be made a day or so in advance.

FOR THE CHAAT MASALA (see Note)

- 2 teaspoons ground coriander
- 2 teaspoons hot red chile flakes
- 1 teaspoon ground cumin
- 1 teaspoon *amchur* (sour mango powder)
- 1 teaspoon sweet paprika
- 1 teaspoon black salt (optional)
- ½ teaspoon freshly ground black pepper
- ½ teaspoon citric acid

FOR THE APRICOT-TAMARIND CHUTNEY
(makes about 1 cup/240 ml)

- ½ cup (85 g) Turkish dried apricots
- 1 heaping tablespoon tamarind concentrate
- Pinch of salt

FOR THE CILANTRO-MINT CHUTNEY
(makes about ¾ cup/180 ml)

- 1½ cups (60 g) chopped fresh cilantro with tender stems
- ¼ cup (10 g) chopped fresh mint
- ¼ cup (40 g) diced sweet onion
- 1 fresh hot green chile, seeded and chopped
- 1 coin peeled fresh ginger, chopped
- 3 tablespoons fresh lime juice
- 1 teaspoon salt
- 1 teaspoon sugar or agave nectar

FOR THE YOGURT

- 1½ cups (360 ml) plain yogurt
- ¼ teaspoon salt

continued

FOR THE VEGETABLES

- 2½ cups (410 g) cooked and cooled (or canned) chickpeas, drained
- 2½ cups (390 g) diced, cooked, and cooled white potatoes
- 1 cup (130 g) diced cucumbers, or peeled and diced jicama or kohlrabi
- 1 cup (180 g) diced ripe and/or green tomatoes or tomatillos, or halved cherry or grape tomatoes
- ½ cup (80 g) sliced sweet onions, soaked in ice water until ready to serve, then drained
- Thinly sliced fresh hot green or red chiles
- Other fun additions: diced sweet peppers; pomegranate arils; diced apple; diced pineapple; diced, cooked, and cooled sweet potatoes; diced, cooked, and cooled rutabaga

FOR THE CRISPIES

- 1 or 2 bags Indian chickpea-flour snacks, such as *boondi* (little balls, shown below) or *sev* (thin short strands, shown opposite)—go nuts at the Indian grocery
- Other possible additions: roasted or fried chickpeas, pan-fried raw cashews or roasted cashews or peanuts, fried nuts and seeds (see page 190), or spicy Fried Giant White Corn (page 240), Corn Chex cereal, puffed millet or other gluten-free grain, or popped sorghum or popcorn

MAKE THE CHAAT MASALA

In a small bowl, combine all the masala ingredients, using your fingers or a fork to break up any lumps. The spice mixture will keep in an airtight container in the cupboard almost indefinitely.

MAKE THE APRICOT-TAMARIND CHUTNEY

In a small saucepan, combine all the ingredients and 1 cup (240 ml) water and bring to a boil. Lower the heat and simmer until the apricots are very soft, about 15 minutes. Let cool for a few minutes. Transfer the mixture to a blender or mini food processor and puree until smooth and just pourable, adding more water as needed to obtain the desired consistency. The chutney will keep in a clean glass jar in the refrigerator for up to 1 week.

MAKE THE CILANTRO-MINT CHUTNEY

In a blender or mini food processor, combine all the chutney ingredients and pulse to finely mince. The chutney will keep in a clean glass jar in the refrigerator for up to 3 days (though after a day the color will not be as bright).

MAKE THE YOGURT

Whisk the yogurt and salt together until very smooth and loose, adding a little cold water if needed to make it just pourable.

ASSEMBLE THE CHAAT

Put the vegetables, chutneys, yogurt, and crisp toppings in serving bowls.

Invite your guests to assemble their own bowls of chaat: Spoon in a variety of different vegetables, then sprinkle them with chaat masala and a little salt. Dollop generously with the yogurt and chutneys, top with some crispies, and sprinkle again with chaat masala. Make each bowl a little differently.

Note: To make the chaat masala extra special, toast whole coriander and cumin seeds in a dry sauté pan and grind them yourself rather than using preground spices. This combination of spices is especially excellent because it features sour ingredients, which intensify the chaat exponentially, and if you're already heading to an Indian grocery to pick up *sev* or *boondi* you might as well look for the special masala ingredients, too: *amchur*, black salt, and citric acid can be found there. However, you can simply toast some cumin seeds and grind them with some chile flakes and salt instead.

Fresh Herb Omelet and Roasting-Pan Jam

MAKES ABOUT ¾ CUP (180 ML) JAM AND AS MANY OMELETS AS YOU'D LIKE

My daughter, Thalia, has been enthralled by the concept of "breakfast in bed" since she was about three years old. I happened to be in a yes-saying mood one night recently and told her that if she could possibly, please, try to stay in bed past 5:30 the next morning, or at least let her dad and me wake up organically for once, I'd bring her breakfast in bed. She managed it, and I brought her this herb-filled omelet, with a dollop of sweet tomato jam made right in the roasting pan. It was quite special, and it actually isn't that hard to pull off even if you aren't as well rested as I was that morning. You can easily prepare the cheese filling the day before.

FOR THE JAM

- 1 tablespoon olive oil
- 1 pound (455 g) ripe Roma or plum tomatoes (about 5), cored and halved lengthwise
- 1 tablespoon sugar
- 1 teaspoon minced fresh herbs, such as basil, tarragon, or parsley, or a combination
- Pinch of salt

FOR EACH OMELET

- 1 ounce (28 g) soft goat cheese
- 1 heaping tablespoon shredded cheddar or Swiss cheese
- 2 tablespoons minced fresh herbs, such as basil, tarragon, or parsley, or a combination
- Salt and freshly ground black pepper
- 2 large eggs
- ¼ tablespoon unsalted butter

MAKE THE JAM

Preheat the oven to 400°F (205°C). Set a large rimmed baking sheet in the oven while it heats.

When the baking sheet is hot, drizzle it with the oil and arrange the tomatoes on it, cut sides down. Roast until the skins are wrinkled and the tomatoes are very soft, about 30 minutes. Remove the pan from the oven but leave it on. With your fingers or tongs, pull the skins off the tomatoes and discard the skins. Using a metal spatula or an old knife, coarsely chop the tomatoes right on the pan, then sprinkle them with the sugar, herbs, and salt. Return the pan to the oven and roast until the tomato mixture is hot and bubbling at the edges, about 10 minutes. Scrape the jam into a bowl and set aside, covered to keep warm if you'd like. (The jam can be made several days in advance and kept in the refrigerator; serve cold or rewarm it on the stovetop.)

MAKE THE OMELET

In a small bowl, use a fork to mash together the cheeses, half of the herbs, and salt and pepper to taste. (Multiply the quantities if you're making more than one omelet, and divide the mixture into portions.)

In a separate bowl, whisk together the remaining herbs, the eggs, and 2 teaspoons water.

In a small sauté pan, melt the butter over medium-high heat. Lower the heat to medium and pour in the eggs. (If making more than one omelet, just pour in about 2 eggs' worth to cook at a time.) Cook the eggs, undisturbed, for 1 minute, then gently loosen and lift the edges of the omelet with a spatula and tilt the pan to let the uncooked eggs on top run onto the hot pan. When the eggs no longer run, dot the cheese mixture over one half of the omelet, then fold the other half over it. Cook, turning the omelet over once if you'd like, until the cheese is melted and the omelet is cooked to your liking (I prefer fairly well done). The whole omelet-cooking process will take about 5 minutes total.

Transfer the omelet to a plate and serve with a spoonful or two of the jam alongside.

Basil and Seared Pineapple Salsa

MAKES ABOUT 2½ CUPS (530 G)

VEGAN

I'm lucky that my daughter will eat just about any kind of salsa, even if it's a tad spicy, but if you're catering to a mixed crowd (kids, adults, adults with sensitive taste buds) it would be a generous gesture to offer this sweet and mild salsa alongside a tart and spicy one. That said, of course, this salsa is also great with a couple of minced hot chiles thrown in—the sweetness of the fruit helps tame the heat. The basil-fragrant salsa is great with fresh tortilla chips, of course, but also alongside slabs of grilled eggplant and zucchini, or as a topping for warm soba noodles with a soy-peanut sauce.

1 tablespoon vegetable oil

½ pineapple, peeled, cored, and cut into ¾-inch-thick (2-cm-thick) wedges

¼ red onion, finely diced

¼ red bell pepper, finely diced

1 tablespoon minced fresh basil

1 tablespoon minced fresh mint

3 tablespoons fresh lime juice

Salt and freshly ground black pepper

In a large sauté pan, heat ½ tablespoon of the oil over medium-high heat. When it shimmers, add half of the pineapple wedges in a single layer so one flat side of each is in contact with the pan. Sear until nicely browned on the bottom, about 2 minutes, then turn and sear the other flat side, about 2 minutes more. Transfer the seared pineapple to a cutting board and repeat with the remaining oil and pineapple. Let the pineapple cool completely.

In a large bowl, combine the onion, bell pepper, basil, mint, and lime juice. Dice the pineapple and add it and any juices from the cutting board to the bowl. Add about ¾ teaspoon salt and a couple of grindings of black pepper. Toss well, then set aside for at least 1 hour to let the flavors come together and the salt dissolve.

Taste and add more salt, if needed. Serve at room temperature, or refrigerate in an airtight container for up to 4 hours.

Rosemary-Grilled Romaine and Radicchio

SERVES 4

VEGAN

Grilling bitter greens with a generous basting of pounded rosemary, garlic, and olive oil gives them a smoky, intensely herbal flavor that complements the bitterness and mellows it just a tad. Serve this dish as a salad course with steak knives for cutting across the grilled wedges, and perhaps a dollop of good homemade aioli (page 251) alongside.

4 cloves garlic, chopped

2 tablespoons minced fresh rosemary

Kosher salt and freshly ground black pepper

⅓ cup (80 ml) olive oil

1 romaine heart

1 large head radicchio, or 2 small ones

Coarse sea salt

Lemon wedges

Prepare a charcoal fire.

In a mortar, combine the garlic, rosemary, 1 teaspoon kosher salt, and a couple of grindings of pepper and smash to a coarse paste with a pestle. (You can do this in a mini food processor instead, but the mortar is actually easier and more efficient.) Stir in the oil.

Rinse the romaine and radicchio and trim a slice off the bottoms, keeping the cores intact. Cut the heads lengthwise into halves if they're small or quarters if they're larger, keeping the cores on so the leaves stay connected at the bottom. Drizzle the romaine and radicchio with half of the oil mixture. Grill the lettuces over medium-high heat, turning frequently, until browned on all sides and the inner layers are tender, about 5 minutes for the romaine and 8 minutes for the radicchio—if the radicchio starts browning too quickly, move it to a cooler spot on the grill.

FALL

broccoli and cauliflower

Regular old broccoli and cauliflower may well be the easiest vegetables to make taste great. Serve them raw with an easy dip like curried feta (see page 37), steam them and toss them with an herbal vinaigrette, roast them, grill them in long spears or flat slabs (respectively), stir-fry them with aromatics and tamari, simmer them with fresh hot chiles in an Indian-spiced tomato-based sauce (like the one on page 56), or in Red Coconut Curry Sauce Concentrate (page 261) plus a little stock or coconut milk, or blanch, coat in a light *pakora* batter (see page 155), and deep-fry them. There's not much you can do to ruin either vegetable apart from negligent overcooking.

Since moving to Lincoln, where Asian produce is plentiful but I've yet to find a single stem of broccoli rabe (aka rapini), Chinese broccoli (aka *gai lan*, *kai-lan*, or Chinese kale), one of my absolute favorite vegetables, has come to play an outsize role in my cooking. It's similar to rabe, with thick edible stems and small, loosely flowering heads (choose bunches with not too many yellow blossoms, which indicate advanced age). It's a lighter green than rabe, and sweeter, less bitter. If broccoli rabe is easier for you to come by, please go ahead and use it in place of the Chinese broccoli in these recipes. And have an extra helping for me.

Roasted Broccoli with Pomegranate and Tahini

SERVES 4

VEGAN

Roasted broccoli is so easy it certainly doesn't need a recipe, but I think this combination is so amazing—the browned tips of the florets, the tangy-smooth tahini-pomegranate dressing, the sweet and crunchy pome-granate seeds—that I had to include it here so you'd be more likely to try it. Serve it as an appetizer or a substantial side dish.

1 bunch broccoli with stems (about 1¼ pounds/565 g)

2 tablespoons olive oil

Salt and freshly ground black pepper

⅓ to ½ recipe Tahini-Pomegranate Sauce (page 204)

About ½ cup (85 g) pomegranate arils

Preheat the oven to 400°F (205°C).

Cut the broccoli into bite-size florets. Peel the stems deeply and cut them into ½-inch (12-mm) pieces. On a large baking sheet, toss the broccoli florets and stems with the oil, ¾ teaspoon salt, and pepper to taste. Roast until tender and nicely browned at the tips of the florets, about 20 minutes. Transfer to a platter or serving bowl, drizzle with the sauce, and sprinkle with the pomegranate seeds. Serve hot or at room temperature.

Seared Broccoli Hash

SERVES 4

VEGAN

I learned about toasting finely chopped broccoli when I was working on the wacky but fun cookbook *The 4-Hour Chef*, by Tim Ferriss. That recipe came from Karen Liebowitz at Mission Street Food in San Francisco: finely chopped and seared, but almost raw, broccoli, folded into mashed avocado, and topped with broiled *unagi* (eel). It was better than it sounds, I swear. I like to cook

the broccoli a little longer so it gets more tender and even toastier. This is a pretty good substitute for rice, texture-wise if not flavor-wise, and a nutty, green-tasting base for all sorts of saucy dishes. If you have leftovers, there are very few things better for piling into a one-egg omelet the next morning, with or without a few shreds of sharp cheddar.

1 onion, roughly chopped

2 tablespoons olive oil

Salt and freshly ground black pepper

1 bunch broccoli with stems (about 1¼ pounds/565 g)

Juice of ½ lemon

In a food processor, pulse the onion to finely chop it. (Don't wash the bowl of the processor yet.)

In a large skillet or sauté pan, heat 1 tablespoon of the oil over medium-high heat until it shimmers. Add the chopped onion and sprinkle with a pinch of salt and a few grindings of pepper. Cook, stirring occasionally, until translucent and beginning to brown, about 6 minutes.

Meanwhile, roughly chop the broccoli crowns. Peel the broccoli stems and roughly chop them. Put the broccoli in the food processor and pulse to finely chop it; the largest pieces of stem should be the size of peas.

Add the broccoli to the skillet, sprinkle with a generous pinch of salt, and stir to combine it with the onion. Drizzle in the remaining 1 tablespoon oil and spread the vegetable mixture evenly in the pan. Raise the heat to high and cook for 6 to 8 minutes, turning with a metal spatula every minute or two, until the broccoli is nicely toasted in spots but still bright green. Taste and add salt and pepper, if needed. Transfer the broccoli to a serving bowl and sprinkle with the lemon juice at the table.

Simple Braised Broccoli

SERVES 4

VEGAN

Here's an all-purpose broccoli recipe that is equally good with sprouting broccoli varieties, like *gai lan* and broccoli rabe, as it is with heading broccoli. You can blanch the broccoli well in advance and keep it in the refrigerator or freezer for those times when you need a quick, mild-flavored accompaniment; thaw it by running it under cool water in a colander for a minute.

1 pound (455 g) Chinese broccoli (*gai lan*), broccoli rabe, broccolini, or regular broccoli

1 tablespoon vegetable or olive oil

2 cloves garlic, chopped

1 cup (240 ml) vegetable stock, or ¼ cup (60 ml) frozen Roasted Vegetable Stock Concentrate (page 262) mixed with ¾ cup (180 ml) water

2 tablespoons shaoxing (Chinese cooking wine) or dry sherry or white wine

Tamari or salt

Hot red pepper flakes or freshly ground black pepper

Bring a large pot of water to a boil. Fill a large bowl with ice water.

If using Chinese broccoli or rabe, trim the very bottoms of the stems. If using regular broccoli, separate the head into large florets, and trim, peel, and coarsely chop the stems. Drop the broccoli into the boiling water and blanch for 2 minutes. Drain the broccoli in a colander, then transfer it to the ice water to stop the cooking. Pick out the ice and drain the broccoli.

In a large sauté pan, heat the oil over medium-high heat until it shimmers. Add the garlic and cook, stirring, until golden, about 1 minute. Add the stock, wine, and broccoli. Cover and cook, lifting the lid and stirring occasionally (use tongs to turn Chinese broccoli or rabe), until the broccoli is tender but still bright green and firm, 4 to 5 minutes. Taste and season with tamari and red pepper flakes to taste. Serve hot.

Broccoli with Potato, Pine Nuts, and Raisins

SERVES 2

If you're not eating wheat pasta, you might wish to have a few hearty, rib-sticking dishes like this one in your repertoire to keep you carbohydrate-satisfied. Here the potato is cut into pieces that resemble penne and parcooked with broccoli before being sautéed and sprinkled with bright, fresh lemon juice. The dish is studded with plump raisins and toasted pine nuts for a bit of sweetness and crunch.

½ bunch broccoli with stems (about ¾ pound/340 g)

1 large russet potato

Salt

2 tablespoons olive oil

½ onion, diced

2 cloves garlic, minced

Freshly ground black pepper

Pinch of hot red pepper flakes

2 tablespoons pine nuts

1 tablespoon raisins

1 tablespoon fresh lemon juice

Small piece of hard or semifirm cheese, such as Parmesan, aged Asiago, or aged Gouda

Trim, peel, and cut the broccoli stems into penne-size pieces. Cut the rest of the head into bite-size florets. Set aside.

Peel the potato and cut it into penne-size sticks. Put it in a large saucepan and add cold water to just cover the potato, along with ½ teaspoon salt. Set the pan over high heat and bring to a boil; lower the heat and simmer for 2 minutes.

Add the broccoli stems to the saucepan. When the water in the saucepan returns to a full rolling boil, add the florets, cover, and cook until the broccoli and potato are just tender, 5 to 7 minutes. Reserve 1 cup (240 ml) of the cooking water, then drain the vegetables in a colander.

In a large sauté pan, heat the oil over medium-high heat until it shimmers. Add the onion and garlic, a pinch of salt, a few grindings of black pepper, and the red chile flakes. Cook, stirring, until the onion is translucent, 5 to 7 minutes. Add the pine nuts and raisins and stir for 1 minute. Add the broccoli and potatoes, season with salt and plenty of black pepper, and turn them with a metal spatula to coat them with the onion mixture. Add the lemon juice, and a little of the reserved cooking water if the mixture seems too dry, then transfer to serving bowls. Grate some cheese—and maybe grind some more black pepper—over the top. Serve hot.

Broccoli-Lemon Soup
with Garam Masala Cheese Crisps

SERVES 3 OR 4 AS A MEAL

I remember adoring thick, gloppy broccoli-cheddar soup as a kid. Okay, even as a college student, ladling soup into a little waxed paper tub for my lunch at the Caf. This draws on the classic broccoli-cheddar experience, but I've added tangy lemon juice and a healthy dose of nutrition in the form of spinach, and replaced the heavy cheese with beaten eggs, which thicken the soup and contribute a bit of protein without weighing it down. A salty cheese crisp flavored with garam masala makes a tasty and startlingly easy garnish, but is entirely optional.

FOR THE SOUP

1 tablespoon olive oil

½ sweet onion, diced

Salt and freshly ground black pepper

2½ cups (600 ml) vegetable stock

1 bunch broccoli with stems (about 1¼ pounds/565 g), crowns separated into florets, stems peeled and chopped

2 packed cups (60 g) spinach, chopped

2 large eggs, beaten

Finely grated zest of 1 small lemon

2 tablespoons fresh lemon juice

Pinch of garam masala

FOR THE CRISPS

½ cup (65 g) shredded Emmentaler or other semifirm cheese

Pinch of salt

⅛ teaspoon garam masala

MAKE THE SOUP

In a large saucepan, heat the oil over medium-high heat. Add the onion, a pinch of salt, and a few grindings of pepper and cook, stirring frequently, until the onion is translucent, about 5 minutes. Add the stock and broccoli, bring to a boil, then lower the heat and simmer until the broccoli is tender, about 10 minutes. Add the spinach and stir until it has wilted, about 1 minute.

Remove the pan from the heat and puree the soup with an immersion blender. Gradually whisk in the eggs, then whisk in the lemon zest, juice, and garam masala. Taste and season with salt and pepper. Return the pan to medium-low heat and cook, whisking frequently and keeping the soup just steaming but not bubbling, for 5 minutes. Remove the pan from the heat and cover to keep warm while you make the crisps.

MAKE THE CRISPS

Heat a large nonstick pan over medium heat. In a medium bowl, toss together the cheese, salt, and garam masala, then make about 6 little piles of the mixture in the pan, spreading the cheese shreds thinly into lacy rounds. Cook on one side until the cheese is melted, solidified, and golden brown in spots, about 5 minutes. If you'd like, flip them and brown the other side. Remove to a paper towel to cool for a minute.

Ladle the soup into serving bowls and serve with the crisps.

Chinese Broccoli (Gai Lan) with Garlic-Miso Sauce

SERVES 2 OR 3

VEGAN

This is a versatile dish, delicious served as a side to other vegetables (even ones not cooked in an Asian style can complement it nicely)—try herby roasted winter squash, for example, or the black beans on page 226. Or serve it over steamed brown rice as an entrée—just double the quantities for the sauce and add a slurry of 1 teaspoon cornstarch mixed with ¼ cup (60 ml) water at the very end of cooking and bring it just to a boil.

1 bunch Chinese broccoli (*gai lan*; about 1 pound/455 g), trimmed

1 tablespoon olive or vegetable oil

2 cloves garlic, minced

1 coin peeled fresh ginger, minced

2 tablespoons miso paste (any kind)

1 teaspoon agave nectar

½ teaspoon hot red pepper flakes

Cut the bunch of Chinese broccoli into 2-inch (5-cm) pieces, keeping the thick stems—the lower 4 inches (10 cm) or so—separate from the leaves.

In a large sauté pan, heat the oil over medium-high heat until it shimmers. Add the garlic and ginger and cook, stirring, until softened but not browned, 1 to 2 minutes. Add the broccoli stems and ¼ cup (60 ml) water, cover, raise the heat to high, and cook until the stems are almost tender, about 3 minutes. Add the broccoli leaves, cover, and cook for 1 minute more. Uncover, stir the stems and leaves together, and cook, stirring occasionally, until the broccoli is just tender and the liquid has evaporated, about 3 minutes more.

Meanwhile, in a small bowl, whisk together the miso, agave nectar, and red pepper flakes.

Add the miso mixture to the broccoli, stir well, and cook until the miso mixture is evenly incorporated and heated through, 3 to 4 minutes. Serve hot.

Stir-Fried Rice Stick Noodles with Chinese Broccoli (Gai Lan) and Lime

SERVES 3 OR 4 AS A MEAL

This is one of the best dishes I've made with *gai lan* since moving to broccoli rabe–challenged Lincoln, Nebraska: quick-cooking rice noodles, scrambled eggs, tender broccoli stems and ever-so-slightly bitter greens, and lots of lime juice and tamari.

7 ounces (200 g) ³⁄₄-inch-wide (2-cm-wide) rice stick noodles

3 large eggs

Salt and freshly ground black pepper

1 bunch Chinese broccoli (*gai lan*; about 1 pound/455 g), trimmed

3 tablespoons vegetable oil

3 shallots, thinly sliced

1 clove garlic, thinly sliced

1½ tablespoons tamari, or to taste

½ to 1 teaspoon hot red pepper flakes

Juice of 1 lime

Bring a large saucepan of water to a boil. Add the noodles and cook for 2 minutes, just until they're flexible. Drain the noodles in a colander, rinse them under cold running water, and leave them in the colander to drain some more.

In a small bowl, beat the eggs together with a generous pinch of salt and black pepper to taste.

Cut the bunch of Chinese broccoli into 2-inch (5-cm) pieces, keeping the thick stems—the lower 4 inches (10 cm) or so—separate from the leaves.

In a large, deep sauté pan, heat 1 tablespoon of the oil over medium-high heat until it shimmers. Add the eggs and let them spread in the pan for 30 seconds or so. When the bottom is just set, use a metal spatula to gently turn and scramble them, cooking for just 1 or 2 more minutes to set them. Scrape the eggs out onto a plate and set aside.

Return the pan to medium-high heat, add 1 tablespoon of the oil, the shallots, and the garlic, and cook, stirring, until the shallots and garlic are softened but not browned, 1 to 2 minutes. Add the broccoli stems and ¼ cup (60 ml) water, cover, raise the heat to high, and cook until the stems are almost tender, about 3 minutes. Add the broccoli leaves, cover, and cook for 1 minute. Uncover, stir the stems and leaves together, and cook, stirring occasionally, until the broccoli is tender and the liquid has evaporated, about 3 minutes more.

Scoot the broccoli to one side of the pan and add the remaining 1 tablespoon oil into the clear space. When the oil is hot, add the cooked noodles and sprinkle with the tamari, red pepper flakes, and lime juice. Stir and turn the noodles with the spatula for a minute, then incorporate the broccoli. The noodles will stick to the pan a bit, but that's okay: Drizzle in ¼ cup (60 ml) water and use the spatula to scrape up the browned bits. Add the scrambled eggs and turn with the spatula to heat through and combine. If necessary, switch to tongs to get everything mixed together. Taste and add a bit more tamari, if needed, then serve hot.

Roasted Cauliflower
with Kalamata Olives and Almonds

Creamy white, bland cauliflower with dark, intense olives is a natural combination. Here the cauliflower is tossed with a paste of finely minced olives, lots of garlic, and almonds and then roasted on a hot baking sheet until the vegetable is tender and the paste has crisped and browned. As it is, this makes a flavorful centerpiece for a vegetable plate, but you can also fancy it up with a spoonful of finely chopped sweet pickled peppers or Sweet Peppers with Dates (page 85) scattered atop.

1 head cauliflower (about 1½ pounds/680 g)

½ cup (55 g) sliced almonds

¼ cup (40 g) pitted kalamata olives

3 cloves garlic, chopped

4 tablespoons (60 ml) olive oil

Salt and freshly ground black pepper

3 small sweet pickled peppers, minced (optional)

Preheat the oven to 400°F (205°C). Set a large rimmed baking sheet in the oven while it heats.

Break the cauliflower into florets, and trim and roughly chop the core. Transfer to a large bowl.

In a mini food processor, combine the almonds, olives, garlic, 3 tablespoons of the oil, a couple of pinches of salt, and a few good grindings of pepper. Pulse to make a coarse paste. Add the paste to the cauliflower in the bowl and toss to coat fairly evenly—it's okay if the olive mixture clumps here and there.

Transfer the cauliflower and all the paste from the bowl to the hot baking sheet and spread it out in a single layer. Drizzle with the remaining 1 tablespoon oil and sprinkle with salt. Roast the cauliflower, turning it over after about 20 minutes, until it is nicely browned in spots and the olive paste is sizzling and browned, about 30 minutes total. Sprinkle with the pickled peppers, if using, and serve immediately.

Broiled Masala Cauliflower

SERVES 2 TO 4

This is not necessarily an attractive dish, but the classic curry spices and tangy yogurt, and the easy way the dish comes together, make it very much worthy of a place in your rotation. Maybe serve it by candlelight?

> 1 cup (240 ml) plain Greek yogurt, preferably full fat
>
> 1 clove garlic, grated
>
> 2 tablespoons fresh lemon juice
>
> 1 tablespoon olive oil
>
> 1 teaspoon grated fresh ginger
>
> 1 teaspoon hot paprika
>
> ½ teaspoon ground cumin
>
> ½ teaspoon garam masala
>
> Salt
>
> 1 large head cauliflower (about 1½ pounds/680 g), broken into 2-inch (5-cm) florets
>
> Lemon wedges
>
> Fresh cilantro sprigs

Preheat the broiler and set a rack about 6 inches (15 cm) from the heat source.

In a large bowl, add the yogurt, garlic, lemon juice, oil, ginger, paprika, cumin, garam masala, and 1¾ teaspoons salt and whisk until smooth.

Toss the cauliflower florets in the yogurt mixture to coat well. Spread them on a rimmed baking sheet in a single layer. Broil the cauliflower, turning with a metal spatula halfway through the cooking, until very well browned in spots and tender throughout, about 25 minutes. Serve hot, with the lemon wedges and cilantro.

Green Riced Cauliflower

SERVES 2 TO 4

VEGAN

Cauliflower "rice" is a cliché at this point—it doesn't taste like rice, and we know it—but I appreciate the idea of making common and familiar vegetables more interesting simply by cutting them in less familiar ways. If you've only ever prepared cauliflower (or broccoli, for that matter) in floret form, this is a fine way to break out of a rut: The experience of cooking and eating the cauliflower will be substantially different, and you might come up with more creative ways of serving it.

> 1 head green or white cauliflower (about 1½ pounds/ 680 g)
>
> 2 tablespoons olive oil
>
> ½ sweet onion, diced
>
> 1 clove garlic, minced
>
> Salt and freshly ground black pepper
>
> 1 cup (30 g) packed fresh cilantro, finely chopped

Trim the cauliflower and peel the core. Coarsely chop the florets and the core. In a food processor, pulse the cauliflower pieces, in batches if necessary, until very finely chopped.

In a large, deep sauté pan, heat the oil over medium-high heat until it shimmers. Add the onion and garlic and cook until the onion is softened and translucent, about 5 minutes. Add the cauliflower and 2 tablespoons water, stir well, and cover the pan. Cook for 2 minutes, then uncover and stir in ¾ teaspoon salt, pepper to taste, and the cilantro. Cook, stirring frequently, until the largest bits of cauliflower are just tender, about 3 minutes more. Serve hot.

Many-Vegetable Split Pea and Apple Stew

SERVES 4 TO 6 AS A MEAL

VEGAN

This is a hearty one-pot meal, bulked up with yellow split peas, which are available in most good supermarkets. I like these flavors—eastern-Mediterranean spices, prickly-hot ginger, sweet and tangy apple and tomatoes—with cauliflower as the main vegetable, but you can easily mix it up and use cubes of hard squash, root vegetables, broccoli, or whatever's on hand, adjusting the cooking time as necessary. This is a satisfying one-dish stew, but you could ladle it over a pile of brown basmati rice, or offer a simple vegetable salad alongside—try grated carrots, fresh lemon juice, and minced fresh flat-leaf parsley.

1 teaspoon ground cumin

6 green cardamom pods

1 teaspoon Aleppo pepper or sweet paprika

2 cinnamon sticks

1 tablespoon olive oil

1 onion, diced

Salt and freshly ground black pepper

3 coins peeled fresh ginger, minced

2½ cups (600 ml) vegetable stock or water

1 cup (210 g) yellow split peas, rinsed and drained

1 small head cauliflower (about 1 pound/455 g), broken into florets, core peeled and chopped

1 pound (455 g) zucchini and/or yellow squash, cut into large chunks

6 small plum tomatoes, peeled and chopped (canned is fine; reserve the juice)

1 apple, peeled, cored, and chopped

Juice of ½ lemon

Fresh cilantro sprigs (optional)

In a small cup, combine the cumin, cardamom pods, Aleppo pepper, and cinnamon sticks.

In a large saucepan or Dutch oven, heat the oil over medium-high heat until it shimmers. Add the onion and a pinch each of salt and pepper and cook, stirring frequently, until the onion is translucent, about 5 minutes. Add the ginger and the spice mixture and stir for 30 seconds. Add the stock and split peas. Raise the heat to high and bring the mixture to a boil, then lower the heat to medium, cover, and simmer for 15 minutes.

Add the cauliflower, zucchini, tomatoes (and their juices, if using canned), and apple to the split peas. Return the mixture to a simmer and cook, with the lid askew, until the split peas and vegetables are very soft—the apple will likely break down totally, which is fine—about 30 minutes, adding a little water if needed to keep the split peas covered.

Gently stir in salt and pepper to taste and squeeze in the lemon juice. Pull out and discard the cinnamon sticks and as many cardamom pods as you can find, or tell your guests to set them aside as they encounter them. Serve hot, in soup plates, garnished with cilantro, if you'd like.

sweet potatoes and other root vegetables

Glorious sweet potatoes are available year-round, but fall is when they're harvested and when you'll find them at their freshest—with deep orange, almost red, dense flesh and very smooth skin, without a trace of stringiness. Organically grown garnet sweet potatoes are fairly consistently of good quality, so snap them up when you find them. Keep sweet potatoes at cool room temperature in a basket or bowl that allows some air circulation; they'll last for a couple of weeks. Or, if you have a bowlful of especially lovely ones that you won't be able to use in time, boil or roast them and freeze them for later.

Fall-harvested parsnips, carrots, beets, turnips, and rutabagas, of course, are also good "keeping" vegetables, and you'll find them throughout the year—and in spring you'll find beautiful young carrots, baby beets, and small white turnips. They have a special affinity for hearty, chilly-evening meals: roasts and stews and warm spices.

Masala Sweet Potatoes

SERVES 4 TO 6

VEGAN

A masala is simply a spice mixture, so I guess the descriptor *masala* could reasonably be attached to any dish that features a combination of spices. I call out the masala in the recipe title here because it's the main feature of the dish, and because it's actually a "wet masala," which is fun: The spices are all combined and ground up with fresh ingredients—onion, garlic, ginger, chiles—and then briefly fried together before the primary vegetable is added. It's an easy way to make a quick and punchy sauce.

1 sweet onion, chopped

2 cloves garlic, chopped

2 coins peeled fresh ginger, chopped

1 to 2 fresh hot green or red chiles, seeded and chopped

2 tablespoons tomato paste

1 teaspoon ground coriander

1/2 teaspoon ground cumin

1/2 teaspoon turmeric

1/2 teaspoon ground cinnamon

Salt and freshly ground black pepper

1 tablespoon vegetable oil

2 pounds (910 g) sweet potatoes (about 3 large), peeled and cut into 1/2-inch (12-mm) pieces

Juice of 1/2 lemon

1/4 teaspoon garam masala (optional)

In a mini food processor or blender, combine the onion, garlic, ginger, chile, tomato paste, coriander, cumin, turmeric, cinnamon, 1¾ teaspoons salt, a few grindings of black pepper, and 1/2 cup (120 ml) water and puree until smooth.

In a large, deep sauté pan, heat the oil over medium-high heat until it shimmers. Carefully add the masala paste—it will splatter. Cook, stirring constantly, for 2 minutes.

Meanwhile, add about 1/2 cup (120 ml) water to the food processor bowl to rinse out the remaining masala paste and reserve.

Add the sweet potatoes to the pan with just enough of the water from the processor so that the liquid comes halfway up the side of the sweet potatoes. Cover the pan, lower the heat to medium-low, and simmer, stirring occasionally, until the sweet potatoes are very soft, about 30 minutes. Add a bit more water if the sauce starts to stick before the sweet potatoes are tender.

Uncover and cook, stirring frequently, until the sauce is thick and pastelike and coats the sweet potatoes, which should be starting to break down. Squeeze in the lemon juice, sprinkle in the garam masala, if using, and stir well. Taste and add more salt and pepper, if needed. Serve hot.

Clockwise from top: Seasoned Greek yogurt, sliced cucumbers, brown lentils (see page 255), Pressed Japanese Turnips (page 257), and Masala Sweet Potatoes.

Slow-Fried Sweet Potatoes

SERVES 4 TO 6

VEGAN

A while back, I read about (and, I have to admit, scoffed at the idea of) this method for making French fries, which has been written about and popularized by the French chef Joël Robuchon but is apparently an old technique. You put cut potatoes in a heavy pot (like a Dutch oven), pour in enough vegetable oil to just cover them, and slowly cook them until done. Madness. Well, I finally tried it last year, and it's a game changer. Here's why you should try it, too (I'll bullet these points, sales presentation–style, because if you haven't cooked fries like this before you may well need convincing):

- It results in fries—I almost always use sweet potatoes, but russets and even kabocha squash turn out brilliantly too—that are perfectly tender on the inside, crisp-crunchy on the outside, and not at all greasy.
- The fries do not—I repeat: do not—absorb any more oil (in fact, I'm pretty sure they absorb less oil) when cooked in this way than when fried following the traditional two-stage process of blanching in oil and then refrying at a higher temperature. I've tested this many times by measuring the amount of cold oil I poured over the raw sweet potatoes, then measuring the oil after the fries have been skimmed out and the oil's cooled down. Always, there's only a few-tablespoon discrepancy.

- You probably hate splattering oil, right? Splattering just doesn't happen in this method because you're never immersing a cold, wet object into hot oil. The oil and potatoes just happily bubble away on the stovetop while you wander around the house doing other things. And that unpleasant deep-frying aftersmell that invades the house when you fry the normal way is not an issue: Here, you just smell sweet-potato fries.
- Because the oil never gets hot enough to do itself damage, it can be reused more times than oil used to deep-fry at high temperatures. That said, the oil does take on a faint sweet-potato flavor, but that isn't such a bad thing, especially if you'll just use it to make more sweet-potato fries.

> 4 sweet potatoes, garnet, regular, and/or white varieties
>
> About 4 cups (1 L) canola or other neutral vegetable oil
>
> Salt and seasonings (see Note)

Line a baking sheet with a paper towel and set a cooling rack upside down on top so the wire rungs are in contact with the paper (this is an Alton Brown trick that helps to quickly wick any dripping oil away from the fries).

Peel the sweet potatoes and cut them into French fry–size pieces, about ⅛ to ¼ inch (3 to 6 mm) thick. Put them in a wide, heavy pot (a Dutch oven works well) and add enough oil to just cover them. Set the pot over medium heat. When the oil starts to bubble gently all over the surface, lower the heat to medium-low—it should continue to bubble—and cook for

45 minutes, occasionally nudging the fries gently with tongs or a slotted spoon. The sweet potatoes should be very limp and soft. Raise the heat to medium or medium-high, so the oil bubbles more vigorously, and cook until the fries are golden brown and stiffer, 15 to 20 minutes more. (They'll crisp up after they're pulled from the oil.) Use a slotted spoon or wire skimmer to transfer the fries to the prepared rack. While the fries are hot, season them with salt and anything else you'd like. Serve hot or warm (they're good at room temperature, too, but more chewy than crunchy-crisp).

Note: I probably don't have to give you any ideas for seasonings, but in case you're tempted only to do the sugar-salt-and-cinnamon thing (which tends to take good sweet potatoes a bit in the dessert direction), here are some other ideas to consider. The spicy, seedy Kale *Furikake* (page 247) is probably my favorite—it's also gorgeously green against the bright sweet potatoes, whether white or garnet. Simple Chinese five-spice powder mixed with salt is good too. For the more adventurous, try numbing, spicy *Shichimi Togarashi* (page 247). For the traditional, a good homemade Creole or Cajun spice mixture (try 4 parts ground cayenne; 1 part each ground coriander, paprika, and black pepper; ½ part each ground cloves, granulated garlic, and dried thyme; and salt to taste) won't go unappreciated. In any case, you might wish to forgo the ketchup in favor of a garlicky aioli (page 251).

Sweet and Spicy (and Well-Done) Hash

SERVES 4

VEGAN

A good hash should be allowed plenty of time in the skillet—especially when you're starting with uncooked vegetables and not leftovers—so that the result includes deeply browned and crusty parts distributed throughout. (In diners, I used to actually order hash "well-done," as if I were a cowboy ordering a T-bone. I've abandoned this questionable practice after getting one too many orders in which the eggs were well-done instead of the hash.) The other quality of a good hash is that the separate elements are cooked to the point where they're on the verge of becoming one; when you scoop up a forkful, you should get a little of everything and shouldn't have to chase errant cubes of sweet potato or what have you around your plate. In other words, a proper hash, in my opinion, is not just mixed-up vegetables that happen to have been cooked in the same pan at the same time. A proper hash truly is greater than the sum of its parts.

2 tablespoons olive oil

1 pound (455 g) sweet potatoes (about 2), peeled and diced

10 ounces (285 g) parsnips (about 2), peeled and diced (see Note)

1 onion, diced

Salt and freshly ground black pepper

½ teaspoon ground coriander

½ teaspoon dried thyme

½ teaspoon hot or sweet paprika

¼ teaspoon ground cloves

¼ teaspoon ground cayenne, or to taste

1 small bunch (67 g) kale, tough stems removed, leaves chopped or shredded

In a large, deep sauté pan or cast-iron skillet, heat the oil over medium heat until it shimmers. Add the sweet potatoes, parsnips, onion, a good pinch of salt, and several grindings of black pepper. Cook, turning frequently with a metal spatula, until the vegetables are evenly tender and nicely browned, about 20 minutes—turn down the heat or drizzle in a splash of water if they seem to be browning too quickly.

In a small cup, combine the coriander, thyme, paprika, cloves, and cayenne. Sprinkle the spice mixture over the vegetables, then add ½ cup (120 ml) water and quickly scrape up the browned bits from the bottom of the pan. Add the kale, cover the pan, and let steam for 1 to 2 minutes. Uncover the pan and cook, flipping the hash with the spatula and turning down the heat if necessary, until the kale is tender, any excess liquid has evaporated, and the vegetables start to stick to the pan again (until you fear the hash is almost burned), 3 to 5 minutes more. The root vegetables will be very soft and breaking apart, and that's good. Serve hot.

Note: If your parsnips are quite large, with a woody core, cut them into quarters lengthwise and cut out the core with a knife or vegetable peeler.

Lightly Glazed Turnips

SERVES 4

VEGAN

This is a quick side dish with lots of pure turnip flavor. The sugar tempers the natural bitterness of the root vegetable, making this a good choice to serve to newcomers to the exciting world of turnip cuisine. Add the sugar a little at a time, to taste, as you may need less of it with certain varieties of turnip: white Japanese turnips, or *hakurei* turnips, are milder and more naturally sweet.

1 pound (455 g) turnips, peeled and cut into ½- to 1-inch (12-mm to 2.5-cm) pieces

1 tablespoon olive oil

1 tablespoon turbinado or brown sugar, plus more if needed

1 tablespoon fresh lemon juice

Salt and freshly ground black pepper

Place the turnips in a saucepan and add enough water to cover them by 1 inch (2.5 cm). Bring to a boil, then lower the heat and simmer until the turnips are just starting to become tender, 10 to 15 minutes. Drain, return the turnips to the pan, and add the oil, sugar, lemon juice, ½ teaspoon salt, and several grindings of pepper. Set the pan over medium to low heat and cook, stirring frequently with a heatproof spatula, until the turnips are very tender, glossy, and golden, 15 to 20 minutes; lower the heat if they start to stick to the pan, and add a splash of water if needed to keep them from browning too quickly. Serve hot.

THE TURNIP BANDWAGON

Turnips are finally starting to get the respect they deserve, now showing up on fancy farm-to-table menus all over the country. A few years ago, when I started gushing about how much I loved turnips all of a sudden, my mom told me that my late uncle, her brother Roy, a lifelong outdoorsman, used to carry a raw turnip in his coat pocket when he went into the woods as a kid. He'd slice pieces off with his hunting knife to snack on, and everybody thought that was the ultimate in crazy. In fact it's practically a literary trope: One of my daughter's favorite storybooks is Sid Fleischman's rollicking tall tale *McBroom Tells the Truth*. The antagonist, an old geezer named—really!—Heck Jones, first appears on the scene eating a green apple. Something's a little off about this character, you think. Next time you see him he's eating a raw turnip, and that confirms it: He's a bad seed. (Interestingly, he's also seen eating a "quince apple"—another unfairly maligned fruit! And it turns out that Heck Jones's undoing, in the end, comes about because he eats the most likeable fruit of all: watermelon.) But Heck and my uncle knew. Turnips, raw or cooked, are delicious.

Parsnip Nuggets

SERVES 2 OR 3

Okay, I'll admit that this is a weird dish, and it hardly needs a recipe except that why would you make something like this unless you'd seen it in a book? It's just diced and lightly maple-sweetened parsnips roasted on a hot baking sheet until they've shrunk and browned and turned into chewy nuggets that happen to make an awesome snack, maybe something to keep the kids happy while the rest of supper is still in the works. They're also surprisingly good as an hors d'oeuvre, speared on fancy toothpicks and dipped into homemade aioli (page 251)—in that case you should consider pouring glasses of a cold, autumnal white wine for your guests, who'll certainly deserve it for being game enough to try "parsnip nuggets."

1 pound (455 g) parsnips (see Note, page 134—throw in a couple extra if they're large and need to be cored)

1 tablespoon olive oil

1 teaspoon maple syrup

Salt and freshly ground black pepper

Preheat the oven to 400°F (205°C). Set a rimmed baking sheet in the oven while it heats.

Peel the parsnips and cut them into ½-inch (12-mm) pieces. In a medium bowl, combine the parsnip pieces with the oil, maple syrup, salt, and a few grindings of pepper and toss to coat. Spread them in a single layer on the preheated baking sheet and roast, turning with a spatula once or twice during the baking time, until nicely browned and tender, 30 to 35 minutes. Serve hot or room temperature and spear with little skewers as a chewy-sweet snack.

Roasted Carrot and Daikon with Japanese Spices

SERVES 2 TO 4

This is a play on the common Japanese bento dish of *kinpira* simmer-sautéed julienned root vegetables—carrots and burdock or daikon—but here the crisp vegetables are tossed in a maple and tamari marinade and roasted instead of cooked on the stovetop. The lightly caramelized spears are then generously seasoned with a sesame seed–based spice mix. If you have a stash of *furikake* or *shichimi togarashi* on hand, this dish comes together quite easily, and the roasted carrots and daikon, plus some braised sturdy greens and a mound of simply steamed brown rice, would make an elegant and homey dinner to serve to friends. Pass more of the spice mixture at the table, if you'd like.

1 tablespoon tamari

1 tablespoon vegetable oil

2 teaspoons maple syrup

Generous pinch of hot red pepper flakes

Salt

4 large carrots, or 8 small ones

1 small daikon radish

2 tablespoons Kale *Furikake* (page 247) or *Shichimi Togarashi* (page 247), or to taste

Preheat the oven to 400°F (205°C). Set a rimmed baking sheet in the oven while it heats.

In a shallow dish, whisk together the tamari, oil, maple syrup, red pepper flakes, and a pinch of salt.

Cut the carrots lengthwise into wedges ½ inch (12 mm) thick at the wider end. Peel the daikon and cut it into wedges of the same size. Put the carrots and daikon in the tamari mixture and toss to coat.

Spread the vegetables out in a single layer on the hot baking sheet and roast, turning once or twice, until nicely browned and tender, 25 to 30 minutes. Sprinkle with *furikake* or *shichimi togarashi* and serve hot or at room temperature.

Dave's Borscht

SERVES 6 AS A MEAL

This is my dad's easy recipe for borscht, a hot and hearty beet-and-cabbage-loaded soup. Hot borscht is usually built around beef, but Dad and I really don't think it needs meat. The potato gives it heft, and the cold sour cream or yogurt melting into the broth as you spoon it from your steaming bowl makes it plenty rich and filling. One word of advice: Try not to drop a half-gallon of this gorgeous red soup onto the floor of your kitchen at any point. It's a great soup, but no fun to clean from every surface in the room. I've tested this thoroughly.

1 tablespoon unsalted butter

1 onion, diced

2 ribs celery, diced

3 carrots, sliced ¼ inch (6 mm) thick

1½ teaspoons caraway seeds

Salt and freshly ground black pepper

3 beets (about 1¼ pounds/565 g), peeled, quartered, and sliced ¾ inch (6 mm) thick

1 large potato (about ¾ pound/340 g), peeled, quartered, and sliced ¾ inch (6 mm) thick

½ head cabbage (about 1 pound/455 g), cored and cut into 1-inch (2.5-cm) pieces

4 cups (1 L) vegetable stock

2 tablespoons fresh lemon juice

Sour cream or plain Greek yogurt, preferably full fat

Chopped fresh dill

In a large pot or Dutch oven, melt the butter over medium heat. Add the onion, celery, carrots, caraway, a pinch of salt, and a few grindings of pepper. Cook, stirring occasionally, until the onion is translucent but not browned, about 5 minutes. Add the beets, potato, cabbage, stock, and enough water to just barely cover the vegetables. Sprinkle in 1½ teaspoons salt, cover the pot, raise the heat to high, and bring the mixture to a boil. Lower the heat and simmer until the beets and cabbage are tender and the potatoes are falling apart, about 1 hour.

Stir in the lemon juice. Taste and season with more salt and pepper, if needed. Serve hot, topped with sour cream and dill.

Quick Cold Beet Soup

SERVES 1 OR 2

My first job in New York was as an assistant for the cookbook editor at a publishing house on Park Avenue South at 23rd Street. Soon after I started work there, a Russian fast-food restaurant opened diagonally across the corner from the offices. It was clean and bright, but not more than a hole in the wall, with high counters against the front window and walls and usually no available stools or chairs. It was the first Russian fast-food restaurant I'd ever seen—come to think of it, it's still the *only* Russian fast-food restaurant I've ever seen—and it was pretty special to me as a brand-new New Yorker. According to Google street view, it's long gone, but I'll never forget standing at the counter in my editorial-

assistant-appropriate slacks and sensible shoes (it was a long walk to and from my subway stop in Queens), slurping the most incredibly refreshing, most vinegary, *coldest* borscht in the known universe, carefully making sure I saved enough of the stingy sour cream dollop on top to last to the end of the bowl, watching the freak show that was 23rd Street through the picture window. Every day it was the best three dollars I spent—and you can bet I was keeping track.

I still don't know how to make a borscht like that one, and I may never. This beet soup is quite different, but its heart is in the right place: It's simple, cheap, tart (and thus filling), and *ice* cold.

2 baseball-size beets (about 10 ounces/285 g), roasted until very tender, peeled, and cooled (see Note)

1 cup (240 ml) cold plain yogurt, plus more for serving, if you'd like

½ cup (120 ml) cold vegetable stock or water

2 tablespoons rice vinegar or white wine vinegar

Salt

2 teaspoons chopped fresh dill, plus 2 sprigs for garnish

In a high-speed blender, combine the beets, yogurt, stock, vinegar, ¾ teaspoon salt, and chopped dill and blend until very smooth, scraping down the sides of the blender jar a few times if necessary. (Alternatively, coarsely grate the beets into a large bowl and whisk in the remaining ingredients.) Taste and season with more salt, if needed. If the soup isn't cold enough for you, blend in a couple of ice cubes or chill it in the refrigerator for up to 6 hours. Serve the soup in small bowls, garnished with dill sprigs and dollops of yogurt, if you'd like.

Note: When you bring home a bunch of beets from the store or farmers' market, it often makes sense to just go ahead and roast, peel, and stash them in a bag or container in the fridge so you'll have them handy for quick last-minute soups like this one or for sorbets like the one on page 234. Preheat the oven to 400°F (205°C). Wrap 2 or 3 beets in a large piece of aluminum foil (use more pieces of foil for more packets of beets) and put the packets on a baking sheet. Roast until a small knife inserted into a beet (through the foil) slides out easily, 45 to 60 minutes for baby beets, longer for larger beets. Let cool for a few minutes, then rub off the skins (or use a vegetable peeler or paring knife to peel them).

Rutabaga with Nutmeg Cream

SERVES 4

I spent about a week trying to come up with an unusual rutabaga recipe. Many large rutabagas were harmed in the process, and at a certain point I just started to feel like a jerk. Why was I trying to do something *fancy* with rutabaga? It's perfectly likable just as it is. I finally wrote to my mom, a known admirer of this vegetable, and asked her what I should do with it. The answer: Cook it, puree it (but know that it'll stay pretty chunky), maybe add some cream. And there you have it.

1½ pounds (680 g) rutabaga

Salt

½ cup (120 ml) half-and-half or heavy cream

Pinch of freshly grated nutmeg

Freshly ground black pepper

Peel the rutabaga fairly deeply and cut it vertically into several wedges 1 inch (2.5 cm) thick in the center (you may be using only part of a rutabaga—they can get huge!), then cut the wedges crosswise into ¼-inch (6-mm) slices.

Place the rutabaga in a large saucepan and add water to cover until the pieces float. Add 1 teaspoon salt and bring the water to a boil. Lower the heat and simmer until the rutabaga pieces are tender, about 20 minutes. Drain them and transfer to a food processor or blender. Add the half-and-half, nutmeg, ½ teaspoon salt, and a grinding of pepper. Pulse to make a chunky puree. Return the puree to the pan and reheat gently over low heat, stirring with a heatproof spatula, until heated through and steaming. Serve hot.

leeks, shallots, and onions

I use alliums—onions, shallots, or garlic, sometimes all three—in nearly every main dish I make, and when Thalia comes into the kitchen and says something smells good, it's usually onions cooking slowly in butter. (I remember reading somewhere when I was a kid—and I can't find reference to this now so I may be making it up—that in the Middle Ages people would cook onions in butter, even if they had nothing else to eat, so that their neighbors within olfactory range would think they had a much more special meal in the works than they actually did.) This is a testament to the power of cooking alliums, the Latin name of the genus that encompasses these root vegetables, which comes from the Greek for "avoid," due to their smell when raw.

Still, when the sweet onions come in, I don't hesitate to use them raw, and when the onions are especially good I'll even make whole salads of them (see page 145). Before adding raw onions to a dish, soak them in ice water for a few minutes to crisp and chill them—it also takes a bit of the bite out. Red and white onions can be easily quick-pickled and kept in the fridge for a couple of weeks: Just pour a hot, salty vinegar solution over them (and maybe some whole spices and a pinch of sugar), let cool, then refrigerate for a few hours before serving. Preserve onions or shallots by making them into refrigerator jams, cooking them down with sugar, vinegar, salt, and maybe some thyme until they can be spread on crusty bread and topped with a slice of aged cheddar. Or cook loads of them for hours in the slow cooker until they're like velvet, and freeze them to use as a base for deeply flavorful soups.

Find leeks in farmers' markets as they're harvested in the cool months, or even sometimes in Asian grocery stores, and they'll be less expensive than in regular supermarkets. To save space in your refrigerator, where they'll keep for a couple of weeks, cut off the tops (put the tops in the freezer to use in stock) and keep the light green and white bottoms in a plastic bag in the crisper drawer.

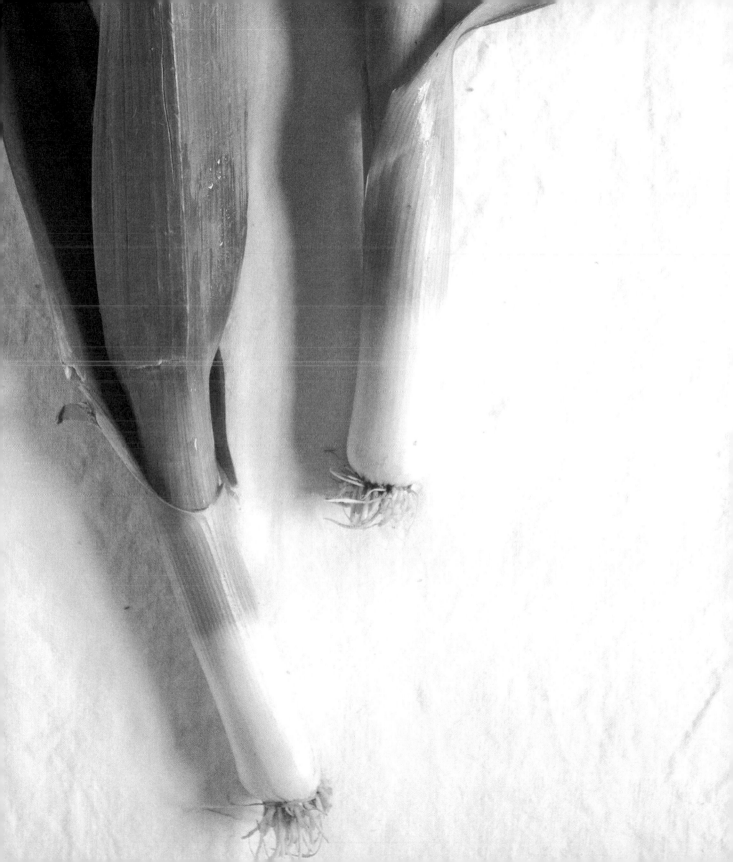

Leek and Mushroom Broth with a Little Egg Salad

SERVES 4 OR 5 AS A MEAL

This is a much-simplified version of a beautiful, fancy salmon dish in one of my most-used cookbooks (actually, my mom owns the book, and I often call her up and ask her to dictate recipes from it because it's out of print and I don't have a copy): Linda Dannenberg's *Fresh Herb Cooking*. If you're looking for an opportunity to use your best vegetable stock (page 262), this is it. Sliced tender leeks, good mushrooms of any kind (in spring, morels would be well showcased here), and squares of sweet pepper crowd the light, flavorful broth topped with a loose and herby egg salad. Served in small bowls, it'd make a fine appetizer for six to eight people.

1 ¼ pounds (565 g) leeks (about 6 medium)

6 cups (1.4 L) vegetable stock

8 ounces (225 g) mixed shiitake and cremini mushrooms, or any nice mushrooms

2 tablespoons olive oil

1 red bell pepper, stemmed, seeded, and cut into ½-inch (12-mm) pieces

Salt and freshly ground black pepper

2 hard-cooked eggs, peeled

2 teaspoons fresh lime juice

1 tablespoon chopped fresh dill

2 teaspoons minced fresh chives

2 tablespoons mayonnaise or aioli (page 251)

Cut the tops off the leeks, rinse the tops well under cold running water, coarsely chop them, and put them in a medium saucepan. Add the stock and bring it to a boil, then lower the heat and simmer gently as you prepare the vegetables, 10 to 20 minutes.

Cut off and discard the roots of the leeks, leaving about 4 inches (10 cm) of white and light green. Cut each leek in half lengthwise and rinse them well under cold running water, separating the layers a little with your thumbs to make sure you get any sand out from between them. Cut the leeks crosswise into ¼-inch (6-mm) slices. Cut off the stems of the shiitake mushrooms (trimming them if they're dirty) and put them in the simmering stock. Cut the shiitake and cremini mushroom caps into quarters if large, halves if smaller, and reserve.

In a Dutch oven, heat the oil over medium-high heat. Add the sliced leeks, mushrooms, bell pepper, a pinch of salt, and a grinding of black pepper and cook, stirring frequently, until the leeks are just starting to brown at the edges, about 5 minutes. Hold a very-fine-mesh sieve (or a regular sieve lined with two layers of rinsed and squeezed cheesecloth) over the pot and strain the leek and mushroom stock; discard the solids. Bring the mixture to a boil, then lower the heat and simmer until the mushrooms and bell pepper are tender, 3 to 5 minutes.

Meanwhile, coarsely grate the eggs into a small bowl and stir in the lime juice, dill, chives, and mayonnaise. Taste and season with salt and black pepper, if needed.

Taste and season the broth with salt and black pepper, if needed. Ladle it into wide serving bowls, top each with a spoonful of the egg salad, and serve immediately.

Olive Oil-Braised Leeks and Chard

SERVES 2 TO 4

CAN BE VEGAN

Leeks and chard are quickly braised in an oil-enriched light tomato sauce until silken and tender, then tossed with feta and dill to make a dish that's surprisingly substantial for having so few ingredients. Serve it with Spiced Brown Rice (page 219) or simply stewed lentils (see page 225). Feel free to leave out the feta for a less intrusive side dish. For the crushed tomatoes, you can also just coarsely grate a halved small tomato into the pan, discarding the skins and core when they reach the grater holes.

½ pound (225 g) leeks (about 2 large)

1 bunch (162 g) Swiss chard

3 tablespoons olive oil

Salt and freshly ground black pepper

¼ cup (60 ml) crushed tomatoes

⅓ cup (50 g) crumbled feta cheese (optional)

2 tablespoons chopped fresh dill, plus more for garnish

Cut off and discard the tops and roots of the leeks, leaving about 4 inches (10 cm) of white and light green. Cut each in half lengthwise and rinse them well under cold running water, separating the layers a little with your thumbs to make sure you get any sand out from between them. Cut the leeks crosswise into ¼-inch (6-mm) slices. Gather the chard leaves together and cut the stems into ½-inch (12-mm) pieces; roughly chop the leaves, keeping separate from the stems.

In a large sauté pan, heat the oil over medium-high heat. When it shimmers, add the leeks, chard stems, a pinch of salt, and a grinding of pepper and cook, stirring frequently, until the leeks are just starting to brown at the edges, 4 to 5 minutes. Add the chard leaves, ½ cup (120 ml) water, and the tomatoes and cook, stirring frequently, until the chard stems and leeks are very tender and most of the liquid has evaporated, 8 to 10 minutes. Season lightly with salt and pepper. Remove from the heat and gently stir in the feta and dill.
Serve hot.

Hot Potato, Leek, and Thyme Soup

SERVES 4 TO 6 AS A MEAL

VEGAN

Many years ago, when an acquaintance of mine told me that leeks were her favorite vegetable, I couldn't imagine such a thing. I thought maybe it was because she was from England and didn't know any better vegetables. (Do they have sweet corn in England?) Aren't leeks just very expensive scallions or onions? Well, no. I've finally realized that the leek is a vegetable entirely worthy of adoration. There's nothing that can replace them in this classic potato and leek soup, where their fragrance and green flavor play off the creaminess of the potatoes.

1¼ pounds (565 g) leeks (about 6 medium)

2 tablespoons olive oil

4 shallots, thinly sliced

Salt and freshly ground black pepper

3 russet potatoes (about 2 pounds/910 g), peeled and chopped

3 cups (720 ml) vegetable stock

2 teaspoons fresh thyme leaves

Cut off and discard the roots and dark green tops of the leeks, leaving about 4 inches (10 cm) of white and pale green. Cut the leeks in half lengthwise and rinse them well under cold running water, spreading the layers apart with your thumbs to get any sand out from between them. Cut the leeks crosswise into ¼-inch (6-mm) slices.

In a Dutch oven or large saucepan, heat the oil over medium heat until it shimmers. Add the leeks and shallots and a pinch of salt. Cook, stirring frequently, until tender and translucent, about 10 minutes. Add the potatoes, stock, thyme, and 2 cups (480 ml) water and raise the heat to high. Bring to a boil, then lower the heat and simmer until the potatoes are very tender, 25 to 30 minutes.

Working in batches, puree the soup in a blender, venting the lid and covering it with a towel to avoid splattering; be careful not to overfill the jar. (Alternatively, use an immersion blender to puree the soup right in the pot.) Return the soup to the pot and set it over medium heat to just heat through, adding a little more water, if necessary, to thin it to a thick but soupy consistency. Season with salt and pepper and serve hot.

Roasted Shallot Salad

SERVES 4 TO 6

VEGAN

I went through a phase when I was reading a lot about Turkish food and cooking plenty of it. It seems my main takeaways were in the allium-as-main-ingredient arena, as evinced by this shallot salad and the sweet onion and apple salad on page 146.

1 pound (455 g) shallots (see Note)

3 tablespoons olive oil

Salt and freshly ground black pepper

2 tablespoons fresh lemon juice

½ teaspoon Aleppo pepper

¼ teaspoon sumac

1 tablespoon minced fresh flat-leaf parsley

Preheat the oven to 400°F (205°C).

Leave gumball-size shallots whole; halve jawbreaker-size ones; quarter any that are larger. Spread them in a single layer on a rimmed baking sheet and drizzle with 1 tablespoon of the oil. Sprinkle them with salt and a few grindings of black pepper and toss to coat. Roast, shaking the pan once or twice during the cooking time, until tender and nicely browned, about 30 minutes. Let the shallots cool on the pan while you make the dressing.

In a large bowl, whisk together the lemon juice, Aleppo pepper, sumac, and ½ teaspoon salt. Add the remaining 2 tablespoons oil in a thin stream, whisking to emulsify.

Add the roasted shallots to the bowl with the dressing and toss to coat. Taste and season with more salt and pepper, if needed—it should be nice and flavorful. Sprinkle with the parsley and serve warm or at room temperature. Store leftovers in the refrigerator for up to 1 week.

Note: Peeling shallots is, hands down, my least favorite kitchen task (they're small and fussy, with thin, stubborn peels), and it galls me all the more because I can't quit shallots—I enjoy them too much. When you have to peel a lot of them, as here, do yourself a favor: Put a kettle of water on to boil and put the shallots in a heatproof bowl. Pour the boiling water over them and let stand for 30 seconds or so, then drain them in a colander and rinse under cold running water. To peel a small one you want to leave whole, slice off the ends, then score the top layer of peel and use the slit as leverage to slip off the outer peel. It's much easier (and the teary-eye effect much lessened) when the outer layer has been softened in the water. For larger ones you're going to halve or quarter anyway, just trim the ends and then cut them in half and peel.

Sweet Onion and Apple Side Salad with Sumac

SERVES 4

VEGAN

Shaved onions with lemon and sumac is a Turkish thing, a bracing salad often served with kebabs, but as I was making this variation on the classic dish here in Lincoln I realized that it happened to have a decidedly Southern aspect. I can easily imagine a home cook in Georgia slicing up some sweet onions and "mountain apples" (as some Georgians call the good crisp apples from North Carolina) and sprinkling them with the sour dried and ground berries of *Rhus glabra*, the common roadside sumac once used to make false lemonade in the absence of actual lemons—the ripe berries are coated with a fine white powder: ascorbic acid, or vitamin C! If you're not the foraging sort, you can find ground sumac, always mixed with some salt to keep it from clumping, in Middle Eastern grocery stores and online—Penzeys' sumac is excellent. Look for Maui or Walla Walla onions in early fall, or Vidalia or Texas Sweet in spring and summer.

Try this refreshing salad as an accompaniment to baked rice balls (stir an egg, some hard cheese, and some oat flour into leftover cold risotto, form into balls, and bake until crisp and nicely browned) or any grilled vegetables, or in sandwiches.

1 large sweet onion

1 crisp sweet apple, such as Winesap or Gala

2 tablespoons fresh lemon juice

Salt and freshly ground black pepper

¼ teaspoon ground sumac, plus more for garnish

2 tender sprigs fresh mint

Cut the top and root ends off the onion and cut it in half vertically. Cut each half crosswise into paper-thin slices. Cut the apple into quarters, cut out the core, and cut each quarter crosswise into paper-thin slices. Put the onion and apple in a large bowl and add the lemon juice, ½ teaspoon salt, a couple grindings of peppers, and the sumac and toss well. Cover and refrigerate until chilled, about 30 minutes.

Tear the mint into the bowl, sprinkle with a couple more pinches of salt and sumac, and maybe another grinding of pepper, and serve cold.

greens

This section may well constitute the heart of this book, and I really had to be strict and curatorial in choosing greens recipes to include. Sturdy greens like kale, collards, beet and bitter turnip tops, and spicy mustard greens, as well as tender cool-season greens like spinach and chard—I truly love them all. And I use them constantly, tossing them into hash, stir-fries, and rice noodle dishes, stuffing them into tacos, enchiladas, and omelets, pureeing them in soups, and of course serving them as salads—rubbing the sturdier ones like collards and kale with salt to tenderize them first.

Lacking a green vegetable for supper, I'll often simply cook a pile of greens the way I learned to cook them at the restaurant where I worked after college. First, olive oil and garlic went on the hot griddle over the broiler station. Then spinach, escarole, collards, even romaine when we ran out of the others, were thrown on top and sprinkled with a giant pinch of salt and pepper. The leaves would sear and stick to the griddle, and I'd scrape at them with tongs and toss them around just until they wilted. I'd taste, season again, and pinch them all up and onto a plate hot from the dishwasher. Diners would tell us our greens were the best they'd ever had, and they were right, or at least they were the best I'd ever had too. I can't get the same kind of heat in the pans on my burners at home, but Derek and Thalia seem very happy with the results.

Grilled Coconut Collards

SERVES 4

VEGAN

With friends and family scattered all over, Derek and I haven't been to a whole lot of weddings. But we made darn sure we got to his college friend Eve's shindig in her adopted hometown of New Orleans. Eve is passionate about eating locally and responsibly, and when we got into town we spent an early evening sitting in the big, lush, and slightly crazy garden she shares with the neighbors, talking about, among other things, food systems and the ethics of what we eat. In the sultry fall twilight I came to no real personal conclusions that I remember except that the mulberries Thalia was eating straight off the trees were amazing, and so were the drinks in our glasses, and that as long as we're doing the best we can to be fair and enjoying ourselves at the table we're probably making the right choices.

As you might imagine of a backyard wedding in New Orleans, there was a lot of music and a hell of a lot of food—extremely fresh, most of it hyperlocal, and clearly cooked by people who know their way around a grill. The Gulf shrimp were outstanding, and I wasn't surprised by that. I was stunned, though, when big platters of oversize collard leaves, flat and ridiculous like palm-leaf fans in an old cartoon, were set down on our dinner table. They were flavored with little more than salt and oil and were grilled to a crisp, almost like smoky kale chips. They were unwieldy and awkward and absolutely delightful.

I vowed to grill collard greens at home, but the size of the leaves and the size of my home grill made it seem too time consuming and costly. It wasn't until three long years later that I hit on the idea of rolling them up and skewering the rolls to conserve precious grill space.

⅔ cup (165 ml) can unsweetened coconut milk

2 tablespoons fresh lemon juice

1 tablespoon tamari

1 tablespoon vegetable oil

¾ teaspoon ground coriander

½ teaspoon ground cumin

½ teaspoon hot paprika

¼ teaspoon turmeric

Salt and freshly ground black pepper

1 bunch (about ¾ pound/340 g) young collard greens

Prepare a medium-hot charcoal fire. Soak 8 bamboo skewers in water for 30 minutes.

In a wide, shallow dish (a baking dish works well), stir together the coconut milk, lemon juice, tamari, oil, coriander, cumin, paprika, turmeric, ½ teaspoon salt, and a few grindings of pepper.

Cut the collard leaves in half lengthwise and slice out the tough center rib. Working from the top, roll up each leaf half into a loose cigar shape and skewer it with two skewers—one at each end. Load 4 or 5 leaf rolls onto each set of skewers. Dip the skewered collards into the coconut milk mixture and turn to coat as completely as possible. Reserve the remaining coconut milk mixture.

Grill, turning once or twice with tongs, until the collards are browned in spots and tender, 8 to 10 minutes; try to keep them on the grill as long as possible before they brown, moving them to cooler parts of the grill if they brown too quickly and covering with the grill lid to prevent flare-ups. Transfer the collards to a serving platter and drizzle with the reserved coconut milk mixture. Serve hot.

Collard Greens Tart with Instant Almond Crust

SERVES 6

This recipe is based on one by Mario Batali for Swiss chard pasticcio, and despite changes I've made due to various exigencies of time and availability—more or less of this or that, different cheeses, different oven temperatures and cooking times—it never fails. I make it with whatever greens are looking good (so far collards have been my favorite in this dish), and it's become a true workhorse that my family can expect to enjoy at least a couple of times a month in the fall and winter.

The crust is not really a crust: All you do is oil the baking dish, sprinkle in some grated cheese and almond flour, and then spoon in the greens and egg mixture. As it bakes, the bottom darkens and firms up into something *resembling* a crust.

2 tablespoons olive oil

1 onion, diced

Salt and freshly ground black pepper

¾ pound (340 g) collard greens, thick stems removed, leaves chopped

¼ cup (25 g) almond flour

3 ounces (85 g) semifirm cheese, such as Gruyère, aged Gouda, or Asiago, grated

4 large eggs

½ cup (20 g) chopped fresh flat-leaf parsley or other herbs

In a large, deep sauté pan, heat 1 tablespoon of the oil over medium-high heat. Add the onion and a pinch of salt and cook, stirring frequently, until translucent, 5 to 7 minutes. Add the collards and 1 cup (240 ml) water. Cover the pan and cook for 5 minutes, lifting the lid once to turn the collards over with a spatula or tongs so they cook evenly. Uncover the pan and cook, stirring occasionally, until the thicker ribs of the collards are tender and most of the water has evaporated, 8 to 10 minutes. Season lightly with salt and pepper. Pour off any excess water and set aside to cool.

Preheat the oven to 350°F (175°C).

Put the remaining 1 tablespoon oil in a 7-by-10-inch (17.5-by-25-cm) baking dish (ideally glass) and rub it all over the bottom and up the sides. Sprinkle the almond flour and one-third of the cheese evenly in the bottom of the baking dish.

In a large bowl, using a fork, whisk together the eggs, parsley, ½ teaspoon salt, several grindings of pepper, and half of the remaining cheese. When the collard mixture has cooled to near room temperature, stir it into the egg mixture. Use the fork to carefully transfer the collard mixture, a little bit at a time, to the prepared baking dish, being sure not to disrupt the almond flour and cheese on the bottom, as they will form the crust. Gently pat down the collards into an even layer, then sprinkle the remaining cheese evenly on top. Bake until the edges are sizzling, the center is firm, and, if you used a glass baking dish and can see the bottom, the crust is browned, 45 to 50 minutes. Let stand for 10 minutes, then cut into squares and serve warm.

Pan-Fried Tofu and Garlic Collard Greens with Tamari and Nutritional Yeast

SERVES 2

VEGAN

Tofu dredged in nutritional yeast and pan-fried is an old-school staple of vegetarian cooking, but I never really appreciated the concept until I tasted the dish at a party in Athens: tiny nubbins of tofu coated with nutritional yeast and intensely seasoned with soy sauce. The concentrated burst of salty umami was something I hadn't experienced in a tofu dish before, and it stuck with me. Here, small cubes of brown-crusted tofu nestle in shredded collard greens, which get a quick sauté, just till they're barely tender and have turned bright green.

1 (15-ounce/425-g) block firm or extra-firm tofu, drained, patted dry, and cut into ¾-inch (12-mm) cubes

2 ½ tablespoons vegetable oil

About 1 tablespoon powdered nutritional yeast (see Note)

1 bunch collard greens, tough stems and ribs removed

3 cloves garlic, minced

About 1 tablespoon tamari

In a large sauté pan, heat 2 tablespoons of the oil over medium-high heat until it shimmers. Add the tofu in a single layer (do this in two batches if your pan isn't big enough) and cook, undisturbed, for about 2 minutes. Use a metal spatula to turn the cubes, which should be golden brown on the bottom, and continue to cook, turning occasionally, until most of the surfaces of the tofu are deeply browned and crisp, 8 to 10 minutes total. Sprinkle with half of the nutritional yeast and toss to coat the cubes well. Transfer the tofu to a plate and wipe out the pan.

Stack the collard leaves and cut them in half lengthwise, then crosswise into ¼- to ½-inch-wide (6- to 12-mm-wide) ribbons.

Return the pan to medium-high heat and add the remaining ½ tablespoon oil and the garlic. Cook, stirring, until the garlic is golden, about 1 minute. Add the collards and cook, stirring frequently, until just tender, 4 to 8 minutes, depending on how old the greens were. Add the tamari and the remaining nutritional yeast and stir well. Taste and season with more tamari and nutritional yeast, if needed. Return the tofu to the pan and toss to combine it with the collards; cook until heated through, about 2 minutes. Serve hot.

Note: Nutritional yeast, which is an inactive yeast grown on sugarcane, is not the same as brewer's yeast or the active dry yeast you'd use to make bread. Look for it in natural foods stores, sometimes in the bulk bins, and with the other yeasts in supermarkets. Check the label if you're strictly vegan, as some brands are made with whey. Nutritional yeast is available in flakes or as a finer powder, and either will work fine here. If using flakes, double or triple the quantity.

Salt-Wilted Kale with Chile and Sesame

SERVES 3 OR 4

This is a virtuous salad, it's true, but also a completely satisfying one—it has quite a bit more substance than most lettuce salads. Rubbing coarse salt into the kale leaves draws some of their water out, wilting and tenderizing them enough to be eaten—nay, *enjoyed*—raw. It may seem like a lot of salt and chile, but you want an intense hit of flavor with every bite; if you like, add them a little at a time as you taste.

Instead of the kale, you can also use mixed baby winter greens (kale, tatsoi, arugula, red mustard, mizuna, etc.), in which case you don't even have to bother slicing them.

2 bunches (about 1¼ pound/565 g) kale, preferably a flat-leaf variety

1 carrot (optional)

Salt

1 teaspoon grated ginger

1 clove garlic, grated

1 tablespoon sesame seeds, toasted

1 to 1½ teaspoons hot red pepper flakes

1 teaspoon sesame oil

1 lemon

Pull or cut out the kale's tough center ribs. Wash the leaves and spin them dry. Stack a handful at a time together on a cutting board and slice into ¼- to ⅛-inch-wide (6- to 3-mm-wide) strips. Put the kale in a large bowl. Shave the carrot, if using, with a vegetable peeler, stack the shavings, then thinly slice them into slivers and add them to the kale. Sprinkle the kale and carrot with 1 teaspoon salt and rub it into the kale with your hands for a couple of minutes, until it's uniformly wilted and wet.

Add the ginger, garlic, sesame seeds, red pepper flakes, and sesame oil. Cut the lemon in half and squeeze in most of the juice. Toss well. Taste and add more red pepper flakes or lemon juice, if needed. Serve. Leftovers will keep in an airtight container in the refrigerator for 1 day, but the kale will soften a bit more and you might have to add a little more salt and lemon juice to revive the flavors.

Variations

Omit the carrot, ginger, and sesame seeds. Instead of shredding the kale, just tear it into bite-size pieces. Replace the sesame oil with 2 tablespoons olive oil. Finish with ¼ cup coarsely grated Parmesan (Don't skimp: You're eating *raw kale*—you deserve as much Parmesan as you want).

Omit the carrot, ginger, sesame seeds, and oil. Instead of shredding the kale, just tear it into bite-size pieces. Use a lime instead of the lemon and add a pinch of ground toasted cumin seeds. Pit, peel, and roughly dice 2 ripe Hass avocados and fold them into the kale. Add a minced seeded fresh jalapeño or serrano chile, if you like, and sprinkle with toasted pepitas and/or oven-crisped corn tortilla pieces (for that matter, this salad is also excellent just rolled up in soft warm corn tortillas).

Curly Kale Pakora

SERVES 4 TO 6

VEGAN

I wouldn't suggest you deep-fry something unless it was really worth it. This kale—lacy and crisp in a light chickpea-flour batter flavored simply with garam masala—is worth it. My husband, Derek, who is not, let's say, part of kale's natural audience, was delighted by the lightness of these *pakora*, which in other renditions can be dense and soggy. Some leaves will remain covered with the thin batter as they fry, some will bare their surface to the hot oil, but every piece will be delicious. (See photo on page 172.)

½ bunch (about 5 ounces/140 g) curly kale (red looks especially nice), tough stems and center ribs removed, leaves chopped

1½ cups (180 g) chickpea flour (*besan*)

1 teaspoon garam masala

1 teaspoon salt

1 tablespoon vegetable oil, plus more for deep-frying

Juice of ½ lemon

Apricot-Tamarind Chutney and Cilantro Mint Chutney (page 000; optional)

Rinse the kale and spin it dry in a salad spinner to extract all the excess water.

Sift the chickpea flour, garam masala, and salt together onto a piece of waxed paper, then transfer to a blender. Add the oil and lemon juice, pulse the blender a few times, then add 1 cup (240 ml) water and blend until very smooth. (You can do this in a bowl with a whisk, but it'll take some time and effort to get all the lumps out manually.) Set aside to rest at room temperature for 10 to 20 minutes (this allows time for the flour to absorb the water), then blend again. The batter should be about the consistency of buttermilk; blend in a little more water if necessary to achieve the desired consistency. Pour the batter into a large bowl.

Line a baking sheet with a paper towel and set a cooling rack upside down on top so the wire rungs are in contact with the paper. In a large, heavy pot or Dutch oven, heat at least 1 ½ inches (4 cm) of oil until it registers about 375°F (190°C) on a candy/deep-frying thermometer.

Put a couple of handfuls of kale in the batter and stir to coat well. When the oil is hot, use tongs to lift a small bunch of the leaves from the batter, letting excess batter drip back into the bowl for a moment, then carefully put the mass of battered leaves in the oil—stand back, as it will spatter a bit. Repeat with a few more bunches of leaves; don't overcrowd the oil. Cook, turning occasionally with a slotted spoon, until nicely browned and crisp, 1½ to 2 minutes; the oil should stay around 350°F (175°C) as the *pakoras* cook. Transfer the cooked *pakoras* to the wire rack to drain. Allow the oil to come back up to 375°F (190°C) and repeat with the remaining kale and batter. Stop making *pakoras* when there is not enough batter to coat the kale thickly—poorly coated kale *pakoras* tend to spatter much more, and absorb more oil.

Serve immediately with the chutneys alongside, if desired, or keep at room temperature up to several hours. You can reheat the *pakoras* on a wire rack set on a baking sheet in a 300°F (150°C) oven, or serve them at room temperature.

Red Coconut Curry Kale

SERVES 2 TO 4

VEGAN

This creamy, bold-flavored braised kale using super-convenient frozen curry concentrate (you can take it straight from freezer to pan) makes a substantial addition to a vegetable plate—try it with rice or another grain, grilled or roasted eggplant, and a baked sweet potato. If you'd like it to be saucy, to serve on its own over a grain or with noodles, perhaps, use a little more coconut milk and add a bit more curry concentrate.

1 tablespoon vegetable oil

2 shallots, thinly sliced

Salt

1/2 cup (120 ml) Red Coconut Curry Sauce Concentrate (page 261), frozen or thawed

1 large bunch kale (about 14 ounces/400 g), tough stems removed, leaves cut into 1-inch (2.5-cm) pieces

2/3 cup (165 ml) can unsweetened coconut milk

Lime wedges

In a large sauté pan, heat the oil over medium-high heat until it shimmers. Add the shallots and a pinch of salt and cook, stirring frequently, until very well browned, about 2 minutes. Add the curry sauce concentrate and stir for 1 minute (or until it's thawed and boiling, if you start with frozen).

Add the kale, 1 cup (240 ml) water, and a generous pinch of salt and stir until the kale is evenly wilted. Cover and cook, stirring occasionally, for about 5 minutes. Stir in the coconut milk and cook, uncovered, until the sauce is fairly thick and the kale is tender. Taste and add more salt, if needed. Serve hot, with lime wedges for squeezing over it.

Maple-Cumin Kale with Buttered Garlic

SERVES 3 OR 4

The hint of sweetness from a half-drizzle of maple syrup, plus a knob of cream cheese, smoothes out the rough edges of bitter kale, making this a good dish to serve to those who might not be sure they like this green just yet.

2 tablespoons unsalted butter or ghee

6 cloves garlic, thinly sliced

1 teaspoon cumin seeds

2 coins peeled fresh ginger, minced

2 bunches kale (about 1 1/2 pounds/680 g), tough stems removed, leaves chopped

1 1/2 teaspoons maple syrup

2 tablespoons (1 ounce/28 g) cream cheese

Salt and freshly ground black pepper

Minced hot fresh green or red chiles (optional)

In a large, deep sauté pan, melt the butter over medium-high heat. Add the garlic and cook, stirring constantly with a slotted spoon, until golden brown and tender, about 2 minutes. Use the slotted spoon to remove the garlic and set it on a paper towel–lined plate to drain, leaving the butter in the pan.

Return the pan to medium-high heat and add the cumin and ginger. Cook, stirring, for 1 minute, then add the kale. Cook, turning the kale over constantly, until it is just wilted, about 2 minutes. Add 2 tablespoons water and continue to cook until the thicker ribs are just tender but still have a bit of crispness, about 5 minutes more; add a little more water if the pan is dry before the kale is tender. Stir in the syrup, cream cheese, and salt and pepper to taste and cook for about 1 minute more, until the cheese is melted and thoroughly incorporated into the greens. Spoon the kale into a serving bowl and top with the sautéed garlic and chiles to taste, if using. Serve hot.

Coconut Kale Chips

SERVES 1 OR 2

VEGAN

You know about kale chips, right? Kale roasted until the leaves are so crisp and delicate you could easily eat a whole bunch's worth in a single sitting? Of course you do—but have you tried them with coconut milk and curry powder? Or with a drop of sesame oil and a shower of sesame seeds? The possibilities are endless. If, by some freak accident, you have leftovers of either version, grind them up to make the Kale *Furikake* on page 247.

½ bunch (about 5 ounces/140 g) kale

¼ cup (60 ml) unsweetened coconut milk

½ teaspoon salt

1 ½ teaspoons unsweetened shredded coconut

¼ teaspoon Madras (hot) curry powder (optional)

Variation
Sesame kale chips: Replace the coconut milk, coconut, and curry powder with 1 tablespoon vegetable oil, a few dashes of sesame oil, and 1 teaspoon sesame seeds. Reduce the salt to ¼ teaspoon and the baking time to 15 to 20 minutes.

Preheat the oven to 350°F (175°C).

Cut out the tough center stems of the kale and tear the leaves into large pieces. In a large bowl, combine the leaves with the coconut milk and salt and toss with your hands to coat the leaves thoroughly. Spread the leaves in a single layer on a rimmed baking sheet, then sprinkle them evenly with the shredded coconut and curry powder, if using. Bake for 20 to 25 minutes, flipping the leaves halfway through the cooking time so they dry and crisp evenly. Turn off the oven and leave the kale in the oven for another 10 to 20 minutes to cool and crisp up. Serve within the day.

Lemony Kale and Apple Soup
with White Beans and Toasted Fennel Seeds

SERVES 4 AS A MEAL

VEGAN

My six-year-old, despite trending toward typical American kid tastes in recent months (in a school paper she wrote that her favorite food is Pop-Tarts even though she's *never eaten a Pop-Tart*), is a huge fan of this bright, citrusy soup. Adding apple to it was her idea, and it was a good one: The sweetness complements the toasty fennel seeds and bitter greens quite nicely.

1 lemon

About ½ cup (20 g) fresh flat-leaf parsley leaves

1 tablespoon olive oil

1 sweet onion, chopped

2 cloves garlic, smashed

Salt

1 sweet crisp apple, such as Winesap or Gala, cored and chopped

6 cups (1.4 L) vegetable stock, or half stock and half water

1 teaspoon fennel seeds, toasted and coarsely ground

1 bunch (10 ounces/285 g) kale, tough stems removed

2 cups (345 g) cooked and drained white beans (see page 226)

Freshly ground black pepper

Using a zester or vegetable peeler, remove the zest from the lemon and then finely mince it together with the parsley. Squeeze the lemon juice into a small bowl and pick out the seeds. Set the lemon zest–parsley mixture and the lemon juice aside.

In a Dutch oven or large saucepan, heat the oil over medium-high heat until it shimmers. Add the onion, garlic, and a pinch of salt. Cook, stirring frequently, until the onion is just starting to brown, about 8 minutes. Add the apple and cook until it just starts to soften and take on some color, about 5 minutes. Add the stock and half of the fennel, bring to a boil over high heat, then add the kale, pushing it down into the liquid as it wilts. Return the mixture to a simmer and cook until the kale is tender but still has some bite, 8 to 10 minutes. Add the reserved lemon juice, beans, and salt and pepper to taste. Heat through. Fish out and discard the garlic, if you'd like. Ladle the soup into bowls and top with the lemon zest–parsley mixture and a sprinkle of the remaining fennel. Serve hot.

Swiss Chard and Ricotta Frittata

SERVES 4

Of course any winter greens would be lovely here, but this frittata is an ideal vehicle for Swiss chard, with its thick stems that become tender with a bit of heat and give the frittata substance and heft. Serve with a green salad, or simply steamed or sautéed tender green beans, a white- or black-bean salad with sweet cherry tomatoes and basil, or just a hunk of good bread.

1 tablespoon olive oil, plus more for the pie plate

1 sweet onion, diced

Salt and freshly ground black pepper

8 ounces (225 g) Swiss chard, stems and leaves chopped

4 large eggs

¼ cup (170 g) best-quality ricotta, or half ricotta and half cream cheese

1 tablespoon chopped fresh basil

Preheat the oven to 400°F (205°C). Oil a 9- to 10-inch (22.5- to 25-cm) glass pie plate.

In a large sauté pan, heat the oil over medium-high heat until it shimmers. Add the onion, a pinch of salt, and a few grindings of pepper. Cook, stirring frequently, until translucent and nicely browned, about 8 minutes. Add the chard and ¼ cup (60 ml) water, cover, and cook for 2 minutes. Uncover and cook, stirring frequently so the chard cooks evenly, until the chard is tender and all the excess liquid has evaporated from the pan, 5 to 7 minutes. Spread the chard mixture evenly in the prepared pie plate.

In a medium bowl, whisk together the eggs, ricotta, basil, and ½ teaspoon salt. Pour the egg mixture over the chard and gently jostle the chard with a spatula so the egg mixture sinks down into it evenly. Bake until set in the center and light golden brown around the edges, about 25 minutes. Let stand for 5 minutes, then cut into wedges and serve warm.

Spinach Yogurt Soup

SERVES 2 TO 4

This is a sort of *kadhi*, the Indian tangy yogurt-based hot soup with mild spices. You can leave all the spices out, if you'd like, flavor it with a teaspoon or so of crushed dried mint, and sprinkle the finished soup with Aleppo pepper and ground sumac for a Turkish-style dish.

1 cup (240 ml) plain full-fat yogurt

¼ cup (30 g) chickpea flour (*besan*)

2 tablespoons dried fenugreek leaves (*kasoori methi*; optional)

¾ teaspoon turmeric

½ teaspoon sweet paprika

1 tablespoon unsalted butter

½ sweet onion, diced

1 clove garlic, minced

1 coin peeled fresh ginger, minced

½ teaspoon cumin seeds

Salt and freshly ground black pepper

¼ to ½ teaspoon hot red pepper flakes

4 packed cups (about 5 ounces/140 g) spinach, chopped

In a large bowl, whisk together the yogurt, chickpea flour, fenugreek, if using, turmeric, and paprika. Gradually whisk in 2 ½ cups (600 ml) water, whisking until smooth. Set aside.

In a large saucepan, melt the butter over medium heat. Add the onion, garlic, ginger, cumin, a pinch of salt, and a grinding of black pepper. Cook, stirring frequently, until the onion is tender and just starting to become golden, 6 to 8 minutes. Add the red pepper flakes and spinach and cook, stirring frequently, until the spinach is wilted and tender, 2 to 3 minutes.

Add the yogurt mixture to the spinach and cook over medium-low to medium heat, stirring occasionally, to slowly bring the soup to a simmer; do not let it boil. It will thicken somewhat as it nears a simmer; this could take 10 to 15 minutes. Keep the mixture at a bare simmer, stirring more frequently now, until the soup is slightly thick and the flavors have come together, 5 to 10 minutes. If you'd like, hit it with an immersion blender for a few seconds. Season generously with salt and black pepper. Serve hot.

Spinach and Raisin Enchiladas

SERVES 4 AS A MEAL

There's something about corn tortillas that to me signals comfort food, and the feeling is even more pronounced when they're covered in a toasty chile sauce and melted cheese. In these easy enchiladas, just a few main ingredients come together to make a truly satisfying and impressive Mexican-style meal. The bite of fresh spinach in the filling is tempered by sweet, plump raisins (dark and golden will both work). Serve the enchiladas with Black Beans with Epazote (page 226) and some long-grain brown rice tossed with minced fresh cilantro. Sprinkle the whole thing with some crumbled cotija or other aged Mexican cheese, and maybe offer a bowl of cold sliced radishes on the side for some palate-cleansing crunch.

The entire casserole is a perfect party dish to make ahead of time; consider, too, doubling the sauce and saving half of it in the freezer for the next time. If you want to use leftover cooked greens for the filling (chard or kale would work in place of spinach), you'll need about 1½ firmly packed cups (375 g) cooked greens; you'll only need to sauté the raisins and add them to the greens before filling the enchiladas. If you'd like, you can add a couple of fresh or canned tomatoes to the sauce for tartness, to stretch it a bit, and to make it slightly less intense.

FOR THE CHILE SAUCE

- 3 ounces (85 g) mixed dried mild and hot chiles (see Note)
- 1 tablespoon vegetable oil
- 1 onion, chopped
- Salt and freshly ground black pepper

FOR THE ENCHILADAS

- 1 tablespoon vegetable oil, or more if needed
- 3 tablespoons raisins
- 1 clove garlic, minced
- 10 ounces (285 g) stemmed mature or baby spinach
- Salt and freshly ground black pepper
- 8 or 9 corn tortillas
- 8 ounces (225 g) Monterey Jack cheese, grated
- 2 ounces (55 g) feta cheese, crumbled

continued

MAKE THE CHILE SAUCE

If the chiles are dusty, wipe them off with a damp cloth or paper towel. Break off and discard the stems, then tear or break the chiles into several pieces and shake out and discard as many of the seeds as you can.

In a large, deep sauté pan, heat the oil over medium-high heat until it shimmers. Add the onion and a pinch of salt and pepper and cook, stirring frequently, until softened and nicely browned, 5 to 7 minutes. Scrape the onion into a blender.

Wipe out the pan and return it to medium-high heat. Add the dried chiles and toast, pressing down on them with a metal spatula to flatten them onto the hot surface of the pan and turning frequently, until all are blackened in spots and fragrant, 2 to 4 minutes total. Carefully add 3½ cups (840 ml) water to the pan (it will splatter). Bring to a boil, then lower the heat and simmer for 20 minutes. Using a slotted spoon, transfer the chiles to the blender with the onion, then pour in the liquid from the sauté pan. Let cool for a bit before blending, venting the lid and covering with a towel to prevent splattering. Blend until very smooth, then blend some more. If you'd like, push the sauce through a sieve to remove any stray seeds or bits of chile skin (I don't usually do this, but it's a generous gesture if you're serving to company). The sauce should be thick but still pourable. Taste and season with salt and pepper. (The sauce can be kept in an airtight container in the refrigerator for up to 4 days, or frozen for up to 6 months.)

MAKE THE ENCHILADAS

Preheat the oven to 350°F (175°C).

In a large, deep sauté pan (you can use the chile pan, wiped out), heat the oil over medium-high heat until it shimmers. Add the raisins and cook, stirring constantly, until they're puffed and lightly browned, about 2 minutes. Using a slotted spoon, transfer the raisins to a medium bowl.

Set the pan back over medium-high heat and add a little oil if it looks dry. Add the garlic and stir for 1 minute. Add the spinach and a pinch of salt and pepper and cook, turning the spinach with tongs, until it is wilted and has released some of its liquid, 3 to 5 minutes. Transfer the spinach to the bowl with the raisins. Using tongs or a slotted spoon, press down on the spinach and tip the bowl to drain off any excess liquid. Taste and season with salt and pepper, if needed. Toss to incorporate the raisins.

Pour about ⅔ cup (160 ml) of the sauce into a 9-by-13-inch (22.5-by-23.5-cm) baking dish and spread it over the bottom. Gather the tortillas, cheeses, spinach mixture, and sauce. Reserve 1 cup (115 g) of the Monterey Jack for topping. Set a plate next to the stovetop.

Heat a clean sauté pan or skillet over medium-high heat. Put a tortilla in the pan and cook until pliable and starting to puff, 30 seconds or so per side. Transfer the tortilla to the plate and top it with a bit of the Monterey Jack and some of the spinach mixture. Roll up the tortilla and place it in the baking dish, seam side down. Repeat with the remaining tortillas, Monterey Jack, and filling, nestling the filled tortillas close together in the dish. If you have leftover spinach mixture, tuck it into the baking dish around the tortillas. Spoon sauce over the filled tortillas, spreading it to cover them evenly and completely; you may not need all of it. Spread the reserved Monterey Jack and the feta evenly on top. (At this point, you can cover the dish with aluminum foil and refrigerate for up to 4 hours before baking.)

Bake until the cheese on top is melted and the enchiladas are heated through and melty in the centers, about 25 minutes. (If the dish goes straight from the fridge to the oven, cook it covered in foil for the first 20 minutes, then uncover and bake until heated through and melty, about 15 minutes more.) Serve hot.

Note: I like the combination of three kinds of dried chiles in this sauce: about 8 guajillos for mild bulk, about 5 pasillas for a dark, winey undertone, and just 2 arbol chiles for heat.

squash

Though these cucurbits are characterized by their hard skins and excellent keeping properties (stored at room temperature under no special conditions, they'll usually last for weeks), some varieties need not be peeled: Dark green kabocha and long yellow-and-green-striped delicata squash, for example, have perfectly edible peels that soften nicely when cooked. These are the ones I most often turn to, because I'm incredibly lazy and if given the choice between the blush-colored butternut, which is lovely but must be peeled, and a kabocha, which is ready to go, I'll go with the latter pretty much every time. When I'm feeling more capable, though, I'll gladly attack a butternut or one of the other more challenging varieties—sugar (or pie) pumpkin (not the kind used for jack-o'-lanterns, which are grown for size and not for the quality of their flesh), acorn squash, the giant Hubbard—with a peeler and my heavy chef's knife. Note that some squash seeds are good for roasting, especially pumpkin and butternut squash: Scoop them into a colander and rinse well, removing all the stringy squash bits, then pat as dry as possible with a paper towel. Toss with a drizzle of olive or nut oil, a good pinch of salt, and whatever spices smell interesting to you, then spread them on a baking sheet in a single layer and roast at 400°F (205°C), stirring once or twice, until golden and crunchy, 10 to 15 minutes.

Basic Roasted Butternut Squash Soup

SERVES 2 OR 3

> CAN BE VEGAN

Everyone needs an easy winter squash soup in their back pocket (figuratively), and this is mine. You should definitely try the variations and suggestions for simple toppings, which in my opinion are the reason for this soup's existence. It's basic in the purest sense, in that it's a reliable base upon which dozens of other interesting dishes can be built.

1 medium-large butternut squash (about 1 pound/455 g), well scrubbed

1 tablespoon olive oil, plus a little more

Salt and freshly ground black pepper

About 2½ cups (600 ml) vegetable stock

¼ teaspoon hot paprika, or ⅛ teaspoon ground cayenne

⅓ cup (80 ml) buttermilk or heavy cream (optional)

Preheat the oven to 400°F (205°C).

Peel the squash and cut off the stem. If your peelings are very thin and wispy, reserve them. Separate the long neck from the bulb-shaped part, then cut each part in half lengthwise. Scrape out the seeds, rinse them in a colander, discard the pulp around them, and pat dry. Chop the squash into 1-inch (2.5-cm) chunks and put them in a single layer on a baking sheet. Drizzle with the oil and sprinkle with salt and pepper. Toss to coat. Toss the seeds and peelings, if using, with a little additional oil, salt, and pepper, and put them on a separate baking sheet. Roast the seeds and peelings until crisp and golden, 5 to 10 minutes, tossing halfway through the cooking. Roast the squash, shaking the pan once or twice while cooking, until tender and starting to turn golden in spots, about 40 minutes.

Transfer the squash to a blender, add the stock and paprika, and puree until very smooth. If you'd like, blend in the buttermilk. Taste and add salt and pepper as needed. If you prefer a thinner soup, add stock or water to achieve the desired consistency. Pour the soup into a saucepan. (If you want an extra-smooth soup, push it through a mesh sieve when you transfer it from the blender to the saucepan.) Set the pan over medium-low heat, and cook, stirring frequently with a heat-proof spatula, until steaming but not boiling. Serve topped with the roasted seeds and peelings, if you haven't already eaten them.

Variations

Add ¼ cup (30 g) masa harina or 1 soaked and drained corn tortilla, a squeeze of lime juice, and ½ teaspoon ground cumin and puree them with the soup in the blender. Garnish with a drizzle of Mexican crema or whisked sour cream, torn cilantro, and maybe some fried corn tortilla strips, too.

Coarsely chop some Roasted Shallot Salad (page 145) and toasted walnuts together and put a heaping table-spoonful in the center of each serving.

Put a dollop of plain Greek yogurt in the center of each serving. Sprinkle in a few drops of toasted walnut oil and a pinch each of Aleppo pepper and sumac.

Add a squeeze of lemon juice and ⅓ teaspoon grated fresh ginger to the blender. Sprinkle each serving with a pinch of chaat masala (a spice mix for chaat; page 109), chopped fresh cilantro, and a little pile of crunchy-crisp *sev*—the chickpea-flour chaat toppings you can find in the snack aisle of Indian grocery stores.

Use half sweet potato and half butternut squash and garnish with a crumble of goat cheese, a drizzle of extra-virgin olive oil, and a few spicy candied pecans.

Pile a few chunks of Perfectly Sautéed Zucchini with Cracked Coriander Seeds and Mint (page 51) in the center of the bowl and drizzle the whole thing with very good olive oil.

Halloween Stew
(Butternut Squash and Black Bean Stew)

SERVES 4 TO 6 AS A MEAL

VEGAN

My friend Marisa Bulzone sent out a recipe for an African-spiced stew with sugar pumpkin and black beans in her weekly newsletter about local foods, *150ish*. Marisa says her recipe was based on one published on a healthy-eating blog by Kathy Nichols, who writes that *her* recipe came from one by Renee Kiff, of the *Healdsburg Tribune* (California), which neither Marisa nor I have been able to track down. In any case, its spirit lives on, sort of. My adulterated version of it—simplifying and changing the spice profile a little, and using any winter squash but pumpkin—has become a favorite in our house for its sweet spiciness (me), Halloween color scheme (Thalia), and chunky texture (my husband loves this stew, but probably wouldn't if it were more souplike).

The hearty stew is great just on its own, but Marisa suggests serving it with crushed roasted peanuts or toasted pine nuts and couscous—quinoa (page 228) or polenta (page 206 or 224) would be fine accompaniments too.

1 large butternut squash (about 2 pounds/910 g)

1 tablespoon olive oil

1 onion, diced

2 fresh hot green or red chiles (optional)

1 clove garlic, minced

½ teaspoon ground cumin

½ teaspoon ground cinnamon

¼ teaspoon ground cayenne

Salt

1 (15- to 19-ounce/425- to 540-g) can black beans, drained and rinsed

1 packed teaspoon finely grated orange zest

Peel the squash and cut off the stem. Separate the long neck from the bulb-shaped part, then cut each part in half lengthwise. Scrape out the seeds (reserve them for roasting, if you'd like; see page 164). Chop the squash into ½-inch (12-mm) pieces.

In a Dutch oven or large saucepan, heat the oil over medium heat until it shimmers. Add the onion and cook, stirring, until softened and translucent, about 8 minutes. Add the chiles, if using, the garlic, cumin, cinnamon, and cayenne and stir for 1 minute. Add the squash, 2 cups (480 ml) water, and 1¾ teaspoons salt. Raise the heat to high and bring the mixture to a boil, then lower the heat and simmer, stirring occasionally, until the squash is tender and beginning to break apart, 15 to 20 minutes. Add a little more water if necessary; the stew should have a little liquid but not be too soupy.

Gently stir in the beans and orange zest, cook for about 5 minutes to heat through, and serve hot.

Delicata Squash Soup with Herbs and Lemongrass

SERVES 2 OR 3

This is one of my favorite soups: a spicy, sour, salty broth—and creamy if you add the coconut milk—with chunks of sweet, dense delicata squash and tart pieces of tomato that burst with flavor as you eat them. Pour the broth over trembling cubes of soft silken tofu to make it a completely satisfying meal.

2 hot fresh chiles, such as serrano, jalapeño, or Thai

2 Kaffir lime leaves

1 stalk lemongrass

4 cups (1 L) vegetable stock

1 delicata squash

1 teaspoon agave nectar, or to taste

Salt

2 tablespoons fresh lime juice, or to taste

1 small (5.6-ounce/165-ml) can or ½ (13- to 15-ounce/ 385- to 445-ml) can unsweetened coconut milk (optional)

2 or 3 large sprigs fresh basil

2 or 3 large sprigs fresh mint

½ dry pint (5 ounces/140 g) grape tomatoes, halved, or 1 cup (180 g) diced tomato

6 ounces (170 g) soft silken tofu, gently cut into small cubes (optional)

Slit 1 of the chiles in half from the bottom, keeping the stem end intact. Tear the lime leaves in a few places, keeping them whole. Cut the top two-thirds of the lemongrass stalk off and trim the bottom. Bruise the lemongrass with the bottom of a large saucepan but keep the stalk whole. In a saucepan, combine the slit chile, lime leaves, lemongrass, and stock and bring to a boil. Lower the heat and simmer for 10 minutes.

Meanwhile, trim and cut the squash in half lengthwise and scrape out the seeds (you can rinse, dry, oil, and roast these like butternut squash or pumpkin seeds; see page 164). Cut each half in half lengthwise, then crosswise into ¼-inch (6-mm) slices.

Remove and discard the chile, lime leaves, and lemongrass from the saucepan. To the simmering stock, add the squash, agave nectar, and 1 teaspoon salt. Bring to a boil over high heat, then lower the heat and simmer until the squash is tender, about 10 minutes. Stir in the lime juice and coconut milk, if using. Taste and add more salt and/or agave nectar, if needed. Bring just to a simmer.

Thinly slice the remaining chile. Put a few chile slices, a basil and a mint sprig, a handful of the tomatoes, and some tofu cubes, if using, in each serving bowl. Ladle in the hot broth and squash and serve.

Herb Custard-Filled Acorn Squash

SERVES 2 TO 4

Cute little acorn squash halves make ideal single-serving-size vessels for a quivering custard that separates as it bakes into a smooth bottom layer and an herby, cheesy top crust. With a simple green salad or a pile of roasted Brussels sprouts, you've got a meal.

1 acorn squash

Salt and freshly ground black pepper

2 large eggs

1 tablespoon grated Parmesan cheese

¼ cup (60 ml) plain yogurt

1½ teaspoons chopped assertive fresh herbs, such as thyme, oregano, and tarragon, or a combination, plus more sprigs for garnish

Olive oil

Preheat the oven to 400°F (205°C).

Cut the squash in half lengthwise, cut out the stem, and scrape out the seeds. Cut a thin slice off the outside-bottom of each half so it sits flat with the cavity up, like a bowl, and doesn't wobble. Set the squash halves on a small baking sheet or in a baking pan and sprinkle the cavities lightly with salt and pepper.

In a bowl, whisk together the eggs, cheese, yogurt, chopped herbs, a scant ½ teaspoon salt, and a few grindings of pepper. Pour the mixture into the squash cavities, leaving about ½ inch (12 mm) empty at the top (the custard will puff up a bit in the oven).

Carefully transfer the squash halves to the oven and bake until the custard is golden and the squash is tender, about 1 hour. The custard should be just cooked through—you can test it by pushing a skewer from the edge of the custard into the center; it should come out with just a bit of solid custard attached, not wet. Let the squash stand for 5 minutes. Drizzle each half with a little oil, scatter herb sprigs over the top, and serve. If you'd like to serve four people, just cut each half in half—this will reveal the pretty layers of custard inside.

Warm Roasted Kabocha Squash Salad

SERVES 4

Kabocha squash, fresh out of the oven, is tossed with a tangy dressing, pinches of goat cheese, and loads of fresh herbs.

1 kabocha squash (about 2⅓ pounds/1.1 kg)

2 tablespoons olive oil

Salt and freshly ground black pepper

2 tablespoons freshly squeezed lemon juice

1 teaspoon honey or agave nectar

½ cup (20 g) fresh flat-leaf parsley leaves

½ cup (20 g) fresh mint leaves

2 ounces (55 g) soft goat cheese (about 1½ inches/ 4 cm of a log)

Preheat the oven to 425°F (220°C).

Scrub the squash well. Cut it in half through the stem end and scrape out the seeds. Cut each half into quarters lengthwise and trim off the hard stem and blossom ends. Keeping the skin on, cut each wedge crosswise into ¼- to ½-inch-thick (6- to 12-mm-thick) slices. Spread the slices in a single layer on a rimmed baking sheet and drizzle them with 1 tablespoon of the oil. Sprinkle with ½ teaspoon salt and a few grindings of pepper and toss to coat the slices with the oil. Bake until tender and lightly browned at the edges, about 25 minutes.

In a large bowl, whisk together the lemon juice, honey, ½ teaspoon salt, pepper to taste, and the remaining 1 tablespoon oil. Add the warm roasted squash, the parsley, and the mint and toss to combine. Crumble the cheese over the top and serve warm.

Spiced Winter Squash Mash

SERVES 2 TO 4

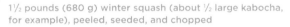

This is one of the best side dishes in the book, I think. Infuse a slick of oil with whole spices, then coarsely mash in cooked winter squash and loosen the mash with naturally sweet coconut milk. You can serve the mash with just about anything: If summer squash is still available where you live, try the Gingery Zucchini on page 56.

One-Baking-Sheet Tomatoes and Chickpeas on page 69 would provide a tart and nutty contrast to the unctuous winter squash. Or you could pull some spiced tomato sauce (see page 56) from the freezer and simmer cauliflower in it until tender; spoon the sauce alongside the squash so they mingle a bit.

1½ pounds (680 g) winter squash (about ½ large kabocha, for example), peeled, seeded, and chopped

1 tablespoon vegetable oil

1 teaspoon cumin seeds

1 teaspoon black or brown mustard seeds

½ cup unsweetened coconut milk, plus more for serving

Salt

¼ teaspoon ground cayenne

Put the squash in a large pot and add enough water to cover by 1 inch (2.5 cm). Bring the water to a boil, then lower the heat and simmer until the squash is very tender, 15 to 20 minutes. Drain well.

In a large sauté pan, heat the oil over medium-high heat until it shimmers. Add the cumin and mustard seeds, then lower the heat to medium and cook until the seeds begin to pop, about 1 minute. Carefully—it'll splatter—add the coconut milk, then add ¾ teaspoon salt and the cayenne. Cook, stirring, until the oil separates, 1 to 2 minutes. Add the squash and cook, turning and mashing it gently with a heatproof spatula or metal turner to incorporate the spiced coconut milk evenly, until heated through, 2 to 3 minutes. Taste and add more salt and/or cayenne, if needed. Scrape the squash into a serving bowl and drizzle very lightly with coconut milk. Serve hot.

With Curly Kale Pakora (page 155) and baby greens with Tangerine Vinaigrette (page 260).

Spaghetti Squash, Pesto, and Cherry Tomatoes

SERVES 2 OR 3 AS A MEAL

Spaghetti squash is a cinch to cook: Just roast it whole, cut it open, seed it, and scrape the pastalike strands out, still hot, into a bowl with flavorful seasonings. As the friendly cashier at my local Indian grocery says of eggplant, it's just a matter of taking away the parts you don't eat and mixing the rest with whatever you like. I've seen a lot of recipes that have you treat the cooked spaghetti squash similarly to actual pasta, mixing it into a sauce in a pan on the heat. I wouldn't recommend doing this, as the distinct strands can quickly turn to mush. Instead, tip it into a raw sauce and let the heat of the squash do the work.

1 (2½-pound/1.2-kg) spaghetti squash

½ dry pint (about 5 ounces/140 g) cherry or grape tomatoes, quartered

2 tablespoons prepared pesto, or 3 tablespoons Arugula Pesto (page 256)

1 tablespoon olive oil, plus more for drizzling

Salt and freshly ground black pepper

Parmesan or other hard cheese

Preheat the oven to 400°F (205°C). Stab the squash deeply with a small, sharp knife five or six times to allow steam to escape as it bakes. Put it on a baking sheet or in a baking pan and bake for about 1 hour, until you can feel that it has softened when you press on the outside.

Meanwhile, put the tomatoes in a large bowl with the pesto and oil. Gently stir to combine.

Halve the squash lengthwise. Scrape out and discard the seeds and gooey part in the center. Holding one half with a kitchen towel to protect your hand, use a spoon or fork to gently scrape the stringy flesh out of the peel and into the bowl with the pesto and tomatoes, taking care to keep the strands of squash as intact as possible. Sprinkle generously with salt and several grindings of pepper and quickly toss to combine. Shave some cheese over the top, drizzle with a little more oil, and serve warm.

WINTER

celery, celery root, and fennel

Cut into lengths, the convex side gently shaved with a vegetable peeler to remove the tougher strings, plain old celery can be simply braised, much like leeks, with butter and a little white wine, or sliced on a sharp diagonal and stir-fried over high heat in vegetable oil (a few drops of sesame oil, too) with ginger and shallots, fresh chiles or a pinch of hot red pepper flakes, a splash of tamari, and maybe a sprinkling of dulse flakes or toasted sesame seeds: celery transformed. Of course celery sticks submerged in cold water in the refrigerator are delicious for snacking—they emerge dripping, extra-crisp, and perfectly refreshing—I like to sprinkle a little salt or Kale *Furikake* (page 247) on them. Keep celery in a plastic bag or other airtight container in the crisper drawer; if it's too long for the drawer (darn those shallow drawers!), cut the bunch in half first. It'll keep for weeks in the bag, but trim the dried-out ends before using it.

Celery root (aka celeriac) is related to but not from the same plant as regular celery. The knobby, strange-looking root is, along with similarly Germanic kohlrabi, one vegetable that is more readily available in my new home of Lincoln, Nebraska, than it has been anywhere else I've lived. It's relatively cheap here, too, which is a real boon to me because I have always been a huge fan of its light, almost artichokelike flavor and smooth texture but have been loath to purchase it in large quantities when it is priced like a specialty item. Keep it refrigerated (it'll last for a couple of weeks), and use a chef's knife to peel it deeply—don't even bother with the vegetable peeler.

Crunchy fennel is a cold-weather treat that takes especially well to roasting on a searing-hot baking sheet; caramelizing the surfaces brings out some of the sweetness and rounds off the edges of its often sharp licorice flavor.

Celery, Black Mission Fig, and Gorgonzola Salad

SERVES 4

The National, one of the best restaurants in Athens, Georgia—its chef is the brilliant Peter Dale—has a celery- and Manchego-stuffed date appetizer on its menu that has acquired near-totemic significance to me. When I moved halfway across the country I wondered how I would survive without those dates. Luckily Hugh Acheson, who's an owner of the restaurant, published a similar recipe in his book *A New Turn in the South*, so I can have them whenever nostalgia overtakes me. This shaved celery salad is inspired by those dates: The sweet elements (I've swapped in figs instead of dates) and saladlike elements have been reversed—here lemon-dressed shaved celery is the star, while sweet strips of sticky dried figs and crumbles of salty blue cheese turn up just in every other forkful or so.

1½ tablespoons fresh lemon juice

Salt and freshly ground black pepper

Pinch of hot red pepper flakes

¼ cup (60 ml) olive oil

4 dried Black Mission figs, stemmed and thinly sliced

1 small shallot, very thinly sliced

¾ pound (340 g) tender celery with leaves

1 cup (40 g) fresh flat-leaf parsley leaves

1½ ounces (43 g) Gorgonzola or other blue cheese

⅓ cup (35 g) walnut halves, toasted

In a large bowl, combine the lemon juice, ½ teaspoon salt, a few grindings of black pepper, and the red pepper flakes and whisk to dissolve the salt. Gradually whisk in the oil until emulsified. Add the figs and shallot to the bowl with the dressing.

Pull the leaves from the celery and set them aside. Remove and discard any tough stems from the parsley. Rinse the celery and parsley leaves and pat them dry. Very thinly slice the celery ribs on an angle—the slices should be paper thin; use this opportunity to practice your knife skills, or drag out a mandoline for the job. Add the celery, along with the celery and parsley leaves, to the bowl with the dressing and toss well. Crumble in the cheese and walnuts and toss. Taste and season with salt and pepper, if needed. Divide among serving plates and serve immediately.

Celery Extravaganza!

SERVES 4 TO 6 AS A MEAL

Did your mom ever make cream of celery soup just so she could use it as an ingredient in a casserole? Mine did, and that's basically what's going on in this gratin, for which you make a simple, creamy sauce that will bind very thinly sliced celery root and potato together as they sink into one another and settle and bubble under a crust of Parmesan. A mandoline will make quick work of the celery root and potato, but you can just use a sharp chef's knife to cut them into slices a bit less than $1/8$ inch (3 mm) thick.

1 tablespoon unsalted butter, plus more for the baking dish

2 cups (270 g) diced celery (from about 4 ribs)

1 onion, diced

½ teaspoon dried thyme, or 1 teaspoon chopped fresh thyme leaves

Salt and freshly ground black pepper

¼ cup (60 ml) white wine

¾ cup (180 ml) heavy cream

½ large celery root (about 13 ounces/370 g), peeled, halved, and thinly sliced

1 large russet potato (about 13 ounces/370 g), peeled and thinly sliced

½ cup (50 g) finely grated Parmesan or other hard cheese

Preheat the oven to 350°F (175°C). Generously butter a 7-by-11-inch (17.5-by-27.5-cm) or similar-size baking dish.

In a medium saucepan, melt the butter over medium heat. Add the celery, onion, thyme, a pinch of salt, and several grindings of pepper. Cook, stirring occasionally, until the celery is very soft but not browned, lowering the heat if necessary to keep it from browning, 12 to 15 minutes.

Add the wine to the celery and onion mixture and cook until it's mostly evaporated, about 2 minutes. Add the cream and ¾ teaspoon salt. Bring the mixture to a simmer, then remove the pan from the heat and puree the sauce with an immersion blender. (Alternatively, transfer the sauce to a regular blender and puree, but take care to vent the lid and cover it with a towel.) Taste and add more salt and pepper, if needed—the sauce should be quite salty and flavorful. Scrape the sauce into a large bowl and add the celery root and potato. Stir to coat the slices as thoroughly as possible.

Spoon about one-third of the vegetable slices into the prepared baking dish. Sprinkle with 2 tablespoons of the cheese. Spoon another third of the slices on top, then sprinkle with another 2 tablespoons of the cheese. Spoon on the last third of the sliced vegetables, then top with the remaining ¼ cup (25 g) cheese. Bake until vigorously bubbly at the edges and golden brown all over the top, about 55 minutes. Let stand for 10 minutes to allow the sauce to thicken and set a bit, then serve hot.

Buttermilk–Celery Root Puree

SERVES 4

Celery root puree, especially with the luxurious addition of dairy—here I use three kinds: butter, tangy buttermilk, *and* milk—is a gift from the gods. Pure white, smooth, and more vegetal than starchy, it's the kind of dish that, like mashed potatoes, can go with anything.

2 celery roots (about 1½ pounds/680 g)

Salt and freshly ground black pepper

1 tablespoon unsalted butter

6 tablespoons (90 ml) buttermilk

About ¼ cup (60 ml) milk or half-and-half

Peel the celery roots—a chef's knife works best; don't worry if there's a bit of brown remaining on the sides, but try to get most of the brown from the bottoms—and rinse them. Quarter the celery roots, then cut each quarter into ½-inch (12-mm) slices. Transfer the slices to a saucepan and add cold water to cover by 1 inch (2.5 cm). Add ½ teaspoon salt, bring the water to a boil, then lower the heat and simmer until the celery root pieces are tender and slide easily off the tip of a knife when stabbed, about 15 minutes. Drain in a colander and rinse briefly.

In a blender or food processor, combine the cooked celery root, butter, buttermilk, milk, ½ teaspoon salt, and a few grindings of pepper and puree until very smooth, scraping down the sides frequently and adding a little more milk if necessary to get it going. Taste and season with salt and pepper, if needed. Rinse out the saucepan and return the puree to it; reheat over low heat, stirring frequently with a heatproof spatula. Serve hot.

Celery Root Pancakes with Fried Eggs

SERVES 4

Just about any firm, not-watery root vegetable can be made into latkelike pancakes. Celery root, because it's not as starchy as white potatoes, makes a lighter version that I find most appealing in the morning. To get those crisp edges, toss the shreds with chickpea flour. Adding the beaten egg to the celery root mixture before cooking is optional; it helps to hold the mixture together. If you leave it out, you can just spread the mixture in the pan and cook it like hash browns, turning it with a spatula to brown both sides.

1 celery root (about 1 pound/455 g)

5 large eggs

½ cup (60 g) chickpea flour (*besan*)

½ teaspoon garam masala (optional)

Salt and freshly ground black pepper

Vegetable oil

Using a sharp, heavy knife, cut the top and bottom off the celery root and stand it upright on the cutting board. Slice off the peel, then rinse well. Cut the celery root into thick wedges and coarsely grate them into a large bowl. Whisk one of the eggs and add it to the celery root, along with the chickpea flour, garam masala, if using, ¾ teaspoon salt, and a couple of grindings of pepper. Stir well with a rubber spatula.

Preheat the oven to 200°F (95°C).

In a large sauté pan, heat 1 tablespoon oil over medium-high heat until it shimmers. Add one-quarter of the celery root mixture, either in loose little clumps (like latkes) or hash brown–style, sprinkled all over the surface of the pan. (No matter how you cook it, you'll need to fry it in batches.) Cook, undisturbed, until the bottom is nicely browned, about 3 minutes, then flip with a metal spatula and cook until the other side is browned, about 3 minutes more. As they finish cooking, transfer them to a heatproof plate and keep them warm in the oven. Repeat with the remaining celery root, adding more oil as needed.

Wipe out the pan if necessary and heat a final 1 tablespoon oil over medium heat. Crack in the remaining eggs, sprinkle with salt and pepper, and cook until done to your liking, about 5 minutes for sunny side up (flip them, if you'd like). Serve the eggs atop the celery root pancakes.

Roasted Fennel with Marjoram and White Beans

SERVES 2 TO 4

VEGAN

Roasting fennel makes it sweeter, and gives it lovely crisp edges that contrast nicely with the creamy white beans—green-tinted, slender flageolets are especially good here. Fresh marjoram has a faint but not overpowering anise flavor, and is a good match for fennel (which is also sometimes called anise), but you could also use oregano, rosemary, thyme, or tarragon—whatever's good and fresh.

1 bulb fennel

2 tablespoons olive oil

1 teaspoon minced fresh marjoram

Salt and freshly ground black pepper

1½ cups (265 g) cooked white beans (see page 226), cooled and drained

1 tablespoon fresh lemon juice, or to taste

Preheat the oven to 400°F (205°C). Set a baking sheet in the oven while it heats.

Cut the top off the fennel bulb (reserve a few of the fronds for garnish) and trim the bottom and any dark spots from the outside of the bulb. Cut the bulb vertically into 8 or 10 wedges, leaving the core intact. Put the fennel in a large bowl and drizzle it with 1 tablespoon of the oil. Add the marjoram, ½ teaspoon salt, and a grinding of pepper and toss well. Spread the wedges on the hot baking sheet, cut sides down, and roast, flipping the wedges once about halfway through, until tender, browned, and crisp at the tips, about 30 minutes.

Meanwhile, put the beans in the same bowl (no need to rinse the bowl), add the remaining 1 tablespoon oil, the lemon juice, about ¼ teaspoon salt, and several grindings of pepper and toss.

Transfer the roasted fennel to a cutting board and coarsely chop it, then add it to the beans. Toss, taste, and season with salt, pepper, and lemon juice, if needed. Serve warm or at room temperature, garnished with chopped fennel fronds.

cabbage, brussels sprouts, and kohlrabi

Cabbage, Brussels sprouts, and kohlrabi (along with turnips, broccoli, and cauliflower) are all part of the *Brassica* genus, and thus it makes sense not only to group them together here but to think of them as being culinarily similar. They take to sweet-and-sour flavors well, and to eastern European spices like caraway and juniper. Their flavors are mild and a bit bland, however, making them ideal candidates for taking into spicy-hot territory. Any of the recipes in this section would work with any kind of cabbage (Napa or Chinese cabbage, green or purple), or Brussels sprouts or kohlrabi with just a little adjustment.

If you happen to see Brussels sprouts being sold still attached to their stalk, buy them. The ones on the stalks are usually very fresh and sweet tasting. They'll keep like that for about a week at cool room temperature (sometimes I'll put the end of the stalk in a pitcher of water, but I'm not convinced it makes a difference—it's pretty in your kitchen, though)—just trim off as many as you need. One full stalk will give you enough for about six to eight servings (it can be hard to estimate quantities when you're looking at such a strange vegetable).

You've probably seen kohlrabi if you have a CSA share and get a weekly box of "whatever we've got"—it's relatively easy to grow. The best ones for eating raw are the pale green, baseball-size ones that are ready in the late fall and early winter. The beautiful purple-skinned kohlrabi can be a bit tough and are better for cooked applications.

Cabbage and Lentil Gratin

SERVES 4 TO 6 AS A MEAL

Hearty, comforting dishes like gratins and casseroles have taken on more significance to me since I moved to blustery Nebraska and had to give up the year-round grilling season I'd begun to take for granted in the southeast. This extra-creamy one, I'm sure, will crop up multiple times next winter. Keep plenty of cooked lentils in the freezer—or in the garage, if you winter in the upper Midwest—for layering into baking dishes and covering with cream and cheese. Even if you're not serving a crowd, this gratin is worth making in a large dish, as it reheats perfectly and makes a fine lunch for several days.

Olive or vegetable oil

2 cups (about 15 ounces/425 g) cooked lentils of any kind (see page 225)

1 tablespoon unsalted butter

½ onion, chopped

1 clove garlic, chopped

Salt and freshly ground black pepper

½ cup (120 ml) dry white wine

1½ pounds (680 g) green cabbage, cored and chopped

½ cup (120 ml) vegetable stock or water

1 cup (240 ml) heavy cream

Freshly grated nutmeg (about ¼ of a nutmeg seed)

½ cup (55 g) shredded Gruyère or Emmentaler cheese

Preheat the oven to 400°F (205°C). Lightly oil a 7-by-11-inch (17.5-by-27.5-cm) baking dish. Spread the lentils evenly in the baking dish.

In a large, deep sauté pan or Dutch oven, melt the butter over medium heat. Add the onion, garlic, a pinch of salt, and a grinding of pepper. Cook, stirring frequently, until the onion is just tender but not browned, about 5 minutes. Add the wine and cook until it's mostly evaporated, about 2 minutes. Add the cabbage, stock, and ½ teaspoon salt. Cook, with the lid askew, stirring occasionally so the cabbage cooks evenly and the layers of leaves separate, until the cabbage is tender, the thinner leaves are translucent, and the liquid is almost gone, about 15 minutes. Spoon the cabbage mixture over the lentils and gently press the pieces so they lie flat.

Return the sauté pan to medium-high heat and add the cream and nutmeg. Bring to a boil and boil for 1 to 2 minutes to reduce slightly. Pour the cream evenly over the cabbage. Sprinkle the cheese evenly over the cabbage. Bake until the cream is bubbling and the cheese is melted and lightly browned in spots, 20 to 25 minutes. Let stand for a few minutes, then serve hot.

Tart-Sweet Braised Cabbage

SERVES 4

VEGAN

This easy side dish takes its cue from the classic sweet-and-sour cabbage, but the flavors are more complex: The tartness here comes not from vinegar but from thick pomegranate molasses. Add the brown sugar a little at a time, stopping when it's just sweet enough for you.

With a hit of ginger, tamari, and sesame, the dish has a vaguely Asian sensibility. Try it alongside the Dry-Fried Green Beans with Garlic Chips and Peanut Sauce (page 60) and steamed brown jasmine rice.

2½ tablespoons pomegranate molasses

¼ cup (55 g) packed brown sugar

2 tablespoons tamari, or to taste

A few dashes of toasted sesame oil

1 tablespoon vegetable oil

1 clove garlic, minced

3 coins peeled fresh ginger, minced

1 head purple cabbage (about 2½ pounds/1.2 kg), cored and cut into 1-inch (2.5-cm) pieces

Salt

In a small bowl, combine the pomegranate molasses, brown sugar, tamari, and sesame oil and set aside.

In a large, deep sauté pan or wok, heat the vegetable oil over medium-high heat until it shimmers. Add the garlic and ginger and cook, stirring, for 30 seconds. Add the cabbage and 1 cup (240 ml) water and stir well. Cover and cook, stirring occasionally, until the cabbage is quite tender, 10 to 12 minutes. Uncover and cook, stirring, for 2 minutes to boil off some of the liquid. Pour in the pomegranate molasses mixture and stir well; cook for about 5 minutes, until most of the liquid has evaporated. Taste and season with salt or more tamari, if needed. Serve hot.

Thalia's Cabbage Soup

SERVES 3 OR 4 AS A MEAL

CAN BE VEGAN

Once when my daughter was about four years old and Derek was out of town, she and I made a very basic cabbage soup (like this one) and shared it for supper every day until he got home. She's adored it ever since, and it's really not hard to understand why: The cabbage, cooked until the leaves are silky and soft, is buttery and mild—totally kid friendly. Thalia is almost seven now, and recently we had a lovely, slow afternoon in the kitchen together, me chopping cabbage while she sautéed the mirepoix of onion, carrot, and celery in butter (she insisted on butter, but of course oil would be perfectly fine) and told me what else she wanted in her soup.

1 tablespoon unsalted butter or olive oil

½ sweet onion, coarsely diced

1 carrot, chopped

1 rib celery with leaves, chopped

Salt

1½ pounds (680 g) green cabbage, cored and chopped

1 (14-ounce/400-g) can whole tomatoes with their juices

3 cups (720 ml) vegetable stock or water

Fresh lemon juice (optional)

In a large saucepan or Dutch oven, melt the butter over medium heat. Add the onion, carrot, celery, and a good pinch of salt. Cook, stirring frequently, until the vegetables are soft and the onion is translucent and just starting to brown, about 8 minutes. Add the cabbage and stir it into the other vegetables, then add the tomatoes and their juices and the stock. Bring to a boil, then lower the heat and simmer, with the lid askew, until the cabbage is very tender and silky, about 30 minutes. Stir occasionally, breaking up the tomatoes with a spoon (or use shears to just cut them apart as they cook in the soup). Taste and season with salt, and add a squeeze of lemon juice, if you'd like. Serve hot, maybe with crackers and a glass of cold milk.

Roasted Baby Choy Sum

SERVES 4

VEGAN

Look in Asian grocery stores or the specialty produce section of a good supermarket for heads of baby *choy sum*: two or three inches long with ruffled dark green leaves and crunchy, bright white stems, sometimes with a bit of yellow blossom in the center of the head. If you can't find *choy sum*, baby bok choy works just as well, though it contains more liquid and will take a little more time in the oven.

1 pound (455 g) baby *choy sum*

2 tablespoons olive or vegetable oil

2 cloves garlic, minced

1 coin peeled fresh ginger, minced (optional)

Salt or tamari

Freshly ground black pepper

Lemon wedges

Preheat the oven to 450°F (230°C). Set a large rimmed baking sheet in the oven while it heats.

Trim a sliver off the bottom of each head of *choy sum*, keeping the leaves attached at the bottom as much as possible. Put them in a large bowl of water and swish them around to loosen any sand from the wrinkly leaves and crevices, then gently lift them out (leaving any sand behind—there isn't much, usually) and spin them dry in a salad spinner. Set aside in a large bowl.

In a cup, combine the oil, garlic, and ginger, if using. Drizzle the mixture over the *choy sum*, tossing to coat. Season with several pinches of salt or a sprinkle of tamari, and a few grindings of pepper.

Spread the *choy sum* heads in a single layer on the preheated baking sheet and roast for 5 minutes. Use tongs or a metal spatula to turn the heads over and roast for 5 minutes more, until the leaves are crisped and browned in spots and the stems are tender. Serve with lemon wedges.

Shredded Brussels Sprout and Sweet Apple Salad

SERVES 2 TO 4

VEGAN

Simple, tangy, and a little sweet: Serve this salad as you would a slaw.

2 tablespoons fresh lemon juice, or more if needed

1 teaspoon agave nectar or honey

1 teaspoon grainy mustard

Salt and freshly ground black pepper

¼ cup (60 ml) olive oil

1 pound (455 g) Brussels sprouts

2 small sweet, crisp apples, such as Winesap or Gala

In a large bowl, combine the lemon juice, agave nectar, mustard, ¾ teaspoon salt, and several grindings of pepper and whisk to dissolve the salt. Gradually whisk in the oil until emulsified.

Trim the bottoms of the Brussels sprouts and very thinly slice the sprouts with a sharp knife. (If you have a food processor with a slicing or shredding blade, you can use it here.) Add the Brussels sprouts to the bowl with the dressing and coarsely grate in the apples (unpeeled is fine), turning each apple as you grate and stopping when you get to the core. Toss well and let stand for 30 minutes. Taste, season with lemon juice and/or salt, if needed, and serve, or refrigerate in an airtight container for up to 2 hours before serving.

Brussels Sprouts with Tamarind-Ginger Dressing

SERVES 4

VEGAN

I think I must've been dreaming about this dish, because I woke up one morning and made it for myself for breakfast. I ate the entire bowl over the course of the morning—a second breakfast, then an early lunch. (It's a good thing I work at home.) Roasted Brussels sprout halves—any loose leaves almost blackened by the heat of the oven, the cut sides caramelized almost to the point of stickiness—are far removed from the soft, boiled mini cabbages you may know, and they become all the more irresistible when drenched in a dressing tangy with dark tamarind concentrate.

continued

FOR THE BRUSSELS SPROUTS

1 pound (455 g) Brussels sprouts, trimmed and halved lengthwise

2 tablespoons olive oil

Salt and freshly ground black pepper

FOR THE DRESSING

2 tablespoons agave nectar or honey

2 tablespoons warm water

2 teaspoons tamarind concentrate (see page 80)

2 teaspoons grated fresh ginger

Salt

Pinch of hot red pepper flakes

2 tablespoons olive oil

MAKE THE BRUSSELS SPROUTS

Preheat the oven to 400°F (205°C). Set a large rimmed baking sheet in the oven while it heats.

In a large bowl, toss the Brussels sprouts with the oil, salt, and a couple of grindings of pepper. Spread them (and any loose leaves) on the hot baking sheet in a single layer. (Don't wash the bowl.) Roast, shaking the pan once or twice, until tender and nicely browned, about 20 minutes.

MAKE THE DRESSING

Meanwhile, in the same bowl, combine the agave nectar, water, tamarind concentrate, ginger, ½ teaspoon salt, and the red pepper flakes and whisk to dissolve the salt. Gradually whisk in the oil until emulsified.

Scrape the roasted Brussels sprouts and leaves into the bowl with the dressing and toss to coat. Lift them out into a serving bowl and drizzle with some of the dressing remaining in the bowl. Serve warm.

Winter Salad with Green Tea Leaf Dressing

SERVES 3 OR 4 AS A MEAL

VEGAN

There's a sizeable Burmese population in Lincoln, many of them Karen (pronounced kuh-RINN) refugees from a part of the country that borders Thailand. The co-op grocery store in our neighborhood sells Burmese green tea leaf salads in its prepared foods case: Very finely shredded green cabbage topped with crisp and none-too-ripe tomato slices fill one half of the takeout container, and the other half is filled with a mixture of crunchy fried peanuts and seeds. A small cup of fermented green tea leaves (called *laphet*) is included for mixing in yourself. Those tea leaves taste like nothing I'm familiar with: just a tad sour, very salty, with a funki-

ness that one can quickly grow to love. I got to reading about Burmese food soon after we arrived in Lincoln, and of course that meant Naomi Duguid's *Burma: Rivers of Flavor*. Duguid's introduction to the classic tea leaf salad says that including fermented tea leaves in her recipe is "an act of optimism," as they're difficult to find. I just had to go a few blocks, to the Karen grocery store, to pick some up (how I love Lincoln!), but I know that's not an option for most. So instead, I've come up with a green tea leaf dressing that in no way replicates the odd and wonderful real thing, but is still delicious—and likely just as strange.

continued

Brussels Sprouts with Tamarind-Ginger Dressing, served with Steamed Millet (page 228)

FOR THE GREEN TEA LEAF DRESSING

- 2 tablespoons good-quality loose green tea leaves
- Boiling water
- 3 coins peeled fresh ginger, chopped
- 6 tablespoons (90 ml) vegetable oil
- ¼ cup (60 ml) fresh lime juice, or more if needed
- 1 tablespoon red miso paste (see Note)
- 1 tablespoon tamari, or more if needed
- ¼ teaspoon sesame oil

FOR THE FRIED NUT MIXTURE

- 2 tablespoons vegetable oil
- ½ cup (75 g) unsalted peanuts and/or raw cashews
- ¼ cup (35 g) shelled sunflower seeds
- 2 tablespoons sesame seeds
- 1 tablespoon pepitas
- 3 tablespoons dried *urad dal* or dried yellow split peas
- 3 cloves garlic, minced
- Salt

FOR THE SALAD

- 4 ounces (113 g) dried soba noodles (see Note)
- 1 teaspoon plus 1 tablespoon vegetable oil
- 6 cloves garlic, thinly sliced
- 1 large kohlrabi bulb, peeled and grated (about 2 cups/ 180 g)
- 2 carrots, grated (about ⅔ cup/70 g)
- 1 cup (100 g) mixed sprouts
- ½ dry pint (about 5 ounces/140 g) grape tomatoes, halved (optional)
- 6 thin coins peeled fresh ginger, stacked and cut into thin julienne strips
- ¼ cup (10 g) fresh cilantro leaves
- 1 fresh hot green or red chile, sliced

MAKE THE GREEN TEA LEAF DRESSING

Put the tea in a heatproof bowl and add boiling water to cover. Let steep for 10 minutes or so, until the tea leaves have expanded and are tender—taste one to check. If your tea has any little tough stems or twigs in it, add enough water to make those float, then carefully scoop them out and discard. Drain the leaves in a sieve and squeeze to extract most of the water.

Transfer the leaves to a mini food processor and add the ginger, vegetable oil, lime juice, miso, tamari, and sesame oil and process until the tea and ginger are finely chopped and the dressing is a little creamy. Taste and add more tamari or lime juice, if needed—it should be quite salty and sour. Transfer to a small serving bowl and set aside.

MAKE THE FRIED NUT MIXTURE

Line a bowl with a paper towel.

In a large sauté pan, heat the oil over medium heat until it shimmers. Add the nuts, seeds, split peas, garlic, and a pinch of salt. Cook, stirring constantly, until the split peas have darkened a shade and the nuts are golden and very fragrant, about 5 minutes. Transfer to the paper towel–lined bowl to drain. Taste and season with more salt, if needed. Set aside.

MAKE THE SALAD

Bring a large pot of water to a boil. Add the noodles and cook, stirring occasionally and watching to be sure the pot doesn't boil over, until just tender, 7 to 8 minutes. Drain the noodles in a sieve and rinse them well under cold running water; drain again and toss them with 1 teaspoon of the oil.

In a small sauté pan, heat the remaining 1 tablespoon oil over medium heat until it shimmers. Add the garlic and cook, stirring with a slotted spoon and tipping the pan a bit so the oil pools at one side and the garlic lightly fries, until golden, about 3 minutes. Using the slotted spoon, transfer the garlic to a folded paper towel to drain.

Divide the noodles among three or four serving bowls. Distribute the kohlrabi, carrots, sprouts, tomatoes, if using, ginger, cilantro, fried nut mixture, fried sliced garlic, and fresh chiles among the bowls. Serve with the dressing on the side for drizzling over.

Note: If you're keeping it gluten free, look for soba noodles that are 100 percent buckwheat—check the ingredients label to make sure there's no wheat flour listed.

Dean Neff's Kohlrabi Salad

SERVES 2 TO 4

Dean was the executive chef at the Five & Ten, the anchor of the world-class restaurant scene in Athens, Georgia, and is now the chef at Cornucopia, a couple of hours north in Cashiers, North Carolina. He serves a small pile of this kohlrabi alongside an egg salad and thin buttered toasts.

½ cup (120 ml) full-fat plain Greek yogurt (see Note)

3 to 4 tablespoons fresh lemon juice

2 to 3 tablespoons fresh lime juice

¼ teaspoon salt, or to taste

1 teaspoon tahini, or to taste

2 heads green kohlrabi without tops (about 1½ pounds/ 680 g), deeply peeled and cut into ¼-inch (6-mm) cubes

1 teaspoon sesame seeds

1 teaspoon cumin seeds

2 ounces (about 3 cups/55 g) tender baby greens, such as watercress, arugula, miner's lettuce, purslane, or sweet pea shoots, or a combination

In a large bowl, whisk together the yogurt, most of the lemon and lime juice, the salt, and tahini until smooth. Taste and season with more lemon or lime juice, salt, or tahini, if needed.

Put the kohlrabi in the bowl with the dressing and toss well. Set aside to marinate for 10 to 30 minutes.

In a small sauté pan, toast the sesame seeds and cumin seeds, stirring constantly with a heatproof spatula, until a shade darker and very fragrant, 1 to 3 minutes. Scrape them into a mortar and pound with a pestle to coarsely grind (or chop them coarsely on a cutting board).

Taste the kohlrabi for seasoning (it should be quite salty and tangy), then add the greens and toss to coat. Divide among serving plates, sprinkle lightly with the sesame and cumin mixture, and serve immediately.

Note: If you have only nonfat Greek yogurt—this is what I usually keep in the house—whisk in a tablespoon of olive oil, cream, or half-and-half: You need the fat to balance the tangy citrus in the dressing.

With black (beluga) lentils (see page 225) and a Seedy Quinoa Cake (page 222).

Shaved Kohlrabi with Lemon and Mustard

SERVES 2 TO 4

VEGAN

This is a good dish to serve on one of those days when spring seems near. It's refreshing and light, a fine complement to a heartier dish like the brown-basmati biryani on page 218 or a topping for the Seedy Quinoa Cakes on page 222.

Juice of 1 lemon

1 generous teaspoon good-quality grainy mustard

Salt and freshly ground black pepper

2 tablespoons olive oil

1 bunch young (small) green kohlrabi (about 14 ounces/ 400 g), tops removed, very thinly sliced (see Note)

1 tablespoon chopped fresh flat-leaf parsley

In a large bowl, combine the lemon juice, mustard, ¾ teaspoon salt, and several grindings of pepper and whisk to dissolve the salt. Gradually whisk in the oil until emulsified.

Add the kohlrabi to the bowl with the dressing and toss well to combine. Scatter the parsley over the salad and serve. The salad can also be refrigerated in an airtight container for up to 2 hours; add the parsley just before serving so it stays bright and fresh.

Note: Using a sharp knife or a mandoline works well to shave the kohlrabi extra thin. If your knife skills, like mine, are rusty and you don't have a mandoline or don't want to bother dragging it out from underneath the waffle iron or whatever, try this trick, which I learned from working on Tim Ferriss's book *The 4-Hour Chef*: Cut the kohlrabi in half or quarters so that you have a piece no wider than the blades of your Y-shaped vegetable peeler. Holding the vegetable peeler horizontally just above the work surface, with the sharp blades up, swipe a kohlrabi piece over the blades to thinly shave slices. In other words, turn your peeler into a mandoline.

Buttered Kohlrabi with Golden Raisins and Paprika

SERVES 2 TO 4

I almost always use kohlrabi raw, but some kohlrabi (especially the purple-skinned variety) is too tough for that purpose. In that case, it should be cooked—a quick sauté will do it.

1½ tablespoons unsalted butter

1½ pounds (680 g) kohlrabi, tops removed, bulbs peeled and diced

2 tablespoons golden raisins

½ teaspoon sweet paprika

Salt

¼ teaspoon ground cinnamon

Pinch of ancho or other hot chile powder

In a large sauté pan, melt the butter over medium-high heat. Add the kohlrabi, raisins, paprika, ¾ teaspoon salt, cinnamon, and chile powder. Cook, stirring frequently, until the kohlrabi is tender, 6 to 8 minutes. Add 2 tablespoons water and cook for 2 minutes longer. Taste and season with more salt, if needed. Serve hot.

potatoes

My friend Regan told me to make sure that there was a section, in this book of all-vegetable meals, of comfort food. I realized that, basically, as soon as white potatoes are involved that's what you've got: comfort food. (If my editor were as unpragmatic as I am, that's what this section would be called. Thankfully, she's not, and these potato recipes will be easier for you to find.) Potatoes are not incredibly nutritious on their own, and should be considered more of a starch, like bread, than a vegetable, so I use them sparingly—when warm, easygoing hominess is needed.

Potato and White Bean Cutlets

SERVES 4 TO 6

VEGAN

My mom used to make fried mashed potatoes for me and my brother for breakfast (it was what she called potato pancakes; we didn't know from latkes back then). Here I use white beans in the potato mixture—more nutrition can't hurt—and some cumin and paprika to make the patties a bit like Indian *aloo tikki*, or "potato cutlets." To make the exterior extra crisp, try dredging both sides in dehydrated potato flakes (look for a brand that contains only that ingredient, if possible).

1½ cups (265 g) diced, cooked, and cooled russet potatoes

1½ cups (265 g) cooked and cooled drained cannelini or other white beans (see page 226)

3 tablespoons vegetable oil

¼ cup (30 g) diced sweet onion

1 clove garlic, minced

Salt and freshly ground black pepper

½ teaspoon ground cumin

½ teaspoon sweet or hot paprika

½ cup (30 g) dehydrated potato flakes (optional)

Optional toppings: Cilantro-Mint Chutney (page 111), Apricot-Tamarind Chutney (page 111), whisked yogurt, thinly sliced fresh hot chiles, fresh cilantro leaves

In a large bowl, combine the potatoes and beans and mash them with a potato masher or fork to a chunky but well-integrated consistency. (Alternatively, pulse them together in a food processor, scraping the sides of the bowl frequently.)

In a small sauté pan, heat 1 tablespoon of the oil over medium-high heat until it shimmers. Add the onion, garlic, and a pinch of salt and cook, stirring frequently, until the onion is golden, about 5 minutes. Stir in the cumin and paprika, then immediately scrape the mixture into the bowl with the potato mixture and stir gently to combine. Taste and add salt and pepper, if needed. Shape the mixture into golf-ball-size balls.

Put the potato flakes, if using, in a shallow bowl. Put a potato ball in the potato flakes and gently flatten it to about ½ inch (12 mm) thick, then turn it over, press the other side into the flakes, and flatten it to ¼ inch (6 mm) thick. Place the potato "cutlet" on a plate and repeat with the remaining balls. If not using potato flakes, just flatten the balls between your palms. If the cutlets are very soft, refrigerate them for 15 to 30 minutes to firm up before proceeding.

Preheat the oven to 200°F (95°C).

In a large sauté pan, heat 1 tablespoon of the oil over medium heat. Carefully add about half of the cutlets; don't overcrowd the pan, or they'll be hard to turn. Cook until the bottoms are deeply browned, about 3 minutes, then use a metal spatula to gently turn them over—careful, they're delicate—and cook until the other side is browned, about 3 minutes more. Transfer the cooked cutlets to a serving platter and keep them warm in the oven. Repeat with the remaining cutlets, wiping out the pan if necessary, and adding the remaining 1 tablespoon oil to cook the remaining cutlets. Serve warm, topped with chutneys and such, if you'd like.

Chipotle Potato Tacos

SERVES 2 OR 3 AS A MEAL

For me, food does not get any more comforting than this. Spicy, smoky chipotles and plenty of the vinegary sauce they're canned in are worked into slightly mashed, skillet-crisp potatoes and spooned into warm tortillas with a few simple garnishes. It's an excellent use for leftover baked or boiled potatoes.

2 large russet potatoes (about 1 ½ pounds/680 g), peeled and cut into ¾-inch (2-cm) chunks

3 tablespoons vegetable oil

1 large white or sweet onion, diced

2 cloves garlic, minced

Salt

¾ teaspoon ground cumin

½ teaspoon dried Mexican oregano

1½ to 2 tablespoons minced canned chipotle chiles in adobo sauce (see Sidebar)

4 to 6 corn tortillas

⅔ cup (100 g) crumbled queso fresco or feta cheese (optional)

½ pint (140 g) grape tomatoes, halved

Lots of fresh cilantro sprigs

Put the potatoes in a large saucepan and add cold water to cover them by 1 inch (2.5 cm). Bring the water to a boil, then lower the heat and simmer until just tender, 10 to 15 minutes. Drain the potatoes and set aside.

In a large, deep sauté pan, heat 2 tablespoons of the oil over medium-high heat until it shimmers. Add the onion, garlic, and a pinch of salt and cook, stirring frequently and lowering the heat if necessary to keep the onion and garlic from burning, until tender and nicely browned, about 5 minutes. Stir in the cumin, oregano, the remaining 1 tablespoon oil, the potatoes, and 1 teaspoon salt. Cook, turning frequently with a metal spatula, until the potatoes are nicely browned and crisp in spots—they'll begin to break apart at the edges, but that's fine. Stir in the chipotle. Taste and season with more salt or adobo sauce, if needed. Set aside, covered, while you warm the tortillas.

Heat a heavy skillet or cast-iron griddle over high heat. Heat the tortillas one at a time in the skillet, turning each over twice and pressing down on the surface with a spatula or spoon so they puff a bit, and stacking them on a plate as you go. Serve the tortillas with the potatoes, cheese, if using, tomatoes, and cilantro, filling the tacos to taste.

A CHIPOTLE TIP

When you first open a can of chipotles, go ahead and fish out all the chiles with a fork and plop them on your cutting board. You almost never need to use a chipotle whole, so mince them all, and scrape them, along with the sauce from the can, into a clean glass jar. They'll keep for months in the refrigerator, during which time you'll be spared the hassle of mincing—and the mess of an opened can covered haphazardly with foil or plastic wrap—so any time you want to add instant tangy, smoky spice it'll be at the ready. Try it on eggs, in a dressing or sauce (see page 259 for one), in a marinade, in a chili or stew, or in a pot of black beans.

SHOPPING THE MEXICAN GROCERY STORES

We live in extraordinary times, when just about anything you could need for a reasonably authentic Mexican or South American dish might, just *might*, be available at your local supermarket. For better value and more fun, though, head to a Latin grocery store. A list:

- **Corn tortillas and/or masa harina,** a fine flour made of nixtamalized (lye- or lime-treated) corn. The masa can be used to make your own tortillas (just add water—really) or to thicken soups and stews (see page 166). Yes, at a Mexican grocery you'll probably have to buy a very large quantity of readymade tortillas if you buy any at all, but go ahead: They keep, in the refrigerator or even just in a cool spot in the house (I keep ours in the mudroom), for weeks and weeks, and stale ones are the best for chilaquiles and fried tortilla strips or chips anyway because they have less moisture and so better retain crispness. The best widely available brand, to my taste, is Guererro, and I know this by dint of a very scientific taste test.

- **Dried giant white corn.** Use them just like dried beans, and in the Spicy Fried Giant White Corn on page 240. (Note that this isn't dried hominy, which is corn that's been nixtamalized—that is, soaked in an alkaline solution to remove the hulls—but you'd do well to bring home some canned or dried hominy, too.)

- **Dried chiles, chiles, chiles.** Start with guajillo (mild) and arbol (hot), and branch out into pasilla, ancho, and more.

- **Sesame seeds,** if you haven't yet stocked up at the Asian grocery. Pepitas (hulled pumpkin seeds) and other nuts and seeds can be had here too, but they'll likely be fresher at the natural foods store or from the supermarket bulk bins.

- Small cans of **chipotle chiles in adobo.**

- **Limes,** if you need them.

- **Poblano chiles** are usually cheap, firm, and glossy here, better than at the supermarket. Stock up, roast, peel, and seed them all as soon as you can, and stash them in the freezer.

- **Tomatillos** are also much better here than at the supermarket. Make an easy roasted salsa for the freezer, if you'd like, when you get home: Pull the papery husks off, rinse, and broil them with some garlic, onion, and chiles on a rimmed baking sheet until blackened in spots on both sides and quite soft. Put it all in a blender, including any juices, with lots of fresh cilantro, and puree. Season with salt and pepper, let cool, and use or freeze for later.

- **Cilantro.**

Rustic Tortilla Espagnola

SERVES 8

This pairing of a classic potato-and-egg tortilla with a pepper jam was inspired by a lunch I was once served from the lovely Farm Cart, a warm-weather food truck that world park outside the dear, departed Farm 255 restaurant in Athens, Georgia. Cut into bite-size pieces, it makes an attractive and crowd-pleasing appetizer or hors d'oeuvre. You could also top the pieces with dollops of the garlicky aioli on page 251. This tortilla is also wonderful made with half potatoes and half sweet potatoes.

1½ pounds (680 g) Yukon Gold potatoes, unpeeled

3 tablespoons olive oil

1 large onion, diced

6 large eggs

Salt and freshly ground black pepper

Red Pepper and Apple Jam (page 253) or a few pinches of paprika (optional)

Scrub the potatoes, put them in a large pot, and add cold water to cover by 1 inch (2.5 cm). Bring the water to a boil, then lower the heat and simmer until the potatoes are tender, about 20 minutes—a knife stuck in the center should slide out easily. Drain in a colander and set aside.

Meanwhile, in a 10-inch (25-cm) sauté pan, heat 1 tablespoon of the oil over medium heat until it shimmers. Add the onion and cook, stirring frequently, until soft and just starting to brown, about 8 minutes. Remove the pan from the heat and set aside.

In a large bowl, whisk together the eggs, 1 teaspoon salt, and several grindings of pepper.

Cut the drained potatoes—while still hot—into ⅛- to ¼-inch (3- to 6-mm) slices and add them to the bowl with the eggs. Add the salt, pepper, and sautéed onion and stir gently to combine.

Rinse out the onion pan, return it to the stovetop over medium heat, and heat 1 tablespoon of the oil until it shimmers, swirling to coat the bottom and sides of the pan. Pour in the potato-egg mixture and pat it down into an even layer with a spatula. Cook until the bottom is golden, about 10 minutes. Now here's the tricky part: Put a large plate upside down over the pan, grasp both the plate and pan with pot holders, hold them tightly together (there may be some loose egg that will attempt to flow out), and flip the whole contraption upside down to invert the tortilla onto the plate. Return the pan to medium-low heat, add the remaining 1 tablespoon oil, swirl to coat the pan, then slide the tortilla back into the pan, uncooked side down. Push the edges down underneath the tortilla to make a neat disk and cook until just set throughout (peek with a knife), about 15 minutes more. Invert again onto the plate and let stand for at least 5 minutes, or let cool completely, before slicing into wedges or squares. Serve warm or at room temperature, dolloped with jam or sprinkled with paprika.

Chickpea Crêpes Wrapped around Sautéed Potatoes and Greens

SERVES 1 OR 2 AS A MEAL

VEGAN

This is a surprisingly easy dish to make for a weekend breakfast (or if you happen to be awake too early on a weekday): The filling is designed for leftover cooked potatoes, and the crêpes can be made several days in advance.

1 teaspoon olive oil, or more if needed

¼ cup (30 g) diced onion

Salt and freshly ground black pepper

½ fresh hot green or red chile, seeded and minced (optional)

¾ cup (130 g) diced cooked potato

Handful of cleaned baby spinach or other tender greens

1 to 2 Chickpea Flour Crêpes (page 221), warm or at room temperature

In a sauté pan, heat the oil over medium-high heat. Add the onion, a pinch of salt, and a grinding of black pepper and cook, stirring frequently with a metal spatula, until the onion is golden, about 5 minutes. Add the chile, if using, and the potato. Cook, turning frequently with the spatula and adding a little more oil if necessary to keep it from sticking too much, until the potato is nicely browned, about 5 minutes. Pile in the greens and turn them with the spatula until they're just wilted. Taste and season with salt. Spoon the filling into a crêpe and serve.

Tamari-Butter Potato Wedges

SERVES 4

I'd never thought to roast potatoes with butter until one day when I was roasting a chicken and basting it with this marinade—and I decided to make some more for the potatoes. The butter browns quite enthusiastically, crisping the corners of the potato wedges and any flat sides in contact with the hot pan. Be sure to preheat the baking sheet in the oven before you spread the potatoes on it so they brown nicely.

4 tablespoons (65 g) unsalted butter

3 tablespoons tamari

3 cloves garlic, minced

1 large sprig fresh rosemary, leaves stripped off and minced

Freshly ground black papper

2 pounds (910 g) russet potatoes, peeled if you like, and cut lengthwise into ¾-inch (2-cm) wedges

Preheat the oven to 400°F (205°C). Set a large rimmed baking sheet in the oven while it heats.

In a small saucepan, combine the butter, tamari, garlic, rosemary, and a few grindings of pepper. Cook over medium heat, stirring, until the butter is melted, then remove the pan from the heat.

Put the potatoes in a large bowl, drizzle them with the tamari-butter mixture, and toss well to coat. Spread the potatoes on the hot baking sheet in a single layer. Roast until nicely browned on the bottom, 25 minutes, then turn the potato wedges with a metal spatula and roast until browned on the other side and tender throughout, 15 to 25 minutes more. Serve hot.

Mashed Potatoes and Kale

SERVES 4

Smooth mashed potatoes just don't do it for me. I think they're so much better with texture, and this dish, in which the potatoes are mashed into sautéed kale, takes that to what some people might consider an extreme.

2 large russet potatoes (about 1¾ pounds/800 g), peeled, quartered lengthwise, and cut crosswise into ¾-inch-thick (2-cm-thick) slices

Salt

2 tablespoons olive oil

1 sweet onion, diced

½ bunch (about 5 ounces/140 g) kale, tough stems and center ribs removed, leaves chopped

Pinch of hot red pepper flakes

Freshly grated nutmeg

6 tablespoons (90 ml) half-and-half

Freshly ground black pepper

Put the potatoes in a large saucepan and add cold water to cover by 1 inch (2.5 cm). Add a generous pinch of salt, and bring the water to a boil. Lower the heat and simmer until the potatoes are tender, about 15 minutes. Drain well and set aside.

Meanwhile, in a large, deep sauté pan, heat 1 tablespoon of the oil over medium heat until it shimmers. Add the onion and a pinch of salt and cook, stirring frequently, until the onion is softened and deeply browned, about 8 minutes. Add a splash of water to deglaze the pan, scraping up any stuck-on bits. Add the kale, red pepper flakes, and a good showering of nutmeg and cook, stirring frequently, until the kale is wilted and fairly tender, about 5 minutes. Scoot the kale to the edge of the pan and pour the remaining 1 tablespoon oil into the center. Add the cooked potatoes and mash them coarsely with a metal spatula, a potato masher, the back of a wooden spoon, or a pastry blender. Stir in the half-and-half, then incorporate the kale. Season with plenty of salt and pepper and cook, turning with a metal spatula, until heated through, about 2 minutes. Serve hot.

mushrooms

Every year Carol and Liz, Derek's mom and sister, cook a big Christmas feast—actually at least two, on Christmas Eve and Christmas, and often another a few days later. The first year I spent the holidays with them, Carol cooked a panful of mushrooms, and they were simply extraordinary. Nothing wacky, just a *whole lot* of butter (something for which she's been known all her life, apparently) and plenty of time in the skillet to get them browned and crusty. I'd never thought to cook mushrooms on their own as a side dish before, but I was converted. The only trick with mushrooms is to cook them over a fairly high heat, until (1) they release their liquid and then (2) the liquid has completely evaporated (if you're cooking in a pan rather than on a grill) and (3) the mushrooms have browned—the browning won't happen until after the liquid has evaporated, so give them time.

In spring you might see foraged wild mushrooms at the farmers' market, if it's a good one: honeycomb-looking morels, coral-colored and frilly chanterelles, elegant fresh porcini. Snap up a handful and cook them as simply as possible, in olive oil or butter, with salt and pepper, and *maybe* asparagus or shelled English peas if it's good stuff, and spoon them onto a simple risotto like the one on page 220, which also uses dried porcini.

MUSHROOMS: CLEANER THAN YOU THINK

Most mushrooms need only a quick wipe-down with a paper towel to clean them; don't obsess over it—the "dirt" on commercially grown mushrooms is most likely peat moss and is pretty clean. If you must get them sparkling clean, go ahead and rinse them quickly in a colander—in that short time they won't absorb very much water at all. Wild morels need more care, and you'll likely have to dunk them in water and swish them around with your hands to get the dirt out of the little crevices; the stems should be trimmed at the bottom if they're very dry. Shiitake stems are tough and stringy and should be pulled or cut off completely, but under no circumstances should you throw them out; save them for a wonderful stock, stashing them in the freezer for later if you have to.

Mushrooms and Crunchy Tofu with Tahini-Pomegranate Sauce

SERVES 2 TO 4

VEGAN

What a simple, satisfying lunch this makes! Shallow-fry the tofu until well browned and crisp—a *non*-nonstick pan is best for this—then toss with quickly sautéed mushrooms and a creamy dressing.

- 3 tablespoons vegetable oil, such as grapeseed
- 1 (15-ounce/425-g) block firm or extra-firm tofu, drained, patted dry, and cut into ¾-inch (2-cm) cubes
- 8 ounces (225 g) whole white or cremini mushrooms, bottoms trimmed, halved
- Salt and freshly ground black pepper
- ½ recipe Tahini-Pomegranate Sauce (page 250)
- ½ dry pint (140 g) grape tomatoes, halved
- 2 scallions, thinly sliced
- 1 teaspoon sesame seeds, toasted (optional)

In a large sauté pan (not nonstick, ideally), heat 2 tablespoons of the oil over medium-high heat until it shimmers. Add the tofu in a single layer (do this in two batches if your pan isn't big enough) and cook, undisturbed—this will decrease the likelihood that it'll stick or break apart when you turn it—until golden brown on the bottom, 2 minutes. Use a metal spatula to turn the cubes, and continue to cook, turning occasionally, for 8 to 10 minutes total, until most of the surfaces of the tofu are deeply browned and crisp. Transfer the tofu to paper towels to drain.

Return the pan to high heat. Add the remaining 1 tablespoon oil, the mushrooms, and a pinch each of salt and pepper. Cook, tossing frequently, until well browned all over and just tender, about 5 minutes.

Put the sauce in a large bowl. Taste and season with more salt and pepper, if needed; it should be pretty salty, since the tofu is bland. Add the mushrooms, tofu, tomatoes, and scallions to the sauce and toss to coat. Sprinkle with the sesame seeds, if using, and serve warm.

Sweet Wine Mushrooms

SERVES 2 OR 3

VEGAN

These simple but perfectly satisfying mushrooms, fragrant with sweet wine and caramelized onion, brightened with fresh lemon juice, make a satisfying addition to a vegetable plate—serve them with the greens and beans on page 226, perhaps a square or wedge of the Rustic Tortilla Espagnola on page 198, and a spoonful of sour, thick labneh or plain Greek yogurt.

- 2 tablespoons olive oil
- 1 sweet onion, finely diced
- Salt and freshly ground black pepper
- 8 ounces (225 g) cremini mushrooms, halved
- 1 tablespoon fresh lemon juice
- 2 tablespoons Marsala, cream sherry, or other sweet wine

In a large sauté pan, heat the oil over medium-high heat. Add the onion, a pinch of salt, and a grinding of pepper. Cook, stirring frequently, until the onion is nicely browned, about 8 minutes. Add the mushrooms and cook, tossing occasionally and increasing the heat as they release their liquid, until all of the liquid is evaporated and the mushrooms begin to brown, about 10 minutes. Add the lemon juice and wine and scrape up any browned bits from the bottom of the pan. Taste and season with salt and pepper. Serve hot.

Variation
Increase the lemon juice to 2 tablespoons and omit the wine. Just as the mushrooms are finished browning, add 2 tablespoons Salsa de Semillas (page 248) and roll and toss the mushrooms around in the pan for a few seconds to coat them. Serve in a corn tortilla, topped with Tomatillo and Avocado Salsa (page 71), Cilantro-Lime Yogurt Vinaigrette (page 260), or just a couple of slices of plain avocado and a squeeze of lime juice.

Roasted Mushrooms and Arugula
with Goat Cheese Polenta

SERVES 4

This may be the ideal way to cook a winter meal: Heat up a baking sheet in the oven, toss on some mushrooms and vegetables, and cook a grain on the stovetop that'll be ready when the vegetables are tender and starting to develop a tasty crust. Spoon the grain dish onto a platter, top with roasted vegetables, and serve with a robust red wine.

FOR THE MUSHROOMS

- 1 pound (455 g) small cremini or white mushrooms, or a mix that includes shiitake caps, wiped clean
- 6 mini sweet peppers, or 1 small red bell pepper, seeded and chopped
- 2 cloves garlic, minced
- 1 teaspoon fresh thyme leaves, chopped
- Salt and freshly ground black pepper
- 2 tablespoons olive oil
- 4 cups (about 3 ounces/80 g) baby arugula

FOR THE POLENTA

- Salt and freshly ground black pepper
- 1 cup (125 g) stone-ground polenta (coarse- or medium-grind cornmeal)
- 4 ounces (113 g) soft goat cheese

MAKE THE MUSHROOMS

Preheat the oven to 400°F (205°C). Set a large rimmed baking sheet or baking pan in the oven while it heats.

In a large bowl, toss together the mushrooms, sweet peppers, garlic, thyme, ¾ teaspoon salt, and several grindings of black pepper. Drizzle with 1 tablespoon of the oil and toss to coat. Spread the mushrooms on the hot baking sheet in a single layer. Roast until the mushrooms are tender and the sweet peppers are beginning to brown in spots, about 25 minutes. Pile the arugula on the baking sheet, drizzle it with the remaining 1 tablespoon oil, and toss to combine it with the other vegetables. Return the baking sheet to the oven until the arugula is wilted and tender, 2 to 5 minutes.

MAKE THE POLENTA

Meanwhile, in a large saucepan, bring 4 cups (1 L) water, ¾ teaspoon salt, and a couple grindings of pepper to a simmer. Gradually whisk in the polenta, a little at a time. Lower the heat to medium-low and cook, whisking occasionally and keeping the temperature such that bubbles plop from the surface every few seconds, until the polenta is thick and the individual grains are tender, 15 to 25 minutes. If you prefer a thinner polenta, whisk in a little more water or stock. Remove the pan from the heat, crumble in the cheese, and whisk to incorporate—it's okay if some lumps of cheese remain unmelted. Taste and season with salt and pepper, if needed. Spoon the polenta onto serving plates or a large platter, spoon the roasted vegetables on top, and serve hot.

Mushroom and Black Garlic Terrine

SERVES 6 TO 8

If you're looking for a good online time-suck, I'd recommend the series of master classes featuring the Irish chef Kevin Thornton, who talks a mile a minute as he's cooking, which is not so remarkable except that almost all of what he's saying is actually useful and enlightening. I'd been wanting to make a mushroom terrine and thinking it should be possible to make one that doesn't require baking, when I stumbled on the appropriate episode in the series, and so this terrine is based on Thornton's simple and straightforward method. I use briefly blanched flat kale leaves to wrap the terrine, because I think the min-

eral flavor of the dark greens heightens the meatiness of the sautéed mushrooms, but you could use sheets of nori instead, as Thornton does. The main flavor going on here besides the mushrooms is black garlic, which adds a slightly tangy, deep umami element. Serve slices of the terrine on small plates with a garnish of Pickled Beet Stems (page 254) as an elegant appetizer, or as the main part of a fancy vegetable plate, perhaps with Smoky Yellow Squash (page 55) and Spiced Brown Rice (page 219).

3 tablespoons olive oil

2 pounds (910 g) beautiful mushrooms of just about any kind (shiitake, oyster, chanterelle, morel, porcini), trimmed and thinly sliced

Salt and freshly ground black pepper

2 tablespoons Marsala or other sweet wine

½ cup (60 g) minced shallots

1 to 2 cloves black garlic (see Note, page 81), minced

1 teaspoon chopped fresh tarragon

1 tablespoon unsalted butter, at room temperature

About 8 large whole lacinato kale leaves, tough stems and thick center ribs removed

In a large, deep sauté pan, heat 1 tablespoon of the oil over high heat until it shimmers. Add half of the mushrooms, a generous pinch of salt, and a couple of grindings of pepper. Cook, tossing frequently, until the mushrooms have released their liquid and the liquid has completely evaporated, 12 to 15 minutes. Pour in half of the wine and cook, stirring to scrape up any browned bits, until it's completely evaporated, about 2 minutes. Transfer the mixture to a colander. Repeat with the remaining mushrooms and wine. Stir the mushrooms in the colander a bit to drain off any excess liquid.

In the same pan, heat the remaining 1 tablespoon oil over medium heat. Add the shallots and cook, stirring frequently, until soft and just beginning to brown, 3 to 5 minutes. Scrape the shallots into a large bowl. Add the drained mushrooms, black garlic, tarragon, and butter and toss to combine and melt the butter. Make sure the black garlic is evenly distrib-

uted in the mushrooms—it's pretty sticky. Taste and season with more salt and pepper, if needed—the mixture should be very flavorful.

Put a kettle of water on to boil and fill a bowl with ice water. Put the kale leaves in a flat baking dish or other heatproof container. Pour boiling water over the leaves to cover them and let stand for 2 minutes. Drain and transfer them to the ice water to cool, then gently squeeze out the water.

Line a 4-by-7-inch (10-by-17.5-cm) terrine mold or loaf pan with huge pieces of plastic wrap extending over all edges. Arrange the kale leaves flat in the mold to completely line the bottom and sides and overhang the sides a bit, saving a few leaves for the top. Gently spoon the mushroom mixture into the mold, spreading it evenly and flattening the mushroom slices. Top with the reserved kale leaves and press the mushrooms down a bit, folding the leaves from the sides over the ones on the top. Fold the overhanging plastic wrap over the whole thing and wrap tightly. Put a rigid piece of cardboard directly on top of the wrapped terrine, inside the mold, and weight it down with a heavy object that extends up above the rim of the mold—I use a large can of tomatoes. To press the terrine further, roll and wrap a thin towel around the mold and weight, tie it as tight as possible, then slip a spoon handle or sturdy stick in the knot to twist it even tighter and press the weight down even more firmly. Put the entire assembly in the refrigerator (wedge it so the spoon handle stays twisted tight, if possible) and chill for at least 24 hours and up to 48.

Unwrap, invert the mold onto a serving platter, slice the terrine with a sharp knife, and serve.

THE
PANTRY

lentils, beans, and whole grains

Several the dishes in this chapter—the more complex ones like the Spring Vegetables with Lentils and Quinoa (page 210), Tanya's Brown Lentil Salad (page 212), Makeshift Vegetable Biryani (page 218), and Porcini Risotto (page 220)—are ones that can easily stand alone as whole meals. I've given detailed instructions, but I'd be happier if you approached them more as templates, jumping-off points from which you can create your own pantry-staple–based dishes. Instead of spring vegetables in the first dish, for example, use summery zucchini and roasted peppers; instead of lentils and quinoa, use brown basmati and black-eyed peas.

Following those one-dish meals are several simple dishes using protein-rich lentils, dried beans, and wholesome gluten-free grains that make flavorful, filling bases for creative vegetarian meals. These are the recipes you should turn to if you need a good sauce-absorber, for example.

Finally, you'll find instructions for basic lentil, bean, and grain cooking, including my foolproof method for cooking any variety of long-grain brown rice (yes, you can make perfectly cooked brown rice, and you won't even have to measure anything). These recipes are ones that can be made well in advance, cooled, and refrigerated for several days or frozen for several months. Go ahead and cook plenty, and keep any you don't use right away in heavy-duty quart-size resealable bags in the freezer.

Spring Vegetables with Lentils and Quinoa

SERVES 2 OR 3 AS A MEAL

CAN BE VEGAN

This is one of the most likable one-dish meals in this book, and can be easily scaled up in a larger pan to serve more people (cooking times will increase a bit, so use your judgment to determine when vegetables are done and the rest is heated through). The combination of nutty asparagus with sweet peas, grated carrot, and minerally spinach makes a happy springtime dish, but feel free to substitute any vegetables that look good and are in season. If you have fresh morels or other mushrooms, by all means add them, too, or reconstitute dried mushrooms in hot water, rinse them well to remove any sand, and add them with the vegetables. Keep in mind that adding longer-cooking vegetables—like root vegetables, or especially tough green beans—will require your parcooking (cooking partially in boiling water, then draining) them before adding them to the skillet. Also, substitute the same quantity of other legumes and grains for the lentils and quinoa, if you like.

Gather all the ingredients together and have them ready, because the cooking only takes about ten minutes total.

1 tablespoon olive oil

1 clove garlic, chopped

2 spring onions, white parts thinly sliced, tender green tops cut into 1-inch (2.5-cm) lengths

¼ cup (60 ml) vegetable stock or water

5 ounces (140 g) asparagus, trimmed and cut into 1-inch (2.5-cm) lengths

½ cup (75 g) shelled fresh or frozen English peas

Salt and freshly ground black pepper

Pinch of hot red pepper flakes

1 small carrot, grated

1½ packed cups (2 ounces/57 g) baby spinach

Coarsely grated zest of 1 small lemon

1 cup (210 g) cooked French green lentils or black (beluga) lentils (see page 225)

1½ cups (260 g) cooked ivory quinoa (page 228)

1 ounce (28 g) feta cheese, or a small piece of hard cheese, such as Parmesan or aged Gouda (optional)

In a large sauté pan, heat the oil over medium-high heat until it shimmers. Add the garlic and white parts of the spring onions and cook, stirring, for 1 minute. Add the stock, asparagus, fresh peas (hold off if using frozen), green parts of the spring onions, a generous pinch of salt, several grindings of black pepper, and the red pepper flakes. Cook, stirring frequently, until the asparagus and peas are just tender, about 2 minutes. Add the carrot, spinach, lemon zest, and another pinch of salt (if using frozen peas, add them now). Pile in the lentils and quinoa. Cook, stirring gently to combine, until the spinach is wilted, the frozen peas (if using) are thawed, and the lentils and quinoa are just heated through, about 2 minutes. Crumble or grate in the cheese, if using. Divide among serving plates and serve hot.

Tanya's Brown Lentil Salad

SERVES 4

Last spring we went to southern California to visit my old college roommate and good friend Tanya. Our first evening there, she and her daughter, Ava, took us down to the beach about a mile from their house, where we spread a blanket on the sand (Ava and Thalia spread their own blanket a dozen yards away from us among the smooth rocks, good for climbing and hiding) and had a picnic with a bottle of red wine and a bottle of white and this salad as the sun went down behind the water. It got chilly in the dark, but the girls romped in the waves anyway, and we couldn't bring ourselves to leave.

In college in Virginia, Tanya had seemed to subsist—and indeed thrive as a volleyball star—on a diet of canned vanilla frosting and sprinkles, but now, back in her California stomping ground and hosting us on the beach, she was making dishes like this, which she described as just precooked lentils mixed with premade salsa and a container of cheese. Humble as that might sound, you might find it hard to put down your fork (or tortilla chip or rice cracker, if you're dipping, and you should), even if you're not eating out under the stars, listening to the Pacific Ocean and the cries of delighted daughters.

2½ cups (470 g) cooked, drained, and cooled brown or green lentils (see page 225)

3 Roma or plum tomatoes, finely diced

¼ sweet onion, finely diced

1 fresh hot green or red chile, such as serrano or jalapeño, seeded and minced

½ cup (20 g) chopped fresh cilantro

3 tablespoons fresh lime juice, or to taste

1 tablespoon olive oil

4 ounces (113 g) feta cheese

Salt and freshly ground black pepper

In a large bowl, toss together the lentils, tomatoes, onion, chile, cilantro, lime juice, and oil. Crumble in the cheese, season with salt (about ½ teaspoon) and several grindings of black pepper and toss well. Cover and refrigerate for at least 1 hour or up to 4 hours. Serve cold.

Refried Lentils

SERVES 3 OR 4

VEGAN

Lentils can absolutely be fried up in a skillet as if they were beans, with oregano, cumin, and some chile for heat. Serve these with a fresh tomato salad, or the Grilled Sweet Corn and Feta Salad on page 84, or underneath a stew of chunky vegetables sautéed until just tender and then doused with The Correct Chile Relleño Sauce (see page 250).

- 2 tablespoons vegetable oil
- 1 onion, diced
- 2 cloves garlic, chopped
- Salt and freshly ground black pepper
- ½ teaspoon dried oregano, preferably Mexican
- ¼ teaspoon ground cumin
- ¼ teaspoon dried chipotle flakes
- 2½ cups (470 g) cooked and drained brown or green lentils (see page 225)

In a large sauté pan or skillet, heat 1 tablespoon of the oil over medium heat until it shimmers. Add the onion, garlic, a pinch of salt, and a grinding of black pepper. Cook, stirring frequently, until the onion is very soft, deeply browned but not burned, and no bits of bright white remain, at least 15 minutes; lower the heat and/or add a splash of water if the onion starts to stick to the pan too much or browns too quickly. The onion mixture should be reduced to just a few tablespoons in volume. Stir in the oregano, cumin, and chipotle flakes.

Scoot the onion mixture to one side of the pan and add the remaining 1 tablespoon oil to the empty part of the pan. Dump in the lentils and cook, turning and mashing them with a metal spatula and stirring them into the onion mixture, until they are heated through and starting to stick to the pan and the flavors have developed, about 5 minutes. Drizzle in about 1 cup (240 ml) water, if you'd like a mushier consistency, and heat through, stirring and mashing. Taste and season with salt, if needed. Serve hot.

Red Lentil Sauce-Absorber

SERVES 3 OR 4

VEGAN

This is your all-purpose red lentil dish, which can be seasoned in a wide variety of ways—try stirring in a little Garam Masala (page 247), or a Cajun spice mix, or even a spoonful of Arugula Pesto (page 256)—and spooned onto your plate with the idea that it will soak up cooking juices, salad dressings, and sauces from nearby vegetables.

- 1 tablespoon olive oil
- ½ sweet onion, diced
- 1 small carrot, diced
- 1 clove garlic, minced
- Salt and freshly ground black pepper
- 1 cup (230 g) red lentils (*masoor dal*), rinsed and drained

In a medium saucepan, heat the oil over medium-high heat. Add the onion, carrot, garlic, ½ teaspoon salt, and a few grindings of pepper. Cook, stirring frequently, until the onion is translucent, about 5 minutes. Add the lentils and 2 cups (480 ml) water. Bring to a boil, then lower the heat and simmer, stirring occasionally, until the lentils are tender but still hold their shape and the liquid surrounding them is creamy, about 10 minutes. Serve hot.

SHOPPING THE BULK BINS AND NATURAL FOODS STORES

Not so long ago, the phrase *bulk bin* might have conjured one of two extremes: the discouraging tubs of musty grains and textured vegetable protein in medicinal-smelling "health food" stores, or the barrels of gumdrops, animal crackers, generic shredded wheat, and mixed nuts you might see in larger supermarkets. Today, though, nearly every decent supermarket and natural or whole foods store has an array of products sold in bulk, including spices and dried herbs, and sometimes liquid ingredients like olive oil, tamari, local honey, agave nectar, and maple syrup. Find a shop where the turnover rate seems to be high, and stock up. (Keep in mind that if you're strictly gluten free, you should opt to buy prepackaged goods to avoid the contamination that inevitably occurs among bins.) Here's a list of ingredients you might want to pick up from the bulk barrels and dispensers, as well as the regular aisles, of a whole foods shop:

- **Brown rice:** I use basmati for Indian dishes, jasmine for Thai, regular long-grain for all-purpose use, and short-grain for risottos and anything where you want the rice to stick together a bit.
- **Lentils and peas:** Look for French green (Puy) and black (beluga) lentils, both of which keep their shape and stay firm after cooking—great for salads and for freezing—as well as regular brown or green and red lentils for everyday use. Yellow split peas will come in handy for *khoreshes* (hearty Persian stews) and to bulk up long-cooking vegetable stews.
- **Nuts:** Buy raw cashews for cashew cream and for frying as a snack or topping, as well as whole and sliced "natural" almonds, pecans, walnuts (if they're fresh—smell them), shelled pistachios, and pine nuts as a splurge.
- **Seeds:** Sesame and flax seeds, plus pepitas.
- **Unsweetened grated coconut.**

- **Flour:** It's best to use finely ground store-bought oat flour (as opposed to homemade) for treats like the Lavender-Oat Shortbread on page 237 where the flour is the main ingredient. If it's refrigerated, almond flour is worth picking up here too.
- **Nonfat dry milk powder:** Here's where you find the very fine, powdery stuff you can use to make the Frothy Hot Spiced Milk Mix on page 263. It's also useful for adding to baked goods.
- **Citric acid:** This can often be found among the bulk spice jars; pick some up if you didn't find it at the Indian grocery and want to make the best chaat masala ever (see page 109). Also helpful if you are a tomato canner.
- **Tamari, agave nectar,** and **honey.**
- **Seaweeds:** Nori, dulse, wakame, and so on. Pick up a kind you've never tried before and experiment! If it's stiff, soak it and then add it to a salad. If it's crumbly, you can probably just use it straight. Dulse leaves (not the flakes) are especially nice crisped in a sauté pan with a little oil.

There are countless online sources for dry goods if you can't find the above in a store. One especially reliable retailer offering a wide variety of nuts, seeds, and grains is Nuts.com.

All-Purpose Urad Dal

SERVES 4

VEGAN

Urad dal is a black bean, very common in Indian cuisine, that has been peeled to reveal the white interior and split in half. You'll sometimes see it labeled "peeled black gram" or "white lentils." When it's cooked in water and stirred vigorously (I use a whisk), it becomes creamy and thick. Simply spiced dal, with plain steamed rice or Spiced Brown Rice (page 219), plus a quickly sautéed vegetable with a little sauce, like the Masala Sweet Potatoes on page 131, make a very fine supper. Set a jar of Cilantro-Mint Chutney (page 109) and a bowl of salted and whisked plain yogurt on the table, and it's dinner-party-worthy. The dal can be made well in advance and reheated just before serving, with a splash of extra water stirred in to loosen it.

1 tablespoon vegetable oil

1 shallot, minced

4 coins peeled fresh ginger, minced

2 cloves garlic, minced

Salt

½ teaspoon cumin seeds

½ teaspoon mustard seeds

½ teaspoon *kalonji* (nigella) seeds (optional, but worth seeking out)

1½ cups (270 g) *urad dal* (split and peeled black gram), rinsed and drained

In a large saucepan, heat the oil over medium-high heat until it shimmers. Add the shallot, ginger, garlic, and a pinch of salt. Cook, stirring, until the shallot is just tender, 1 to 2 minutes. Lower the heat to medium-low and add the cumin, mustard, and *kalonji* seeds, if using, and stir until the seeds start to pop, about 1 minute. Add the dal, 3 ½ cups (840 ml) water, and ¾ teaspoon salt. Raise the heat to high and bring the mixture to a boil, then lower the heat and simmer, whisking occasionally (and more frequently toward the end), until the dal is tender but still holds its shape and the liquid is creamy, about 30 minutes. Taste and add more salt, if needed. For a smoother dish, puree the dal with an immersion blender. Add a little water if you'd like a soupier consistency.

The Perfect Black Bean Soup

SERVES 3 OR 4

VEGAN

Most black bean soup, in my opinion, is too thick and too coarse-textured. I think I might as well be eating regular black beans, and enjoying them as such, instead of pretending that this stuff in my bowl is soup. This soup, on the other hand, especially if you go the distance and push it through a sieve (use a medium-mesh one and it won't be that much of a trial—I promise), is a true soup: not a bean puree but a silky and deeply black bean–flavored broth. A soup you could *sip*, in other words. Try it with the tangy, creamy avocado dollop and Salsa de Semillas (page 248), or just pile some diced avocado in the bowl and sprinkle with toasted sesame seeds.

FOR THE AVOCADO PUREE

- 1 large Hass avocado
- 2 tablespoons fresh lime juice
- Salt
- A few drops of hot sauce (optional)

FOR THE SOUP

- 4 cups (440 g) drained cooked black beans (see page 226), plus 3 cups (720 ml) broth from cooked black beans
- Salt and freshly ground black pepper
- 3 tablespoons cream sherry vinegar, or half regular sherry vinegar and half cream sherry or sweet Marsala wine
- Salsa de Semillas (page 248)

MAKE THE AVOCADO PUREE

Using a chef's knife, halve the avocado lengthwise. Remove the pit by holding the pit half in your palm and carefully letting the knife drop partway into the pit; twist the knife to loosen and pull out the pit, then use your thumb and forefinger to pinch the pit off the knife. Scoop the flesh from the peel into a mini food processor. Add the lime juice, ¾ teaspoon salt, and the hot sauce, if using, and process until very, very smooth. Taste and add more salt, if needed. (To store, scrape into a small container and nestle the pit into the center. Cover with plastic wrap pressed directly onto the surface of the puree. The puree will keep in the refrigerator for up to 3 days.)

MAKE THE SOUP

In a large saucepan or pot, combine the beans, broth, a pinch of salt, and a few grindings of pepper and bring to a boil. Lower the heat and simmer for 5 minutes. Puree until very smooth, using either a regular blender (vent the lid and put a kitchen towel over the top to keep it from exploding, and work in batches if necessary) or an immersion blender. To make it "perfect," take the extra step: Pour the soup through a sieve into a clean saucepan, pressing gently with a spatula until the pulp in the sieve (little bits of the bean skins) is the consistency of thick applesauce; discard the solids. Reheat the soup over medium-low heat, stirring constantly with a heatproof spatula. Taste and season with more salt and pepper, if needed. Just before serving, stir in the vinegar. The consistency should be like that of half-and-half or light cream, not too thick and not too watery.

Ladle the soup into wide soup plates. Put a dollop of avocado puree in each serving, and sprinkle each bowl with about 2 teaspoons of the salsa de semillas. Serve.

Warm Borlotti Bean Salad

SERVES 4

VEGAN

Derek makes the absolute best Santa Maria–style grilled tri-tip steak in the world. I usually try to round out the meal with pink beans and a fresh salsa studded with celery and oregano—the traditional accompaniments to tri-tip—which mingle on the plate. Even when Derek's special tri-tip is not in the offing, I'll make this homey dish combining that bright, raw salsa and warm, creamy beans and think of lovely, lazy spring and fall grilling days.

2½ cups (275 g) cooked and drained borlotti (cranberry) beans (see page 226)

2 tender ribs celery, finely diced

4 ripe Roma tomatoes, diced

¼ sweet onion, finely diced

2 scallions, thinly sliced

1 clove garlic, grated

2 teaspoons minced fresh oregano or marjoram

2 tablespoons red wine vinegar

1 tablespoon olive oil

Pinch of ground cayenne

1½ teaspoons tamari, or to taste

Freshly ground black pepper

In a saucepan, combine the beans and ¼ cup (60 ml) water and cook over medium-low heat, stirring gently with a heat-proof spatula, until heated through, 3 to 5 minutes. Add the celery, tomatoes, onions, scallions, garlic, oregano, vinegar, oil, and cayenne, as well as tamari and black pepper to taste. Toss well. Serve warm.

Garlic-Sautéed White Beans and Winter Greens

SERVES 2 OR 3

You couldn't design an easier or more satisfying, comforting, and nutritious dish than beans and greens, and it's one of those dishes that hardly needs a recipe at all. I used to sauté the greens first, then dump in the beans, but my friend Mary Jessica mentioned that she starts with the beans, and I now prefer this order of events, as the beans break up a bit and melt into the greens more. But if you'd like more distinct elements, start with the garlic, then the greens, then the beans, cooking just to heat them through. Serve these with polenta (see page 224), or Sweet Wine Mushrooms (page 205), or fried or poached eggs.

continued

- 2 tablespoons olive oil
- 3 cloves garlic, chopped
- 1½ cups (165 g) cooked and drained white beans (see page 226)
- Pinch of hot red pepper flakes
- 5 cups (190 g) chopped greens, such as beet tops, turnip greens, mustard greens, or kale
- ¼ cup (60 ml) dry white wine
- ¼ cup (60 ml) vegetable stock or water
- Salt and freshly ground black pepper
- ¼ cup (40 g) finely crumbled cotija or freshly grated hard cheese, such as Parmesan or pecorino

In a large sauté pan, heat the oil over medium heat until it shimmers. Add the garlic and cook, stirring frequently, until soft and beginning to turn golden, about 2 minutes. Add the beans and red pepper flakes and cook, stirring, for 2 minutes. Pile in the greens, sprinkle with a good pinch of salt and a couple of grindings of pepper, and drizzle with the wine and stock. Cover the pan and cook, lifting the lid to turn the beans and greens occasionally, until the greens are tender and the beans are starting to fall apart, about 5 minutes. Taste and season with salt and pepper, if needed. Sprinkle with the cheese and serve hot.

Makeshift Vegetable Biryani

SERVES 4 AS A MEAL

VEGAN

My six-year-old daughter, Thalia, is a fantastic eater in most respects, but I'm still searching for a classic Indian dish she'll love. So far the best contender is this mildly spiced mixed-vegetable biryani, basmati rice studded with raisins and cashews—I make it without chiles for her. You can use just about any combination of vegetables you'd like: Carrots, finely chopped cauliflower and broccoli, sweet corn kernels, and zucchini and yellow squash are all great, but you could go further afield and try thinly sliced *gai lan* (Chinese broccoli) or broccoli rabe, or parcooked diced turnips, rutabagas, potatoes, or sweet potatoes.

- 2 tablespoons raisins
- 1 tablespoon vegetable oil
- ¼ cup (30 g) raw cashews, coarsely chopped
- ½ teaspoon cumin seeds
- About 2 cups (300 g) diced raw mixed vegetables
- 2 coins peeled fresh ginger, minced
- 1 fresh hot chile, seeded and minced (optional)
- Salt
- About 3 cups (450 g) cooked and cooled Long-Grain Brown Rice (page 228) or Spiced Brown Rice (page 219; if using spiced rice, eliminate cumin seeds above)
- ½ cup (90 g) halved small cherry tomatoes or diced regular tomatoes
- Chopped fresh cilantro (optional)

Put the raisins in a cup and add hot water to cover; let soak for 5 to 10 minutes, then drain the raisins and set aside.

In a large, deep sauté pan, heat the oil over medium-high heat until it shimmers. Add the cashews and cumin. Cook, stirring frequently, until fragrant and just starting to turn golden, 1 to 2 minutes. Add the vegetables, ginger, chile, if using, and a pinch of salt. Cook, stirring frequently, until the vegetables are just barely tender, 4 to 8 minutes depending on the vegetables; if they start to stick to the pan too much for comfort, add a splash of water. Add the rice, tomatoes, and drained raisins and sprinkle with ½ teaspoon salt. Cook, turning with a spatula, until the rice is heated through and the vegetables are evenly distributed throughout, 2 to 3 minutes. Taste and add more salt, if needed. Transfer to a serving bowl and scatter some cilantro over the top, if you'd like. Serve hot.

Spiced Brown Rice

SERVES 2 OR 3

VEGAN

This is the basic rice to serve with an Indian meal, in which case you should most definitely seek out fragrant brown basmati. If you'd like to make a larger batch, just double the quantities and use a larger saucepan.

1 cup (105 g) brown basmati or other long grain brown rice

1 tablespoon vegetable oil

2 green cardamom pods

2 whole cloves

½ teaspoon cumin seeds

½ teaspoon salt

Variation
If the rice is to accompany a Mexican dish, omit the cardamom and cloves, and fold in 2 tablespoons chopped fresh cilantro just before serving. You can also sauté a little finely minced onion and garlic in the oil before adding the spices.

Put the rice in a medium saucepan and add water to cover by about 1 inch (2.5 cm). Bring the water to a boil, uncovered, then lower the heat and simmer briskly for 15 minutes. Drain the rice in a sieve and rinse it under cold running water to cool; drain well. (At this point you can put the parcooked rice in an airtight container and keep it in the refrigerator for several days, or freeze it for up to 3 months; to thaw it, put it in a sieve and rinse it under cold running water to break up the grains.)

Return the saucepan to medium heat and add the oil, cardamom, cloves, and cumin. Cook, stirring, for 1 minute. Add the drained rice and salt and stir for 1 minute. Add 1 cup (240 ml) water, stir, and raise the heat to high. Bring the mixture to a full boil, then lower the heat to medium-low, cover, and simmer until the rice is tender and all the water has been absorbed, about 15 minutes; fluff the rice with a spatula, cover, and let stand for 5 minutes more. If the rice is tender but there's still water in the pan, just drain the rice in a sieve and return it to the pan, cover, and let stand for 5 minutes. Serve hot.

SPICED BASMATI RICE USING LEFTOVERS

Cooking rice with the whole spices in the water results in a more flavorful dish, as the spices gently infuse the grains as they plump. But you can also just cook a big batch of basic, unspiced brown rice, keep it in bags in the freezer, then thaw what you need for each meal. When ready to serve, heat 2 tablespoons oil in a large sauté pan over medium-high heat until it shimmers, add the whole spices, and cook, stirring, until they're fragrant. Spoon in the thawed rice, sprinkle it with salt and add a glassful of water, cover, and steam, stirring once or twice, until heated through, about 5 minutes.

Porcini Risotto

SERVES 3 OR 4

Making a risotto with brown rice (short-grain rice is best) will take a good hour or so, but the nubby texture and deep flavors are worth the time. I've broken the rice-cooking down into two parts here so you can parcook the rice in a saucepan while the aromatics—onion, garlic, wine, mushrooms—are sizzling in a sauté pan. As the risotto simmers, try cooking up some fresh mushrooms or other vegetables in a bit of olive oil to spoon on top of the finished rice.

1 ounce (28 g) dried porcini mushrooms

1 cup (185 g) short-grain brown rice

1¾ cups (420 ml) vegetable stock

1 tablespoon olive oil or unsalted butter

½ small onion, diced

1 clove garlic, minced

Salt and freshly ground black pepper

½ cup (120 ml) dry white, red, or rosé wine

1 tablespoon cream cheese, or 2 tablespoons heavy cream

Put the porcini in a heatproof cup and add about 1 cup (240 ml) very hot water, or enough to cover. Let soak for 15 to 20 minutes, until soft. Agitate the mushrooms a bit to loosen any sand, then let the water settle. Gently lift out the mushrooms and finely chop them, discarding any very tough bits of stem. Reserve the soaking liquid.

At the same time, in a medium saucepan, combine the rice and stock and bring the stock to a boil, then lower the heat and simmer briskly, uncovered, for 15 to 20 minutes.

Meanwhile, in a large sauté pan, heat the oil over medium-high heat until it shimmers. Add the onion, garlic, a pinch of salt, and a grinding of pepper. Cook, stirring frequently, until the onion is translucent and golden, about 7 minutes. Add the mushrooms and wine and stir, scraping up any bits on the bottom of the pan. When the wine has evaporated, carefully add the rice and its cooking liquid to the mushroom mixture, and stir in ½ teaspoon salt. Bring the mixture to a boil, then lower the heat to maintain a brisk simmer. Stir occasionally and add enough mushroom soaking liquid (poured through a very-fine-mesh sieve or a regular sieve lined with two layers of rinsed and squeezed cheesecloth, or being very careful not to add the grit in the bottom of the cup) to keep the mixture soupy; if the mushroom liquid runs out before the rice is very tender, add plain water. Cook until the rice is tender and the liquid surrounding it is a little creamy, 20 to 30 minutes, letting much of the excess liquid evaporate toward the end.

Stir in the cream cheese and let it melt into the risotto, then taste and stir in more salt, if needed. Serve hot.

Chickpea Flour Crêpes

MAKES ABOUT 8

These light, soft crêpes are pretty much foolproof, especially if you have a good nonstick pan or griddle, in which case you don't even need to oil the surface. Keep a plastic-wrapped stack of these in the fridge for a last-minute meal; you can easily double the batch. Bring them to room temperature and fill with any combination of vegetables you can think of: sautéed chickpeas, sweet peppers, and greens; sautéed chopped asparagus and sweet peas with dollops of ricotta; or warm Black Beans with Epazote (page 226), chopped tomatoes, and sliced avocado. They're especially good for breakfast, filled with sautéed potatoes and spinach (page 200).

> 1 cup (130 g) chickpea flour (*besan*)
>
> Salt
>
> Olive oil, for the pan

If the chickpea flour is lumpy, sift it into a medium bowl. Whisk in a pinch of salt and 1 cup (240 ml) water until smooth. Let stand at room temperature for a few minutes or up to 2 hours, whisk again, and add more water, if needed, until the consistency of heavy cream.

Heat a nonstick griddle or well-seasoned cast-iron skillet over medium heat until a drop of water skids across the surface before evaporating. (If not using a nonstick pan, wipe the pan with an oil-moistened paper towel, and repeat this before making each crêpe.) Pour about ¼ cup (60 ml) of the batter in the center of the pan and tilt the pan to spread the batter as thinly as possible while keeping the pool of batter in an essentially round configuration. Cook until the crêpe is dry on the surface, about 30 seconds; do not flip. Transfer the crêpe to a plate and repeat with the remaining batter. (The crêpes can be kept in the refrigerator, tightly wrapped in plastic, for several days. Pull one out and fill it when you need a quick meal.)

Millet-Parmesan Cake

SERVES 4 TO 6

While plain steamed millet, perhaps with a shaving of Roasted Vegetable Stock Concentrate (page 262) added to the cooking water, makes an ideal sauce-absorber, this firm baked cake of millet with eggs and cheese can serve a similar purpose while providing a more interesting texture. Try it with the root vegetable hash on page 134.

> Olive oil, for the pan
>
> 3 large eggs
>
> ½ cup (50 g) finely grated Parmesan or other hard cheese
>
> Salt and freshly ground black pepper
>
> 3 cups (550 g) Steamed Millet (page 228), cooled

Preheat the oven to 350°F (175°C). Generously oil the bottom and sides of a 9-inch (22.5-cm) round cake pan. If you want to turn the cake out of the pan for serving, line the bottom with a round of parchment and oil the parchment.

In a large bowl, whisk together the eggs, cheese, ¾ teaspoon salt, and several grindings of pepper. Add the millet and use a rubber spatula to thoroughly combine the millet with the egg mixture, then spread it evenly in the prepared pan. Bake until firm in the center, dry on top, and sizzling around the edges, about 35 minutes. Cut into wedges and serve from the pan, or, if you used parchment, invert it onto a platter, peel off the paper, slice, and serve.

Seedy Quinoa Cakes

MAKES ABOUT 8; SERVES 4

CAN BE VEGAN

The mixed herbs are a great way to vary the flavors of these crisp-crusted patties of quinoa and crunchy seeds. Try a combination of equal parts cilantro, Thai basil, and scallion, plus a very finely minced Kaffir lime leaf if serving with, say, Red Coconut Curry Kale (page 156). Or use basil and parsley, decrease the salt, and add a couple of tablespoons of grated Parmesan if you're making the cakes to accompany something Italian-inflected, like Twice-Roasted Eggplant and Red Pepper (page 100) or The Perfect Caponata (page 102). These hold up well in a bento box, too, as they're just fine at room temperature.

Olive or vegetable oil

1 large egg, or 2 tablespoons golden flax seeds plus ¼ cup (60 ml) warm water

3 cups (525 g) cooked and cooled quinoa, any color, or a mixture

3 tablespoons minced herbs and/or scallions (optional)

2 tablespoons pepitas

2 tablespoons sunflower seeds

Salt

About 2 tablespoons oat flour, if needed

Preheat the oven to 350°F (175°C). Oil a baking sheet.

Whisk the egg thoroughly in a large bowl. (If using flax seed instead of egg, grind it finely in a spice mill and put it in a large bowl with the warm water. Whisk well, until it has the consistency of beaten egg whites.)

Add the quinoa to the egg and stir vigorously. Add the herbs, if using, the pepitas, sunflower seeds, and ¾ teaspoon salt and beat well. If the mixture is very loose, beat in the oat flour. Wet your palms and form the mixture into about 8 patties; they won't hold their shape well on their own, so just put each straight on the baking sheet and nudge it into shape, a bit less than ½ inch (12 mm) thick and 4 inches (10 cm) in diameter.

Drizzle the cakes with a little oil and bake until firm and crisp, about 30 minutes, turning them over halfway through the cooking time. If you'd like a browner top, put them under the broiler, about 6 inches (15 cm) away from the heat source, for 3 to 5 minutes. Serve hot or warm.

Variation

If you have a free burner on the stovetop, it's quicker to pan-fry the cakes, and though they do absorb more oil, the finished cakes are more delicate and even crispier: Heat 2 tablespoons oil in a large sauté pan over medium-high heat, add the cakes, and use a metal spatula to flatten them in the pan. Cook, undisturbed, for about 5 minutes, until nicely browned on the bottom, then carefully flip them with the spatula and cook until the second side is browned and the cakes are heated through, about 5 minutes more; if they're browning too quickly, lower the heat. Add more oil and cook the second batch, keeping the first warm on a plate in a warm oven, if you'd like.

Sweet Corn Polenta

SERVES 2 TO 4

VEGAN

Polenta with fresh sweet corn and herbs: It doesn't get much better than this. Serve a scoopful of it underneath the Healing Stew on page 63, or really any stew, or with black beans and a simple green salad—or do as I do and warm some up for breakfast and serve it with half an avocado, sprinkled with lime juice and Salsa de Semillas (page 248).

4 cups (1 L) weak vegetable stock or water, or a little more if needed

1 cup (125 g) stone-ground polenta (coarse- or medium-grind cornmeal)

Salt and freshly ground black pepper

1 tablespoon olive oil

¼ sweet onion, diced

2 cups (330 g) sweet corn kernels (cut from about 3 large ears)

4 small sprigs fresh basil, leaves torn, or 2 tablespoons chopped fresh cilantro

In a large saucepan, bring the stock to a simmer. Add the polenta a little at a time, whisking constantly. Return to a simmer and cook, whisking occasionally and sweeping the whisk around the bottom of the pan to make sure nothing's sticking, until the polenta is thickened and the individual grains are tender, 15 to 25 minutes depending on the grind. Taste and season with salt and a few grindings of pepper. If you'd like a looser polenta, add a little water or stock and taste again.

Meanwhile, in a large sauté pan, heat the oil over medium-high heat. Add the onion and a pinch of salt and cook, stirring frequently, until the onion is translucent, 5 to 7 minutes. Add the corn and cook, stirring frequently, until tender and golden, 4 to 5 minutes. Scrape the mixture into the cooked polenta and stir well. Stir in the basil leaves and serve hot.

pantry basics

Black (Beluga) Lentils

MAKES ABOUT 2 CUPS (415 G)

VEGAN

1 cup (200 g) black (beluga) lentils
Salt

Rinse the lentils in a sieve under cold running water and finger through them quickly to make sure there are no pebbles or other stray non-lentil materials. Transfer them to a medium saucepan and add enough cold water to cover by 2 inches (5 cm). Bring the water to a boil, then lower the heat and simmer, uncovered, until the lentils are tender but still hold their shape and aren't falling apart, 20 to 25 minutes, adding a good pinch of salt in the last 5 minutes. Drain in a sieve. If you're not using the lentils right away, rinse them under cold running water to cool, then transfer them to an airtight container and refrigerate for up to 4 days or freeze in a freezer bag or other freezer-safe container for up to 3 months.

Brown or Green Lentils

MAKES ABOUT 2½ CUPS (470 G)

VEGAN

1 cup (200 g) brown or regular green (not French) lentils
Salt

Rinse the lentils in a sieve under cold running water and finger through them quickly to make sure there are no pebbles or other stray non-lentil materials. Transfer them to a medium saucepan and add enough cold water to cover by 2 inches (5 cm). Bring the water to a boil, then lower the heat and simmer, uncovered, until the lentils are tender but still hold their shape and aren't falling apart, about 20 minutes, adding 1 teaspoon salt in the last 5 minutes. Drain in a sieve. If you're not using the lentils right away, rinse them under cold running water to cool, then transfer them to an airtight container and refrigerate for up to 4 days or freeze in a freezer bag or other freezer-safe container for up to 3 months.

Basic Black Beans with Epazote

VEGAN

1 pound (455 g) dried black beans

1 onion, diced

2 cloves garlic, minced

1 dried arbol or cayenne chile

1 bay leaf

1 teaspoon dried epazote (see Note)

½ teaspoon ground cumin

Salt

Rinse the beans under cold running water. If you have the time, soak them in cold water to cover by at least 2 inches (5 cm) for 8 hours or overnight. If you don't have the time, cover them with water in a large saucepan or pot, bring to a boil, then remove from the heat and let soak for 1 hour.

Drain the beans, return them to the pan, and add the onion, garlic, chile, bay leaf, epazote, cumin, and 8 cups (2 L) water. Bring the water to a boil, then lower the heat and simmer gently, with the lid askew, until the beans are tender, adding 2 teaspoons salt in the last 15 to 30 minutes of cooking (so the salt won't keep the beans from becoming soft) and adding a bit of water every once in a while to keep the water level consistent. Depending on the size and age of the beans, this could take from 1 hour 15 minutes to 1 hour 45 minutes. (Alternatively, use a slow cooker: Cook on the low setting for about 8 hours or on high for about 4 hours, adding the salt toward the end.) Serve, or let cool, then ladle the beans and broth into an airtight container and refrigerate for up to 3 days, reheating on the stovetop before serving. Or see the sidebar at right for more ways to use the beans and broth, either together or separately.

Note: Epazote is a pungent herb that's readily available in dried form in Latin American grocery stores and in the Mexican foods section of many regular supermarkets.

Beans

VEGAN

I've found that the best way to achieve beans that are creamy on the inside and hold their shape nicely is to let the beans cool completely in their cooking liquid.

About 2 cups (1 pound/455 g) dried white beans, such as navy, cannellini, flageolet, or Great Northern beans; dried chickpeas; or dried pink or red beans, such as kidney, borlotti, or cranberry beans

Salt

Rinse the beans under cold running water. If you have time, soak them in cold water to cover by at least 2 inches (5 cm) for 8 hours or overnight. If you don't have time, cover them with water in a Dutch oven or pot, bring to a boil, then remove from the heat, cover, and let soak for 1 hour.

Drain the beans, return them to the pan, and add 8 cups (2 L) fresh water. Bring the water to a boil, then lower the heat and simmer gently, with the lid askew, until the beans are tender, adding 2 teaspoons salt in the last 15 to 30 minutes of cooking (so the salt won't keep the beans from becoming soft) and adding more water as needed to keep the water level consistent. Depending on the size and age of the beans, this could take anywhere from 1 hour 15 minutes to 1 hour 45 minutes. (Alternatively, use a slow cooker: Cook on the low setting for about 8 hours or on high for about 4 hours, adding the salt toward the end.) If you're not serving the beans hot right away, let them cool in their cooking liquid.

Drain the beans in a colander. Serve plain or in another recipe. They'll keep in zip-top bags or other airtight containers in the refrigerator for several days or in the freezer for up to 3 months.

SO YOU HAVE A POT OF BEANS

Once you've cooked a big batch of beans, you have several options for proceeding. Drain the beans in a colander set over a bowl, and use the broth and some of the beans for soup (see page 216); spoon the remaining beans into a freezer bag or other container and freeze or refrigerate for later. Or lightly mash some of the beans with some broth to serve with rice. Or drain in a colander and use the beans in a salad (think salsa), and simmer the broth until it's reduced to a thick sauce consistency, stir in a few drops of cream sherry or agave nectar, and drizzle over grilled vegetables or into the Creamy Cashew Asparagus Soup with Pea Shoots on page 32. Or, of course, skip the draining altogether and serve the beans as they are, with plenty of rice and/or tortillas for sopping up the flavorful broth.

USING YOUR LARGE-BATCH BEANS, LENTILS, AND BROWN RICE

To thaw and reheat frozen beans, lentils, or brown rice, break the frozen mass apart and put it in a pan with a little water. Cover and cook over medium heat, lifting the lid and stirring occasionally, until thawed—it won't take long. If you want to serve them cold, in a salad, for example (French green lentils and black beluga lentils are best because they hold their shape), empty the frozen mass into a colander and rinse under cold running water until the beans, lentils, or grains break apart and separate, gently helping them along with your fingers. Rinse for a minute or so longer to finish thawing, or just let them thaw and drain for a while in the colander while you prepare the rest of your dish.

Long-Grain Brown Rice

MAKES ABOUT 3 CUPS (450 G)

VEGAN

This method can be used for any kind of long-grain brown rice—basmati, jasmine, or regular.

> 1 cup (185 g) long-grain brown rice
> Salt

Put the rice and ½ teaspoon salt in a medium saucepan and add water to cover by about 1 inch (2.5 cm). Bring the water to a boil, then lower the heat and simmer briskly, uncovered, for 15 to 20 minutes—the rice should be a little softened but still raw inside. Drain the rice in a sieve and rinse under cold running water to cool. (At this point you can put the parcooked rice in an airtight container and keep it in the refrigerator for several days, or freeze it for up to 3 months; to thaw it, put it in a sieve and rinse under cold running water to break up the grains.)

Put the parcooked rice in a collapsible steamer basket or a large mesh sieve. Fill a medium or large saucepan with 1 inch (2.5 cm) of water and bring it to a boil. Set the steamer or sieve in the saucepan, ideally so that the rice is not touching the water, cover the pan, and steam until the rice is tender and fluffy, 15 to 20 minutes. Dump it out into a bowl and serve, or let cool and refrigerate for up to 5 days or freeze for up to 3 months.

Quinoa

MAKES ABOUT 3 CUPS (525 G)

VEGAN

> 1 cup (175 g) quinoa, any color
> Salt

Put the quinoa in a fine-mesh sieve and rinse well under cold running water, agitating it with your fingers to remove any traces of soapy-tasting saponin that may be on the grains. (Most packaged quinoa has been prewashed, but you can't really tell with the bulk bins.) Drain well, then scrape the quinoa into a 1½- to 2-quart (1.5- to 2-L) saucepan and add 1½ cups (360 ml) cold water and a good pinch of salt. Bring the water to a boil, then lower the heat to low, cover, and cook until all the water has been absorbed, 15 to 20 minutes. Fluff the quinoa with a spatula. If you're not using it right away, let it cool to room temperature—red or black quinoa is sturdy enough that you can put it in a sieve and rinse it under cold running water to cool it off quickly, but ivory quinoa becomes a bit soggy with rinsing—then transfer it to an airtight container and refrigerate for up to 4 days or freeze in a freezer bag or other freezer-safe container for up to 3 months.

Steamed Millet

MAKES 3 CUPS (600 G)

VEGAN

> 1 cup (200 g) millet
> Salt
> 2 cups (480 ml) vegetable stock or water

In a dry medium saucepan, toast the millet over medium-high heat, stirring frequently with a heatproof spatula, until fragrant and very hot to the touch, about 3 minutes. Carefully pour in the stock (it'll spatter a little at first), add ¼ teaspoon salt, and bring to a boil. Lower the heat to low, cover, and simmer until the water is absorbed and the millet grains are tender, 20 to 25 minutes. Fluff the millet with the spatula. Spread it on a plate to cool if not using right away, and refrigerate in an airtight container for up to 2 days or freeze in a freezer bag or other freezer-safe container for up to 3 months.

Urad dal

French green lentil

SARUDAM (PEARL TAPIOCA)
Distributed By
House of Spices (India) In
O. William Road, East
, MD - 1130
www.hosindia.com
100 GRAMS 1 OZ

polenta

green mango

CHICK PEAS

ORGANIC

Black L

USDA ORGANIC

WHOLE
kist Selects

THE TREATS
CUPBOARD

a few simple desserts and snacks

My dear, sweet daughter, Thalia, somehow got the idea in her head that dessert after supper is an everyday occurrence. Until I can disabuse her of the notion, and instill in her my own belief (belief, yes, but unfortunately not always my practice) that dessert is *for special occasions*, I'll try to make sure the fruit bowl is full and the cupboard stocked with not-too-sweet sweets. Also, because I work at home, I try to keep some sort of snack at the ready for the afternoons—copyediting cookbooks all day can really make a person hungry. So here are a few ideas for easy desserts and somewhat healthful snacks.

I've found that with a decent high-speed blender, a quick, reasonably healthful dessert or vegetable-based pick-me-up smoothie can be ready in just a few minutes. You don't need a Vitamix or Blendtec (I don't have one), just a good, solid, powerful motor and the patience to keep blending until your mixture is absolutely smooth.

A Chocolate Something

SERVES 4 TO 6

VEGAN

Sometimes, don't you just want a *little bite* of something sweet at the end of a meal? Not a full-blown dessert, just a taste of something a bit decadent while you finish your glass of wine? I don't know what to call this simple treat of dense, smooth, very dark chilled chocolate-coconut cream, served in tiny cups, but I can tell you it's delicious.

For a fancy addition, put a can of coconut milk in the refrigerator to chill for a couple hours, then scoop out the thick cream on top and whisk it with an electric mixer until smooth (add a little sugar or maple syrup, if you'd like). Dollop a bit on top of each serving of chocolate and dust with cinnamon or cocoa powder or grated chocolate. Use the thin, watery part left in the can in the Creamy Coconut Water Smoothie on page 243.

4 ounces (113 g) dark chocolate, finely chopped

1 cup (240 ml) coconut milk

2 tablespoons virgin coconut oil

2 tablespoons maple syrup

Pinch of salt

In a small saucepan, combine all the ingredients. Place over medium-low heat and cook, stirring frequently, until the chocolate has melted and the mixture is smooth. Let cool for 15 minutes, then blend with an immersion blender until frothy. (Alternatively, scrape the mixture into a regular blender, let cool, then blend until smooth.)

Find four small, pretty cups or, preferably (because the chocolate is very intense, and a little goes a long way), six tinier, daintier cups. Divide the chocolate mixture among the cups, cover each tightly with plastic wrap, and chill in the refrigerator until firm, at least 1 hour or up to 2 days. Let stand at room temperature for 30 minutes to 1 hour to soften a bit before serving.

Mini Chocolate Shakes

SERVES 2

VEGAN

This shake is thick, creamy, and very chocolatey, sweetened with sugary dates—
serve it in small portions as a special treat.

1 ripe banana

8 small pitted dates, soaked in warm water for
10 minutes to soften, then drained

½ Hass avocado

1 cup ice cubes

½ cup (120 ml) oat milk

1 tablespoon dark cocoa powder

¼ teaspoon pure vanilla extract

Put all the ingredients in a high-speed blender and blend until very smooth, scraping down the sides of the blender jar a few times. Serve immediately.

Quickie Blueberry-Beet Sorbet

SERVES 2 OR 3

VEGAN

Deep purple, smooth, and ever so slightly sweet and tart, this pretty sorbet would be a
perfect light ending to a hearty fall or winter meal.

1 baseball-size roasted beet, peeled and cooled
(see page 139)

½ ripe banana

2 cups ice cubes

½ cup (120 ml) oat or almond milk

½ cup (80 g) frozen blueberries

½ teaspoon pure vanilla extract

Pinch of salt

2 to 4 tablespoons agave nectar or maple syrup

Put all the ingredients, adding sweetener to taste, in a high-speed blender and blend until very smooth, scraping down the sides of the blender jar a few times. Serve immediately, or transfer to a freezer-safe container and freeze until a bit firmer, about 1 hour. If it gets very hard in the freezer, let it sit out on the counter for 10 minutes, then scrape it with a fork or spoon, granita style, to serve.

Easy Little Cheesecakes
with Anise-Grenadine Peaches

SERVES 6

These cheesecakes fall into that beloved category of desserts that basically require little more than mixing a few things together and baking. You can serve them still slightly warm, turned out onto dessert plates, or chill them and serve them in their baking dishes (they're easier to unmold when still warm, but easier to store in the molds). Feel free to experiment with different flavorings, too: a scraped vanilla bean, or lemon juice and some finely grated zest, or sweet spices like cinnamon or cardamom would all be fine additions to the batter.

FOR THE CHEESECAKES

- 1 tablespoon unsalted butter, softened, for the cocottes
- 16 ounces (455 g) cream cheese, at room temperature
- 4 large eggs
- ½ cup (100 g) granulated sugar
- 3 tablespoons fresh lime juice
- ½ teaspoon pure vanilla extract
- Salt

FOR THE PEACHES

- 2 very ripe peaches, pitted and diced
- 3 tablespoons sugar
- 1 tablespoon good-quality (real) grenadine
- 2 teaspoons fresh lemon juice
- ⅛ teaspoon ground aniseeds

MAKE THE CHEESECAKES

Preheat the oven to 350°F (175°C). Generously butter 6 (¾- to 1-cup/180- to 240-ml) cocottes, ramekins, or custard cups and arrange them in a deep baking dish. Put a kettle of water on to boil.

In a blender or food processor, combine the cream cheese, eggs, granulated sugar, lime juice, vanilla, and a generous pinch of salt and process until very smooth. Pour the mixture into the prepared cocottes, filling them no more than two-thirds full. Pour boiling water into the baking dish to come about halfway up the sides of the cocottes. Carefully transfer the baking dish with the cocottes to the oven and bake until the cheesecakes are firm in the center (they should register 155° to 160°F/68° to 70°C on an instant-read thermometer), about 35 minutes. Remove the hot cocottes from the water bath—a canning jar lifter makes this easy. If serving warm, loosen the edges of the cheesecakes with a thin knife, and gently turn them out onto serving plates. If serving chilled, let them cool completely on a wire rack, then cover each with plastic wrap and chill for at least 2 hours or up to 2 days.

MAKE THE PEACHES

In a small saucepan, combine the peaches, sugar, grenadine, lemon juice, and aniseeds and cook over medium heat, stirring frequently, until the peaches are soft and breaking down and their liquid is reduced slightly, about 10 minutes. The peaches can be served warm or chilled. (Store the peaches, if needed, in an airtight container in the refrigerator for up to 3 days—they'll lose some of their bright color after about a day, but none of their flavor.)

Top the warm or chilled cheesecakes with their peaches and serve.

Stewed Stone Fruit with Maple "Cream"

SERVES 3 OR 4

Simply stewed fruit, either baked in crisps and crumbles or just on its own, makes a satisfying dessert that you really don't have to think about too much in advance.

4 to 5 tablespoons (60 to 75 ml) maple syrup, or 3 tablespoons maple syrup plus 1 to 2 tablespoons cane or maple sugar

2 tablespoons well-stirred tahini

2 teaspoons fresh lime juice

¼ cup (60 ml) plain Greek yogurt (optional)

4 ripe plums, peaches, and/or apricots, pitted and chopped

In a small bowl, whisk together 3 tablespoons of the maple syrup, the tahini, lime juice, yogurt, if using, and 2 table-spoons water until very smooth and creamy. Set aside.

In a small saucepan, combine the fruit, ¼ cup (60 ml) water, and 1 to 2 tablespoons maple syrup (or the maple sugar, if preferred). Cook over medium heat, stirring frequently with a heatproof spatula, until the fruit is soft and syrupy, 5 to 10 minutes, depending on the ripeness of the fruit. Taste and add more sweetener, if needed.

Spoon the hot fruit into small serving bowls and top with dollops or drizzles of the maple "cream." Serve.

Sesame-Oat Fruit Crisp

SERVES 4 TO 6

Fruit crisp is the most common and beloved baked dessert around here, and I'll often make just a couple of servings of it at a time, in a small baking dish or in cast-iron cocottes or ramekins. Serve with a drizzle of full-fat yogurt or sour cream whisked with a bit of sweetener (or one of the *sharbets*—citrus-y fruit syrups—on page 264), or follow my friend and Atlanta food blogger Meghan Splawn's lead and put cold heavy cream and a drizzle of maple syrup in a pint-size glass jar, put the lid on, and shake it like a cocktail until you have whipped cream (about 3 minutes).

2½ pounds (1.2 kg) cored or pitted and chopped apples, pears, plums, peaches, or whole fresh or frozen berries, or a combination

1 tablespoon fresh lemon juice

¾ cup (150 g) sugar

6 tablespoons (85 g) unsalted butter or coconut oil, plus more for the dish

½ cup (50 g) oat flour

½ cup (80 g) raw rolled oats

2 tablespoons sesame seeds

1½ teaspoons ground cinnamon

Salt

Preheat the oven to 375°F (190°C). Grease a 10-inch (25-cm) pie dish or 9-inch (22.5-cm) square baking dish.

In a large bowl, toss the fruit with the lemon juice and ¼ cup (50 g) of the sugar, then spread the fruit mixture in the prepared pie dish.

In a medium bowl, combine the butter, flour, oats, sesame seeds, the remaining ½ cup (100 g) sugar, the cinnamon, and a pinch of salt, cutting them together with a pastry cutter or your fingertips until all the ingredients are thoroughly incorporated. Scatter the mixture over the fruit, squeezing some of it into clumps with your fingers. Bake until the fruit is tender (juicier fruits will bubble at the edges) and the topping is golden brown, about 30 minutes. Serve warm.

Lavender-Oat Shortbread

MAKES 16 TRIANGLES

Fragrant dried lavender blossoms are a natural addition to shortbread, here made with oat flour, which makes for an especially melt-in-your-mouth cookie. For this recipe try to find ready-made oat flour, which is very fine and powdery, rather than grinding your own (unless your food processor or grinder is more powerful than mine, or you have a good high-speed blender). You can find oat flour in the bulk bins at most natural foods stores, and packaged in the gluten-free baking section of better supermarkets.

2½ cups (250 g) fine oat flour, plus more for the work surface

½ cup (50 g) plus 1 teaspoon confectioners' sugar

1 cup (2 sticks/226 g), good-quality unsalted butter, cold and cut into small pieces

¾ teaspoon dried lavender blossoms, rubbed between your fingers, plus a pinch

Fine salt

1 large egg, separated

Preheat the oven to 350°F (175°C). Line a baking sheet with parchment paper.

Sift the oat flour and confectioners' sugar into a large bowl or a food processor. Add the butter, rubbed lavender, and a generous pinch of fine salt. Using a pastry blender (or pulsing the food processor), cut the butter into the dry ingredients until the bits of butter are the size of rice grains. Make a well in the center of the mixture (no need to do this if using a food processor) and add the egg yolk and 2 tablespoons cold water. Stir (or pulse) to incorporate. Turn the dough out onto a lightly floured work surface and knead with your hands until the dough is uniform, with some larger pieces of butter remaining; it'll be slightly sticky.

Divide the dough in half and shape it into two balls. Between two pieces of waxed paper, roll out one ball to a disk a little less than ½ inch (1 cm) thick and 7 to 8 inches (17.5 to 20 cm) in diameter. Remove the top piece of paper. If you'd like a clean outer edge, set a 7- to 8-inch (17.5- to 20-cm) plate on top of the disk and use it as a template to cut a perfect circle. Use a metal ruler edge or a knife to score the disk into 8 wedges, pressing about halfway through the thickness of the dough. Prick the wedges deeply with a fork. Tip the disk onto the palm of your hand, peel the paper off the bottom, and place the disk, scored side up, on the prepared baking sheet, leaving room for the second disk. Repeat with the second ball of dough.

Whisk the remaining 1 teaspoon confectioners' sugar together with 1 teaspoon water, then whisk in the egg white. Brush the egg wash over the tops of the disks and sprinkle with just a few lavender blossoms. Bake in the center of the oven for 15 minutes. Lower the oven temperature to 300°F (150°C) and continue to bake until golden brown and firm in the center, 25 to 30 minutes. Let cool on the baking sheet, then use a knife to cut into wedges along the scored lines. Store in an airtight container at room temperature for up to 3 days.

Banana-Cardamom Bars

MAKES 9 LARGE OR 16 SMALL SQUARES

Here, a tender, nutty, coconut-fragrant crust is topped with caramelized spiced bananas and baked until bottom and top sort of meld together. After a half-day or so, the bananas will become a bit brown, as bananas do; sift a bit of confectioners' sugar over the top if aesthetics are a concern. If you want to keep them longer than a day, put the leftovers in a single layer in an airtight container or on a plate covered with plastic wrap in the fridge.

1½ cups (145 g) oat flour

1 cup (90 g) almond flour

⅓ cup (40 g) plus 2 tablespoons confectioners' sugar

Salt

¼ cup (20 g) unsweetened grated coconut

½ cup (1 stick/113 g) plus 1 tablespoon unsalted butter

4 large bananas, cut crosswise into ¼-inch (6-mm) slices

2 teaspoons fresh lemon juice

½ teaspoon ground cardamom

Preheat the oven to 350°F (175°C).

Sift the oat flour, almond flour, ⅓ cup (40 g) of the confectioners' sugar, and a pinch of salt into a medium bowl. Stir in the coconut.

In a small sauté pan, melt ½ cup (113 g) of the butter over medium heat. Pour the butter into the flour mixture and stir well with a spatula. (Don't rinse out the butter pan.) Pat the dough evenly into the bottom of a 9-inch (22.5-cm) square baking pan. Bake for 15 minutes. Keep the oven on.

Meanwhile, in the sauté pan, melt the remaining 1 tablespoon butter over medium heat. Add the bananas, the remaining 2 tablespoons confectioners' sugar, the lemon juice, and the cardamom. Stir until the cardamom and sugar are evenly distributed and the banana slices start to break down, 1 to 2 minutes.

Gently spoon the bananas and their liquid over the crust so the slices are in a single layer. They'll sink down into the surface of the crust a bit. Return the pan to the oven and bake until you can see some caramelized spots at the edges of the pan, about 30 minutes. Set the pan on a wire rack to cool completely. Cut into squares or rectangles and serve. The bars will keep in an airtight container in the refrigerator for up to 2 days.

Variations

To make the crust vegan, use ½ cup (120 ml) melted virgin coconut oil instead of the butter (it also gives the crust a more pronounced coconut flavor—really nice) and increase the oat flour to 2 cups (200 g). Sauté the bananas with 1 tablespoon coconut oil instead of butter. If as a vegan you avoid confectioners' sugar, substitute regular granulated cane sugar; the crust won't be quite as melt-in-your-mouth, but it'll still be tasty.

For a dessert that's more like a tart or pie, with a topping of juicy fruit such as peaches, nectarines, apples, pears, or a combination, use about 1 pound (455 g) fruit, pitted or cored and sliced ¼ inch (6 mm) thick. Sauté the fruit with 2 tablespoons granulated or brown sugar instead of confectioners' sugar, and cook until the fruit is tender but still holds its shape and the liquid is syrupy, about 10 minutes depending on the fruit, its ripeness, and the size of your pan. (You can also, of course, use any other flavoring instead of cardamom: ground cinnamon or the seeds of 1 vanilla bean, for example.) Gently spoon the fruit slices and syrup onto the parbaked crust in a single layer and press down slightly with a spatula. Bake again as directed.

Date Snacks

MAKES 24 SMALL BITES; EASILY MADE ONE AT A TIME

VEGAN

These snack-treats fit very well into a bento lunch (wrap in a little square of dry waxed paper), and I often have one or two myself with tea in the afternoon. They're also nice to serve with cocktails.

24 small pitted dates

About 1 teaspoon rosewater (optional)

About 6 tablespoons (50 g) shelled pistachios (salted or not)

⅓ cup (25 g) grated unsweetened coconut, toasted and finely ground in a spice mill

Cut a slit down one side of each date if there isn't one already. Put the dates in a bowl and sprinkle them evenly with the rosewater; toss. Stuff a few pistachios in each date, close them, and roll them in the coconut to coat. You can do this several hours in advance and keep them on a plate, uncovered, at room temperature. Serve at room temperature.

Cheddar-Seed Crackers

MAKES ABOUT 42 (1½- TO 2-INCH/4- TO 5-CM) CRACKERS

These exceedingly rich and filling flourless cheese crackers are super-easy to make, and very fine with a glass of wine or cocktails on a Saturday afternoon. Go nuts experimenting with the flavorings: Instead of rosemary and dried cranberries, try a couple of minced apricots and ½ teaspoon garam masala (page 247), or minced dates and Madras curry powder. Or replace 1 ounce (28 g) of the cheddar with a grated hard cheese like Parmesan; use pine nuts in place of sesame seeds, and 2 teaspoons minced fresh basil instead of rosemary. You get the idea. Also, if you don't feel like rolling out the dough, you can just pinch off bits, press them as flat and thin as possible between your palms, and slap them onto a baking sheet (no need for parchment or greasing).

1 cup (170 g) raw sunflower seeds

4 ounces (113 g) extra-sharp cheddar cheese, cut into pieces

2 tablespoons unsalted butter

1 tablespoon sesame seeds

1 teaspoon minced fresh rosemary and/or 2 tablespoons dried cranberries

Salt

Preheat the oven to 350°F (175°C).

In a food processor, combine the sunflower seeds, cheese, butter, sesame seeds, rosemary or cranberries, and ¾ teaspoon salt. Process until the sunflower seeds are very finely chopped and the mixture becomes a pasty dough that will hold together when you press it, scraping the side of the bowl as needed. Scoop half of the dough onto a sheet of parchment paper and pat it into a compact shape. Cover with a second sheet of parchment and roll out the dough to less than ⅛ inch (3 mm) thick, flipping over the parchment sandwich and lifting each sheet to loosen it from the dough if it wrinkles.

continued

Lift off the top sheet. Cut the dough into squares of whatever size. (If you'd like, cut off the rough edges and reroll those, but I don't bother.) Transfer the parchment with the dough to a baking sheet. Bake until golden and sizzling, 12 to 15 minutes.

Gently separate the squares with a metal spatula and return them to the oven for about 3 minutes. Transfer the crackers to a wire rack to cool. Repeat with the remaining dough. Store the cooled crackers in an airtight container for up to 3 days.

Spicy Fried Giant White Corn

MAKES ABOUT 4 CUPS (300 G); SERVES 6 TO 8 AS A SNACK

VEGAN

I had a similar snack of fried hominy at one of my favorite restaurants in Athens, Georgia, the Branded Butcher (the chef is vegan, if that helps), and a friend in Atlanta, the food writer Wendell Brock, took it upon himself to figure out the best way to make it at home. It's pretty darn simple: Soak the giant white corn in water overnight, boil it and drain well, then fry it and season it. Super-crunchy, spicy, and salty, it's basically made for a cold beer or even a shrub-and-seltzer on ice (see page 265). A fine thing to have around the house, the corn will keep for at least a couple weeks.

Use the large kernels of dried white corn you can find with the dried beans and rice in the Mexican foods section of some grocery stores, or in Latin grocery stores. It's not hominy, but it's the stuff one treats with lime or lye to make hominy at home. (Incidentally, I would not recommend frying canned hominy: No matter how carefully you dry it off, it spatters like crazy in the oil, and tends to clump together and become a greasy, dangerous nightmare.)

1 pound (455 g) dried giant white corn

Salt

Vegetable oil for deep-frying

¾ teaspoon ground cumin

¾ teaspoon ancho or other chile powder

1 lime

Put the corn in a large saucepan or pot and add cold water to cover by at least 2 inches (5 cm). Soak for 8 hours or overnight.

Drain the corn, return to the pot, and cover again with water. Bring the water to a boil over high heat, then lower the heat and simmer, stirring occasionally, until the corn is tender and no bright white remains in the center when you cut a kernel open with a knife, about 1½ hours, adding several big pinches of salt in the last 30 minutes. Some of the kernels will have

started to split, and that's fine. Drain the corn very well and spread the kernels out on a paper towel–lined baking sheet to air-dry, patting them with another paper towel to get all the excess water off. To be extra-sure you get the corn dry, which will minimize the splattering when you fry it, set the baking sheet in a 150°F (65°C) oven for 15 minutes or so.

Wipe out the pan and fill with 2 inches (5 cm) of oil. Heat the oil until it registers about 375°F (190°C) on a deep-frying or candy thermometer clipped to the edge of the pan. Have a lid ready and line a baking sheet with dry paper towels or a paper bag. In a small cup, combine the cumin, chile powder, and 1¼ teaspoons salt and set the mixture aside with the lime and a grater.

Working in batches so you don't crowd the oil, load up a slotted spoon or a small sieve with a few large spoonfuls of the corn and very carefully lower it into the oil (the spoon helps deliver the corn to the oil safely). Immediately put the lid on,

slightly askew (leave the thermometer in the oil)—the oil will splatter and pop, so be careful to stay back and keep that lid on. When the splattering slows down, lift the lid and stir gently to separate the kernels. Fry the corn until deeply browned, adjusting the heat to keep the temperature as close to 375°F (190°C) as possible; the cooking time will vary from 5 to 10 minutes depending on the size of your pot, the heat source, and how crowded the oil is. With a slotted spoon, scoop the corn onto the paper towels to drain. Transfer the still-hot corn to a large bowl and toss with some of the spice mixture. Grate

some lime zest over it. Taste and add more salt, if needed. Repeat with the remaining batches, adding them to the bowl and tossing as you go.

Cut the lime into wedges and serve with the warm or room-temperature fried corn. The corn will keep in an airtight container at room temperature for at least a couple of weeks, though the kernels will become more crunchy than crisp after a few hours.

Three Fun Green Smoothies

MAKES ABOUT 1¼ CUPS (300 ML) EACH; SERVES 1

Smoothie recipes drive me crazy. First, isn't part of the beauty of the smoothie that you can make it up yourself using produce you already have? Second, so many smoothie recipes call for *far* more fruit than I'd ever want to eat in one sitting, even if the smoothie is serving as a full meal—say, a quick breakfast or lunch. Most smoothies, too, especially ones featuring lots of frozen fruit, are just too filling for me, so I use ice and just a little fruit for sweetness, which makes them light and bracing. Needless to say, these recipes should be considered merely jumping-off points for your own experiments.

The Green Pea Smoothie is slightly sweet, with a hint of vanilla, and makes a fine all-purpose breakfast.

The Creamy Coconut Water Smoothie is a real treat, with maple syrup and pure coconut water (to which I might be addicted, as evinced by the fact that I recently walked, at night, through snow, to the grocery store to re-up my supply). Just don't use anything labeled coconut "juice," and make sure the coconut water is unsweetened—the sweetened ones taste awful. Avocado makes it silky on the palate, and is a good way to add fiber without too much, well, *fibrousness*. The Apple-Mint Smoothie, a bit sweet, very minty, and totally refreshing, is very much like an agua fresca. Think of it as a fresh-pressed juice you can make without a juicer.

PUT AN EGG IN IT

My friend and one-time editor Natalie Kaire tipped me off to the idea of using hard-cooked egg yolks to enrich blended drinks and add a hit of nonvegan protein, and that would be great except what do you do with the hard-cooked whites? I have no separate use for them, although I'm sure our dog would have some ideas. I ignore him and just throw the whole egg in the blender; you won't even notice it with all the other flavors going on in these.

Green Pea Smoothie

1 cup ice cubes

½ cup (65 g) frozen peas

½ peach, chopped

½ cup (120 ml) oat or almond milk

1 rib celery, chopped

1 hard-cooked egg, cooled and peeled

2 dried apricots or prunes, chopped

Handful of spinach

½ teaspoon pure vanilla extract

Juice of 1 lemon wedge

Put all the ingredients in a high-speed blender and blend until very smooth, scraping down the sides of the blender jar a few times if necessary. Serve in a tall glass.

Creamy Coconut Water Smoothie

VEGAN

1 cup ice cubes

1 cup (240 ml) pure coconut water

½ Hass avocado, pitted and peeled

1 tablespoon fresh lime juice

1 tablespoon maple syrup

1 small sprig fresh basil or mint, tough stem removed (optional)

Put all the ingredients in a high-speed blender and blend until very smooth, scraping down the sides of the blender jar a few times if necessary. Serve in a tall glass.

Apple-Mint Smoothie

VEGAN

1 cup ice cubes

½ cup (120 ml) oat or almond milk

1 small apple, cored and chopped

1 rib celery, chopped

Handful of spinach

2 or 3 sprigs fresh mint

1 coin peeled fresh ginger, chopped

1 tablespoon Carrot Marmalade (page 256) or any tart-sweet preserve

Put all the ingredients in a high-speed blender and blend until very smooth, scraping down the sides of the blender jar a few times if necessary. Serve in a tall glass.

MAKE-
AHEADS

spice mixes, condiments, and concentrates

Cooking vegetarian meals, and enjoying not only the results but the process, is so much easier when you have some interesting, intensely flavorful spice blends, condiments, and concentrates already made. I've put together some memorable meals almost entirely from spices I've premixed and ingredients I've pulled from the shelves—frozen cooked beans, frozen blanched broccoli rabe, frozen curry paste or a vinaigrette, and so on. Here are a few make-aheads—including standards like vegetable stock concentrate and vinaigrettes as well as more unusual options, like kale *furikake*, a mixture of seeds, spices, and roasted kale—that you can keep on hand in the spice cupboard, refrigerator, or freezer to use in this book's recipes and in your own innovations.

I've also thrown in a few fun ideas for drinks: a ready-made mix you can use to make a frothy, milky hot drink in cold months (add good cocoa powder to make a hot chocolate mix!) and several ideas for long-keeping fruit syrups (aka *sharbets*) and drinking vinegars (aka shrubs) to mix into plain seltzer or water or to use to create fun summer cocktails.

Three Versatile Spice Mixes

MAKES ABOUT ½ CUP (40 G) EACH

VEGAN

Both of the Japanese spice mixes that follow are based on sesame seeds, and both can be used in similar ways, but the effects of each are so distinctive (nutty heat versus numbing, mouthwatering citrus) that I decided to include both recipes here. *Furikake*, a simple but powerfully flavorful Japanese seasoning, usually contains seaweed of some sort—try nori, hijiki, or dulse—but I also like it made from leftover kale chips; roasted kale has always had a seafoodlike flavor to me anyway. Sprinkle it on noodle dishes, into soups, onto roasted root vegetables, or into stir-fries. Grind it extra-fine, with a little maple sugar, if you'd like, to use as a topping for popcorn. Only a few ingredients off from *furikake*,

seven-spice, or *shichimi togarashi*, is marked by the faint numbing caused by the Szechuan peppercorns and the floral fragrance contributed by the dried orange peel. It can do wonders sprinkled onto any roasted vegetable or an otherwise simple stir-fry.

Garam masala is a combination of peppery, sweet spices used in northern Indian (Punjabi and Kashmiri) dishes. I have always liked the excellent Punjab-style preground blend from Penzeys, so Thalia and I embarked on a mission to copy it one afternoon when it was threatening to run out. It was a fun kitchen project for both of us, sniffing and mixing, and learning a little bit about fractions.

Kale Furikake

VEGAN

- ¼ cup (30 g) sesame seeds
- ½ recipe Sesame Kale Chips (see page 157), cooled
- ½ teaspoon salt
- ½ teaspoon hot red pepper flakes

Combine all the ingredients in a spice mill and pulse three or four times to coarsely grind. (Alternatively, do this in a mortar with a pestle.) Store in an airtight container in the refrigerator for up to 3 weeks or the freezer for several months.

Garam Masala

VEGAN

- 1 tablespoon whole coriander seeds, or 2 teaspoons ground coriander
- 1 tablespoon whole black peppercorns
- 1 teaspoon green cardamom seeds, from about 14 cardamom pods
- 1 teaspoon ground cinnamon
- 1 teaspoon *kalonji* (nigella) seeds
- ½ teaspoon ground cloves
- ½ teaspoon ground ginger
- ½ teaspoon caraway seeds
- ¼ nutmeg seed, crushed

Combine all the ingredients in a spice mill and grind to a fine powder. Store in an airtight container in a dark place for up to a year.

Shichimi Togarashi (Japanese Seven-Spice)

VEGAN

- 3 tablespoons sesame seeds, toasted and cooled
- 1 tablespoon Szechuan peppercorns
- 1 tablespoon dried hijiki or crumbled nori seaweed
- 1½ teaspoons poppyseeds
- 1 teaspoon hot red pepper flakes
- 1 teaspoon minced dried orange or tangerine peel
- 1 teaspoon ground ginger

Put all the ingredients in a spice mill and pulse to a coarse powder. Store in an airtight container in a cool, dark place for up to 3 months.

Salsa de Semillas

MAKES ABOUT 2 CUPS (285 G)

VEGAN

On a hot spring day last year, on a trip to California, Derek and I left Thalia with my old college roommate, Tanya, and her daughter and conducted a surgical strike on the taquerias of Cesar Chavez Avenue in East L.A. In one place—they blur together—we were served, in a little plastic cup, what the woman at the counter called "dry salsa," and it was something like this: crunchy and nutty, smoky, full of deep chile flavor but not very spicy, a crumbly paste of oil-seared and ground-up dried chiles, toasty seeds, and nuts.

Make a nice big batch, keep it in the freezer, and you'll find dozens of uses for it. Two favorites so far are as a topping for perfect black bean soup (page 216), and tossed into a hot pan with dark sautéed mushrooms (see page 205) destined for tacos—spoon in another, fresh salsa, like the creamy and crisp tomatillo and avocado one on page 71, for a meal you won't forget. I've also been known to make a breakfast by reheating some leftover sweet corn polenta in a pan, scooping half an avocado onto the plate next to it, squeezing on some lime juice, and sprinkling large quantities of salsa de semillas straight from the freezer bag over everything.

8 dried guajillo chiles

4 dried arbol chiles

2 tablespoons vegetable oil

½ cup (65 g) sesame seeds

½ cup (65 g) raw pepitas

¾ cup (95 g) raw cashews or unsalted peanuts

Salt

If the chiles are dusty, wipe them off with a damp cloth or paper towel. Break off and discard the stems, then tear or break the chiles into several large pieces and shake out and discard as many of the seeds as you can.

In a large sauté pan, heat 1 tablespoon of the oil over medium-high heat until it shimmers. Add half of the chiles and, using a metal spatula, press down on them to flatten them onto the hot surface of the pan. When they blacken slightly and become fragrant (or you start coughing from the fumes), turn them over and sear the other sides. Cook the chiles for about 2 minutes total, then transfer them to a mini food processor or blender. Repeat with the remaining chiles, using the oil remaining in the pan.

Lower the heat to medium and add the sesame seeds to the pan. Cook, stirring constantly with a heatproof spatula, until golden, about 1 minute. Scrape into a medium bowl. Put the pepitas in the pan and cook until they're lightly browned and popping, 30 to 60 seconds. Scrape them into the bowl with the sesame seeds but don't stir. Heat the remaining 1 tablespoon oil in the pan and add the cashews. Cook, stirring constantly, until golden, about 1 minute, then scrape the cashews and oil into the bowl. Let everything cool for at least 15 minutes.

Pulse the chiles, scraping down the sides as needed, until finely ground—they'll make a loose paste. Spoon in most of the cashews and pepitas (hold back most of the sesame seeds at the bottom of the bowl) and about ¾ teaspoon salt and pulse to combine and grind. Add the remaining cashews, pepitas, and the sesame seeds and pulse just a couple times; the salsa should be dry and crumbly, with some larger chunks of seeds and nuts remaining. Taste and add more salt, if needed. Serve immediately at room temperature, or refrigerate in an airtight container for up to 1 week or freeze for up to 3 weeks.

The Correct Chile Relleño Sauce (i.e., My Mom's)

MAKES ABOUT 4½ CUPS (1.1 L)

VEGAN

This will make enough for two casseroles (see page 86). Freeze the extra! The spicing is simple enough that you could easily add some cumin and coriander, or garam masala, and have an Indian-style sauce for simmering big chunks of vegetables.

> 1 tablespoon olive oil
>
> 1 small onion, chopped
>
> 1 clove garlic, chopped
>
> Salt and freshly ground black pepper
>
> ½ teaspoon ground cloves
>
> Pinch of ground cinnamon
>
> 1 (28-ounce/795-g) can crushed or whole peeled tomatoes with their juices

In a large saucepan, heat the oil over medium-high heat until it shimmers. Add the onion, garlic, a pinch of salt, and several grindings of pepper. Cook, stirring frequently, until the onion is translucent, 5 to 7 minutes. Add the cloves and cinnamon and stir for 10 seconds, then add the tomatoes and their juices and ½ teaspoon salt. Bring to a boil, then lower the heat and simmer, stirring occasionally, until the flavors come together and the tomatoes have broken down somewhat, about 20 minutes. Puree the sauce using an immersion blender. Taste and add more salt and pepper, if needed. Use immediately, or let cool completely, then refrigerate in an airtight container for up to 2 days, or freeze for up to 3 months.

Tahini-Pomegranate Sauce

MAKES ABOUT 1 CUP (240 ML)

VEGAN

Use this on any salad or with any steamed or roasted vegetables. Try it, too, in the mushroom-and-tofu recipe on page 204, and with Herby Falafel (page 106).

> ½ cup (120 ml) well-stirred tahini
>
> ¼ cup (60 ml) pomegranate molasses
>
> 2 cloves garlic, grated
>
> Salt and freshly ground black pepper

In a large bowl, whisk together the tahini, 6 tablespoons (90 ml) water, the pomegranate molasses, garlic, 1¾ teaspoons salt, and pepper to taste. The sauce should be runny, the consistency of heavy cream, and light in color; add a little more water if necessary. The sauce can be stored in a clean jar in the refrigerator for about 2 weeks.

Classic Aioli

Aioli is essentially a garlicky homemade mayonnaise. All you need is a bowl and a whisk; it doesn't have to end up as thick and stiff as the store-bought stuff, and it'll thicken up in the refrigerator if you make it in advance.

3 large egg yolks

3 tablespoons fresh lemon juice

2 to 3 cloves garlic

Salt

¾ to 1 cup (180 to 240 ml) olive oil (see Note)

Variations

Use lime juice instead of lemon and add a spoonful of minced chipotles in adobo (see page 197) and a pinch of ground cumin with the garlic.

Add fresh herbs! Sweet, tender, mild minced herbs like young parsley, basil, chervil, tarragon, or cilantro can be added with abandon. More assertive herbs like thyme, lavender blossoms, rosemary tips, oregano, marjoram, or savory should be added more judiciously.

Add smoked paprika and/or a pinch of cayenne. Sweet paprika can be wan here—stick with the spicier stuff.

Crumble a tiny pinch of saffron threads into the egg yolks for a fragrant, beautifully yellow aioli.

A dollop, a drizzle, a gentle nap of aioli will fancy up any plain steamed vegetables, and a little dipping bowl of chilled aioli served with a plate of raw or blanched crudités makes a nice starter or afternoon snack.

In a medium bowl, whisk the egg yolks and lemon juice. Finely grate in some of the garlic (or smash it to a paste with a heavy knife on a cutting board and add it). Whisk in ¾ teaspoon salt. Whisk in the oil just a few drops at a time, and continue whisking until the sauce is thick—it should have the consistency of cake batter. (You can also do all of this in a mini food processor, adding the oil very slowly through the hole in the lid.) Taste and whisk in more salt and/or garlic, if needed. Serve, or store in an airtight container in the refrigerator for up to 3 days.

Note: If you're using extra-virgin olive oil, you might want to replace half of it with a neutral vegetable oil like grapeseed so the oil flavor isn't overpowering.

Harissa

MAKES ABOUT 1 CUP (240 ML)

CAN BE VEGAN

I've been using harissa, a North African condiment, a lot lately to add a smoky, deep flavor to stews and sauces, and even as a quick spreadable topping for tostadas. This one—based on toasted and reconstituted dried chiles (I like to use mild guajillos or New Mexico chiles with a few of a spicy variety like arbol thrown in, but you can vary it depending on what you have) and spiced with cumin and caraway—is deep and intense. See the variation for a more easygoing version.

5 ounces (140 g) dried chiles, preferably guajillos with 3 or 4 arbol

6 cloves garlic, peeled but left whole

¼ cup (60 ml) olive oil, plus more for storage

1 tablespoon fresh lemon juice

¾ teaspoon cumin seeds

½ teaspoon caraway seeds

Salt

Agave nectar, honey, or sugar (optional)

Variation

For a milder, less assertive version based on fresh red peppers instead of dried, roast 2 or 3 red bell peppers and a few unpeeled garlic cloves. Peel and seed the peppers, peel the garlic, and grind them all to a puree with ¼ to ⅓ cup (60 to 80 ml) olive oil, salt to taste, and a good squeeze of fresh lemon juice. Store leftovers in the freezer for up to 3 months.

If the chiles are dusty, wipe them off with a damp cloth or paper towel. Break off and discard the stems, then tear or break the chiles into several pieces and shake out and discard as many of the seeds as you can.

Heat a large, deep sauté pan over medium-high heat. Add the chiles and garlic and toast them, pressing down on them with a metal spatula to flatten them onto the hot surface of the pan. Turn frequently and cook until all of the chiles are toasted, blackened in spots, and fragrant, 2 to 4 minutes total. Carefully add about 1½ cups (360 ml) water (it will splatter at first). Bring to a boil, then lower the heat and simmer, stirring occasionally, until the chiles and garlic are softened, about 20 minutes. Using a slotted spoon, transfer the chiles and garlic to a blender, then pour in the liquid from the sauté pan along with the oil, lemon juice, cumin, caraway, and ¾ teaspoon salt. Let cool for a bit before blending, or vent the lid and cover with a towel to contain any explosions. Blend until very smooth, then blend some more. If you'd like, push the sauce through a sieve into a bowl to remove any stray seeds or bits of chile skin (discard these). Taste and stir in more salt or a drizzle of agave nectar, if needed.

Scrape the mixture into a very clean glass jar, let cool, then cover the surface with a layer of oil and put the lid on. Use immediately, or store in the refrigerator in the jar for about 2 weeks. Always scoop it out with a clean, dry spoon and cover the surface with more oil as necessary.

Red Pepper and Apple Jam

MAKES ABOUT 2 CUPS (480 ML)

VEGAN

Originally made to accompany the Rustic Tortilla Espagnola on page 198, this radiant and nearly translucent tart and spicy jam has been used in our house on just about everything. Try it on a grilled portobello mushroom with melted cheddar, or dotted onto Roasted Cauliflower with Kalamata Olives and Almonds (page 126).

2 large red bell peppers, diced

1 Granny Smith or other tart apple, cored and diced

3 or more Fresno or jalapeño chiles, seeded and minced

⅔ cup (160 ml) cider vinegar

½ cup (110 g) turbinado or brown sugar

½ teaspoon salt

In a saucepan, combine all the ingredients and bring the mixture to a boil. Lower the heat and simmer briskly, stirring occasionally, until the liquid is reduced and somewhat syrupy and the apple pieces are brown and translucent and starting to break down, about 40 minutes. Let cool to room temperature and serve, or refrigerate in a clean jar for up to 1 month.

Quick-Pickled Beet Stems

MAKES ABOUT 1 PINT (180 G)

Cut the tops off the roots and use the 5 to 6 inches (12 to 15 cm) of stem, just below where the green part of the leaves begins; for a pint- or similar-size jar (a tall jelly jar works well), the stems from about 1 bunch of beets (about 3 beets) will do nicely. See the variations below for springtime ramps and asparagus.

Handful of beet stems, cut to fit in the jar

½ teaspoon allspice berries

½ teaspoon whole black peppercorns

1 cinnamon stick

1 cup (240 ml) brown rice vinegar

1½ teaspoons honey

Salt

Bring a pot of water to a boil, add the beet stems, and blanch until just tender, 2 to 3 minutes. Drain and immediately transfer to a bowl of ice water to chill. Drain well.

Stand the beet stems upright in a heatproof glass jar with a lid—a tall jelly jar or other canning jar. Add the allspice, peppercorns, and cinnamon stick.

In a small saucepan, combine the vinegar, honey, 1¾ teaspoons salt, and ½ cup (120 ml) water. Bring to a boil, then pour the brine into the jar with the beet stems to cover them (it's okay if the ends stick out a bit at the top). Let cool, then put the lid on and refrigerate until chilled, preferably for at least 1 day. The pickles will keep for weeks in the refrigerator.

Variations

For quick-pickled asparagus: Use as many spears as will fit in your jar—the bottoms can be used if they're tender; taste them to make sure they're not too fibrous. Blanch until just bright green, 2 to 3 minutes. Omit the allspice, cinnamon, and honey and add 1 clove garlic and 1 halved small shallot to the jar with the peppercorns. Use 1 cup (240 ml) white wine vinegar, ¼ cup (60 ml) water, and 1½ teaspoons salt for the brine.

For quick-pickled ramps: Use as many ramps as you can fit in your jar—a good-size bunch. Wash them well, trim off the roots, and cut off the leafy green tops (save the tops for sautéing). Blanch the ramps until just floppy, about 3 minutes. Omit the allspice, peppercorns, cinnamon, and honey, and instead add ½ teaspoon hot red pepper flakes and ¼ teaspoon cumin seeds. Use 1 cup (240 ml) cider vinegar, ½ cup (120 ml) water, and 1½ teaspoons salt for the brine.

Carrot Marmalade

MAKES ABOUT 2¾ CUPS (660 ML)

VEGAN

Use this sweet jam in smoothies (straight from the freezer) or mix it with a little oil and use it to glaze grilled or roasted vegetables, or just have it on toasted dark bread with a mug of tea. Stir in a handful of chopped blanched almonds or hazelnuts to make a sweetmeat to serve by the spoonful with wedges of good cheese.

1 navel orange, scrubbed

1 lemon, scrubbed and halved

1 pound (455 g) carrots, chopped

1¼ cups (265 g) turbinado sugar

Cut the orange and half of the lemon into small pieces, peel and all, removing any seeds. Working in batches if necessary, put the carrots and chopped orange and lemon in a food processor and pulse to finely chop. Transfer the mixture to a large saucepan with the juice of the remaining ½ lemon, the sugar, and 1 cup (240 ml) water. Bring to a boil, then lower the heat and simmer briskly until the carrot and citrus peel pieces are tender, glossy, and mostly translucent, about 45 minutes. Transfer to clean glass jars, let cool for a few minutes, then put the lids on and keep in the refrigerator. The marmalade will keep in the refrigerator for up to 1 month or in the freezer for up to 6 months (freezing tablespoon-size mounds on a piece of waxed paper, then storing in a freezer bag, makes the marmalade easy to use a little at a time).

Arugula Pesto

MAKES ABOUT ⅔ CUP (180 G)

VEGAN

All-basil pesto is a luxury when you don't have easy access to loads of the king of herbs. In the winter, when all you might have is a potted basil plant on the kitchen windowsill, stretching it with spicy arugula is most definitely acceptable. And speaking of luxuries, feel free to replace the pine nuts with chopped almonds (blanched or unblanched), chopped walnuts, or pistachios. I've also taken to leaving the cheese out of my pesto, which has so much bright, herby, spicy flavor on its own that the cheese seems unnecessary. Dollop generous spoonfuls of this pesto onto sautéed mixed vegetables to bring otherwise disparate refrigerator stragglers together: the odd carrot, zucchini, broccoli florets, and the like. Or spread a thin layer of ricotta or hummus on a large Chickpea Flour Crêpe (page 221), top with pesto and some fresh lettuces dressed with lemon juice, salt and pepper, and olive oil, and wrap the whole thing up for lunch.

4 packed cups (240 g) baby arugula

½ packed cup (30 g) basil leaves

1 large clove garlic, peeled and left whole

6 tablespoons (90 ml) olive oil

2 tablespoons pine nuts, toasted

Salt and freshly ground black pepper

Fill a large bowl with ice water.

Bring a large saucepan of water to a boil. Add the arugula, basil, and garlic. Cook for 30 seconds, then drain and transfer to the ice water to cool. Pick out the ice cubes and drain in a colander or sieve, squeezing to extract all the excess water from the arugula and basil. Put the greens and garlic on a cutting board and finely chop them. Transfer to a mini food processor and add the oil, pine nuts, ¾ teaspoon salt, and a grinding of pepper. Pulse until finely chopped and combined, scraping down the side of the processor bowl as needed. Use immediately, or store in an airtight container in the refrigerator for up to 3 days or in the freezer for up to 3 months.

Pressed Japanese Turnips

MAKES ABOUT 1 CUP (225 G)

VEGAN

These are quick salted pickles in the Japanese *tsuke-mono* style: They're not sour (though they do take on a slight tang after a few days in the refrigerator), just salty and clean tasting. Serve a couple forkfuls with a rice dish, or even folded into steamed brown rice.

> 1 bunch (about 6 small) white Japanese (*hakurei*) turnips with greens (about 1 pound/455 g)
>
> 2-inch (5-cm) piece dulse seaweed, or 1 teaspoon dulse flakes
>
> Salt

Wash the turnips and their greens in a colander and shake off as much excess water as you can. Cut off the greens, discard the tough lower stems, and slice the leaves crosswise into ½-inch-wide (12-mm-wide) ribbons. Cut the turnips into thin rounds less than ⅛ inch (3 mm) thick, then stack the rounds and cut them into matchstick-size pieces. (Alternatively, leave the trimmed leaves whole and cut the turnips into thin wedges.)

Put the turnips, greens, and dulse in a bowl and toss with 1 teaspoon salt. Let stand until the vegetables release a lot of their liquid, about 5 minutes. Put a clean plate on top of the turnips and greens and weight it down with a couple of full jars or cans. Set aside at room temperature for 1 to 2 hours, until the turnips have softened and expelled much of their liquid. Taste and add more salt, if needed, stirring to dissolve it.

Serve, or transfer the turnips, greens, and liquid to a clean glass jar or other nonreactive container, pressing down so the liquid covers the turnips and greens, put the lid on, and refrigerate for up to 2 weeks.

Three Creamy Vegan Dressings

MAKES ABOUT 1½ CUPS (360 ML) EACH

I will always love a simple, pure vinaigrette gently napping the frilled edges of tender lettuces, but I have to admit that here's something that just feels special about a thick, creamy, cold dressing dolloped on crisp chopped greens. If salads are not a lunchtime staple for you, with one or more of these dressings on hand in the refrigerator they might yet earn a few spots in the weekly rotation.

The first dressing uses the vegan standby raw cashews to achieve creamy liftoff. (The cashew cream itself doubles easily and can be kept in the fridge for a few days. Use it to make creamy soups, milkshakelike smoothies—why not freeze cubes of it?—or sauces.)

The second dressing is based on soft silken tofu, the Japanese-style tofu that comes in an aseptic box. For a delicious potato salad, mix a generous dollop of this spicy cream into a bowlful of sliced, cooked, and cooled potatoes, season with a little more salt, if needed, and coarsely mash some of the potatoes with a fork. Stir in some diced celery, drained capers or chopped Sicilian-style green olives, and some minced fresh cilantro, if you like.

The fragrant orange dressing with tahini is especially good drizzled on grilled vegetables or into a pita sandwich. I've also been known to sauté sliced leftover cooked sweet potatoes with salt and lots of Cajun spice (a mixture of cayenne, black pepper, thyme, dried garlic, ground cloves, and so on; see the note on page 133) until crusty and deeply browned, scrape them onto a plate, and put a little dollop of this dressing nearby—it thickens and firms up in the fridge—for dragging the spicy sweet potatoes through. If this breakfast doesn't wake you up, nothing will.

A BENTO TIP

For all the years I've been packing my daughter's lunches—well, okay, for all the years since she began to accept salad as a part of her lunch—I've struggled to find an appropriate side container for dressings. (A predressed salad will wilt into something sad and awful by lunchtime.) The little sauce bottles from Japan, designed for soy sauce, are fine for a touch of simple vinaigrette, or to hold a couple of pinches of salt and pepper for sprinkling on fresh tomatoes or cucumbers, but they just don't work for thicker mixtures like these. Dip containers are usually too big, and often don't come home with the leftover sauce fully sealed up inside (oh, the mess!).

Finally, toward the end of one especially bad hay-fever season, I hit on a solution: I emptied, de-labeled, and thoroughly washed a wide-mouthed screw-top allergy-medicine bottle, which keeps a nice tight seal even when the cardboard lining is removed from the inside of the lid. We fill up a container with salad greens, chopped vegetables, sunflower seeds, dried cranberries, and so on, and tuck the dressing bottle in among them.

Tangy Cashew-Herb Dressing

VEGAN

FOR THE CASHEW CREAM

1 cup (130 g) raw cashew pieces

FOR THE DRESSING

¾ cup (30 g) chopped fresh herbs (I like a combination of basil, parsley, chives, and tarragon)

½ clove garlic, grated

¼ cup (60 ml) fresh lemon juice, or to taste

3 tablespoons olive oil

Salt and freshly ground black pepper

MAKE THE CASHEW CREAM

Soak the cashews in cold water to cover for 6 hours or overnight at room temperature. Drain them in a sieve, rinse under cold running water, drain again, and transfer to a good blender—a high-speed one is best. Add ½ cup (120 ml) fresh water and blend like crazy, until very, very smooth, scraping down the sides of the blender jar once or twice. When the mixture is smooth, blend some more. Measure out 1 cup (240 ml) of the cashew cream and store the rest for another use. No need to clean the blender jar. (The cream can be made in advance and refrigerated in an airtight container for up to 3 days or frozen for up to 3 months.)

MAKE THE DRESSING

Return the reserved 1 cup (240 ml) cashew cream to the blender, add the herbs, garlic, lemon juice, oil, ¾ teaspoon salt, and a couple of grindings of pepper. Blend until very smooth, adding enough water to make a runny dressing consistency (about 2 tablespoons). Taste and season with more salt and/or lemon juice, if needed. The dressing can be kept in a jar in the refrigerator for up to 1 week.

Variation
To make a nice, thick, simple dip for vegetables or pitas, omit the water and reduce the lemon juice to 2 tablespoons.

Chipotle-Cumin Dressing

VEGAN

12 ounces (340 g) soft silken tofu

3 tablespoons fresh lime juice

1 to 2 tablespoons minced chipotle in adobo (see Sidebar, page 197)

½ clove garlic, grated

½ teaspoon ground cumin

Salt and freshly ground black pepper

Ground cayenne (optional)

Add the tofu, lime juice, chipotle, garlic, cumin, ¾ teaspoon salt, and a few grindings of pepper to a mini food processor or blender. Blend until very smooth. Taste and season with more salt and pepper, if needed, and a pinch of cayenne, if you like. The dressing can be kept in a jar in the refrigerator for up to 3 days.

Orange-Tahini Dressing

VEGAN

1 large shallot, minced

1 teaspoon grated orange zest

⅔ cup (160 ml) fresh orange juice

2 tablespoons sherry vinegar

1 teaspoon Aleppo pepper or hot paprika

Salt

⅔ cup (160 ml) well-stirred tahini

In a medium bowl, combine the shallot, orange zest, orange juice, vinegar, Aleppo pepper, and 1 teaspoon salt and whisk to dissolve the salt. Add the tahini and whisk well; it'll look curdled at first, then smooth out. The dressing can be kept in a jar in the refrigerator for up to 1 week.

A Few Vinaigrettes for the Fridge

MAKES A LITTLE LESS THAN 1 CUP (240 ML) EACH

Following are three dead-simple—but distinctive—vinaigrettes you can mix up in a half-pint canning jar (easily doubled and mixed in a pint-size jar). They'll keep for at least a week in the refrigerator; just shake them up right before using. If the oil in either of the first two recipes has solidified in the cold, set the jar in a pan of hot water for a few minutes to loosen it, then shake well.

The tangerine vinaigrette is great with a salad of tender greens and toasted nuts—walnuts, hazelnuts, almonds. If you'd like, add a tablespoon of the appro-

priate nut oil. Try the almond butter–enriched dressing with sturdier greens like spinach, dandelion, or baby kale, or even with cold rice noodles and raw vegetables like grated carrot, thinly sliced scallions, and sweet corn. Use the yogurt-based cilantro-lime vinaigrette not just with lettuces and sturdier raw greens but also as a sauce to drizzle over grilled summer vegetables, mushrooms, or tofu, or to toss with a mixed-bean and chopped vegetable salad.

Tangerine Vinaigrette

VEGAN

- 3 tablespoons fresh tangerine juice
- 2 tablespoons red wine vinegar
- 1 tablespoon minced shallot
- Salt and freshly ground black pepper
- About ½ cup (120 ml) olive oil

Add the tangerine juice, vinegar, shallot, ¾ teaspoon salt, and several grindings of pepper to a half-pint glass canning jar or other nonreactive container with a tight lid. Swirl around to start dissolving the salt, then add the oil—a little more for a milder vinaigrette, a little less for a tangier one. Put the lid on tightly and shake well. Drizzle on salad or store in the refrigerator for up to 1 week.

Almond-Ginger Vinaigrette

VEGAN

- ¼ cup brown rice vinegar
- 1 tablespoon almond butter
- ½ teaspoon grated fresh ginger
- ½ teaspoon hot red pepper flakes
- Salt
- About ½ cup (120 ml) vegetable oil or mild olive oil

Add the vinegar, almond butter, ginger, red pepper flakes, and ¾ teaspoon salt to a half-pint glass canning jar or other nonreactive container with a tight lid. Put the lid on tightly and shake well, until the almond butter is fully incorporated, then open the jar and add the oil—a little more for a milder vinaigrette, a little less for a tangier one. Put the lid on tightly again and shake well. Drizzle on salad or store in the refrigerator for up to 1 week.

Cilantro-Lime Yogurt Vinaigrette

- 3 tablespoons fresh lime juice
- 2 heaping tablespoons minced fresh cilantro
- 1 scant tablespoon minced shallot
- Salt
- ⅛ teaspoon ground cumin (optional)
- About ½ cup (120 ml) vegetable oil
- ¼ cup (60 ml) plain Greek yogurt, preferably not fat-free

Add the lime juice, cilantro, shallot, ¾ teaspoon salt, and the cumin, if using, to a half-pint glass canning jar or other nonreactive container with a tight lid. Swirl around to start dissolving the salt, then add the oil—a little more for a milder vinaigrette, a little less for a tangier one. Put the lid on tightly and shake well, then open the jar and add the yogurt. Put the lid on tightly again and shake well. Drizzle on salad or store in the refrigerator for up to 1 week.

Red Coconut Curry Sauce Concentrate

MAKES ABOUT 2½ CUPS (600 ML)

VEGAN

Thai curry pastes are staples in my refrigerator. Store-bought ones are often very good, but it can be a challenge to track down vegetarian brands, as they usually contain shrimp paste or dried shrimp. With a few jars of this concentrate in the freezer, the only things you'll need for a quick Thai-style curry dish are a can of coconut milk, some lime juice, and whatever vegetables you'd like. Cook the thawed sauce in a little oil until it's fragrant and the color has darkened a shade, add a bit of coconut milk (and some stock or water to make a soup), then add sliced vegetables to poach (sliced shiitake caps, drained canned bamboo shoots, sliced eggplant, and red bell peppers, for example). Or use it in the thick-sauced stir-fry of bitter greens on page 26.

Due to a child's presence in our household I use milder Fresno chiles in bases like this for more flexibility, and then slice some hot chiles for my own servings, putting them on the table in a tiny, pretty vessel that's been unofficially designated the "chile dish." Of course, you can add some hotter chiles, like red jalapeños or serranos, or go in the opposite direction and use sweet bell peppers with no heat at all.

1 (13- to 15-ounce/385- to 445-ml) can unsweetened coconut milk

2 stalks lemongrass, outer leaves discarded, trimmed, lower 4 inches (10 cm) only, thinly sliced (about ½ cup/50 g)

15 fresh red Fresno chiles (about 4.5 ounces/135 g), or other relatively mild red chile, seeded and chopped

6 fresh Kaffir lime leaves, center ribs removed, minced (about 2 teaspoons)

4 coins peeled fresh ginger or galangal, minced (about 4 teaspoons)

4 cloves garlic, minced

2 teaspoons ground coriander

1½ teaspoons hot paprika

1 teaspoon ground cumin

½ teaspoon turmeric

Salt

Add all of the ingredients and 1½ teaspoons salt to a blender with ¼ cup (60 ml) water (use it to rinse out the coconut milk cans). Puree until very smooth, as smooth as possible. Keep in the refrigerator for up to 5 days, or pour into ½-cup (120-ml) freezer-safe containers and freeze for up to 6 months. Thaw before using to flavor curries and soups.

Roasted Vegetable Stock Concentrate

MAKES ABOUT 1½ CUPS (360 ML); ENOUGH FOR ABOUT 8 CUPS (2 L) STOCK

VEGAN

I am not ashamed to say that I use a commercial vegetable stock concentrate fairly regularly, but I will admit that my brothy soups are always, *always* better when they're based on a homemade stock like this one. I usually make this with whatever vegetable scraps I've squirreled away in the refrigerator or freezer—leek and fennel tops, celery bunch bases, carrot and onion trimmings, and so on. Roast a pound (455 g) or so of trimmings from dense vegetables like carrots and celery; save trimmings from mushrooms, tomatoes, and herbs and add them with the water. If you're working from scratch, the following recipe is a good starting point. I add some tamari to the concentrate for saltiness and even more depth of flavor, but you can leave it out if you'd like.

It's not difficult to boil down a stock until it's concentrated and intense, which saves all-important freezer space. Freeze it in small quantities in containers of any shape or size, then turn the disks or squares out into a freezer bag for long-term storage; the size of the pieces doesn't much matter as you can easily break or slice off what you need, or use more than one piece. I usually reconstitute this concentrate in a ratio of about 4:1 water to concentrate, which makes a weak but still flavorful stock good for cooking grains, using in soups with lots of other ingredients, and so on. Simply use more concentrate for a more robust flavor.

4 ribs celery, coarsely chopped

1 onion, coarsely chopped

3 carrots, coarsely chopped

1 tablespoon olive oil

Salt

Stems from ½ bunch fresh parsley

2 bay leaves

½ teaspoon whole black peppercorns

2 tablespoons tamari (optional)

Preheat the oven to 400°F (205°C).

Put the celery, onion, and carrots on a large rimmed baking sheet. Drizzle them with the oil, sprinkle lightly with salt, and toss. Roast until deeply browned, 50 to 60 minutes.

Transfer the vegetables to a Dutch oven or large saucepan. Deglaze the baking sheet with 1 cup (240 ml) water, scraping up all the browned bits; pour the deglazing liquid into the pot with the vegetables. Add 6 more cups (1.4 L) water, the parsley stems, bay leaves, and peppercorns. Bring to a boil, then lower the heat and simmer, uncovered, until reduced by about half, about 40 minutes. Pour the stock through a fine-mesh sieve into a large bowl, pressing down on the solids to extract as much liquid as possible, and discard the solids. Rinse out the Dutch oven and return the stock to it. Add the tamari, if using, then boil over medium-high heat until reduced to about 1½ cups (360 ml). Pour the stock into a heatproof glass measuring cup and let cool to room temperature. Transfer the cooled stock into smaller freezer-safe containers and freeze; consolidate the frozen disks or cubes into a freezer-safe bag for easy storage, if you like, and store in the freezer for up to 3 months. To use, dissolve the concentrate in hot water to taste (4 parts water to 1 part concentrate is a good place to start).

Frothy Hot Spiced Milk Mix

MAKES ABOUT 1½ CUPS (200 G); ENOUGH FOR ABOUT 8 MUGS

My friend Heidi sent me a canister of salep drink mix she picked up in Turkey, where the hot, thick, very sweet drink is commonly enjoyed around Christmastime. Salep is the ground dried rhizome of a certain variety of mountain orchid and is rare and expensive, so most mixes contain only a very small percentage of true salep. My approximation of the mix, below, contains a whopping zero percent salep. During our first winter in Nebraska, I kept a jar of the mix in the cupboard. When you have as many snow days as we do, the hot, foamy, slightly sweet milky drink is a nice change from hot chocolate for warming up after playing outside.

1 cup (130 g) non-instant nonfat dry milk powder (preferably the very fine powdery kind you can find in health food stores in the bulk bins, not the granular kind)

½ cup (70 g) confectioners' sugar

2 tablespoons cornstarch

½ teaspoon ground cinnamon

⅛ teaspoon ground aniseeds

Put all the ingredients in a mini food processor and pulse to combine. (Alternatively, whisk in a large bowl—but beware of the possible mess!) Store in an airtight container for up to 3 months. To use, put 1 cup (240 ml) water in a saucepan and whisk in 3 tablespoons of the mix. Bring just to a foamy boil over medium-high heat, whisking frequently and removing the pan from the heat just before it foams over the rim. Pour into a mug and drink hot.

Three Sharbets (Fruit Syrups) and a Couple of Shrubs (Drinking Vinegars)

MAKES 2½ TO 3 CUPS (600 TO 720 ML) EACH; ENOUGH FOR 18 TO 20 SMALL DRINKS

Sharbets (the Persian version) and shrubs or squashes (British) are all essentially infused syrups, usually with either citrus or vinegar added to offset the sweetness, that are fun to have on hand to dilute with water, plain seltzer, or club soda for a refreshing warm-weather drink that's only as sweet as you want it. At the brilliant Pok Pok, in Portland, Oregon, shrubs are sold bottled as "drinking vinegars" that can be enjoyed diluted or not. Experiment with using these syrups in cocktails, too, and consider adding a drizzle to your summer sangria. I also suspect that a sip of one of the drinking vinegars, undiluted or in a mug of hot water, would be quite soothing to a sore throat in winter. All of these concentrates will keep for weeks in the refrigerator.

If you decide to make a shrub you are probably already a fan of vinegar, but I feel I should warn you that in these recipes you'll be heating vinegar on the stovetop, and that can result in some vinegar-scented fumes wafting through your living space. Which you might or might not love.

Of course you can use just about any fruit you'd like in the *sharbets* and shrubs, but my favorite *sharbet* is the one based on blackberries, the flavor of which comes through especially well in the syrup even when diluted,

continued

and my favorite fruits to use in a shrub are strawberry and rhubarb, which have a natural tartness that seems of a piece with the acidic vinegar. For an easy frozen treat, whisk about 6 tablespoons of any of the citrus-sour *sharbets* into a cup or so of plain full-fat Greek yogurt, cover, and freeze until firm; let the frozen yogurt sit at room temperature for 15 to 20 minutes before scooping and serving.

Pandan Leaf Sharbet

VEGAN

4 (12-inch/30-cm) frozen pandan leaves (see Note)

1¼ cups (250 g) sugar

½ cup (120 ml) fresh lime juice

1 tablespoon unsweetened dried coconut

In a saucepan, combine the pandan leaves, sugar, lime juice, coconut, and 1 cup (240 ml) water. Bring to a boil, then lower the heat and simmer for 10 minutes. Pour the syrup through a fine-mesh sieve into a heatproof glass measuring cup, discarding the solids. Pour the syrup into very clean glass canning jars. Let cool, then put the lids on and chill in the refrigerator; after a couple of days, strain the syrup again into clean jars to remove any bits of solidified coconut oil, cover, and store in the refrigerator for up to 1 month. Add the *sharbet* to water, seltzer, or other drinks to taste.

Note: Look for pandan leaves, which have a wonderful vanilla-coconut perfume, in the freezer section of Asian grocery stores. They're flat, wide, bladelike leaves, fairly sturdy-looking, and packaged stacked and folded in plastic bags. Another use for pandan leaves: Tie a length of pandan leaf into a knot and drop it into a pitcher of cold water; let it infuse in the refrigerator for a couple of hours before serving the chilled scented water with dinner.

Blackberry Sharbet

VEGAN

2 cups (10 ounces/285 g) fresh or frozen blackberries

1½ cups sugar

¼ cup (60 ml) fresh lemon juice

In a saucepan, combine the blackberries, sugar, lemon juice, and 1 cup (240 ml) water. Bring to a boil, then lower the heat and simmer for 10 minutes. Pour the syrup through a fine-mesh sieve into a heatproof glass measuring cup; save the blackberries to stir into plain yogurt or to spoon onto ice cream, or just eat them straight. Pour the syrup into very clean glass canning jars. Let cool, then put the lids on and store in the refrigerator for up to 1 month. Add the *sharbet* to water, seltzer, or other drinks to taste.

Meyer Lemon–Mint Sharbet

VEGAN

2 Meyer lemons, scrubbed and sliced

4 large sprigs mint

1½ cups (300 g) sugar

In a saucepan, combine the lemons, mint, sugar, and 1½ cups (360 ml) water. Bring to a boil, then lower the heat and simmer for 10 minutes. Pour the syrup through a fine-mesh sieve into a heatproof glass measuring cup, discarding the solids. Pour the syrup into very clean glass canning jars. Let cool, then put the lids on and store in the refrigerator for up to 1 month. Add the *sharbet* to water, seltzer, or other drinks to taste.

Strawberry-Rosemary Shrub

VEGAN

| 1½ cups (9 ounces/255 g) diced strawberries
| 1½ cups (360 ml) cider vinegar
| 1¼ cups (250 g) sugar
| 1 sprig fresh rosemary

In a saucepan, combine the strawberries, vinegar, sugar, and rosemary. Bring to a boil over high heat, then lower the heat and simmer for 5 minutes. Remove the pan from the heat and set aside to cool to room temperature. Pour the mixture through a fine-mesh sieve into a very clean glass jar, discarding the solids. Cover and store in the refrigerator for up to 1 month. Add the shrub to water, seltzer, or other drinks to taste.

Rhubarb Shrub

VEGAN

| 3 cups (24 ounces/680 g) chopped fresh or thawed frozen rhubarb
| 2 cups (480 ml) cider vinegar
| 1½ cups (300 g) sugar

In a saucepan, combine the rhubarb, vinegar, and sugar. Bring to a boil over high heat, then lower the heat and simmer for 5 minutes. Remove the pan from the heat and set aside to cool to room temperature. Pour the mixture through a fine-mesh sieve into a very clean glass jar, discarding the solids. Cover and store in the refrigerator for up to 1 month. Add the shrub to water, seltzer, or other drinks to taste.

seasonality

Depending on where you live, and the practices of the farmers and gardeners in your area, certain vegetables may come into season at slightly different times than listed here and throughout this book. Seasons overlap, seasons can be extended with cold frames and greenhouses, and seasons can vary from year to year. This is a general guide, something to check before you head out to the farmers' market or grocery store, or to photocopy (heck, tear it out of the book, if you want) and tuck in your shopping bag for quick reference.

More detailed information for your specific location can be found online—look for it on the website of your state's university extension office. To find farmers' markets, farm stands, and CSA arrangements near you, which will of course be running with the seasons, check the map at Local Harvest (localharvest.org).

SPRING

- morel and chanterelle mushrooms
- arugula
- escarole
- butter lettuce (aka Bibb or Boston lettuce)
- tender salad greens: mâche, Little Gem, mizuna, watercress, purslane
- watercress
- dandelion greens
- baby spinach
- pea shoots
- English peas
- sugar snap peas
- artichokes
- asparagus
- baby carrots
- baby beets
- radishes: French breakfast, watermelon, red, Icicle white, Easter egg
- new potatoes

SPRING AND SUMMER

- spring onions
- young (green) garlic
- garlic scapes
- sweet onions: Vidalia, Texas Sweet

SUMMER

- zucchini
- yellow squash
- pattypan squash
- green beans
- wax beans
- French beans (haricots verts)
- yard-long beans
- Romano beans
- tomatoes
- cucumbers
- sweet corn
- bell peppers and mini sweet peppers
- hot chiles: jalapeño, serrano, Fresno, habanero, Padrón, poblano, Hungarian wax, banana peppers, finger peppers, Thai and bird's-eye, cayenne, hot cherry, Hatch
- okra
- eggplant: Japanese, Chinese, globe, white, Thai green
- herbs: cilantro, mint, parsley, chervil, sweet basil, Thai and holy basil, marjoram, oregano, thyme, rosemary, summer savory
- porcini mushrooms

SUMMER AND FALL

- broccoli
- broccoli rabe
- Chinese broccoli (gai lan)
- broccolini
- cauliflower
- broccoflower

FALL

- sweet potatoes: garnet and white
- parsnips
- carrots
- daikon
- black radishes
- beets
- turnips: Japanese (harukei), white globe, golden
- rutabaga
- onions: red and yellow
- sweet onions: Maui, Walla Walla
- leeks
- shallots
- garlic (cured)
- fennel

FALL AND WINTER

- collard greens
- kale: curly, lacinato (aka dinosaur, Tuscan, or cavolo nero), red kale, red Russian kale
- spinach
- Swiss chard
- butternut squash
- delicata squash
- sugar (pie) pumpkin
- acorn squash
- kabocha squash
- Hubbard squash
- spaghetti squash

WINTER

- celery
- celery root (celeriac)
- cabbage: green, purple, Savoy, Napa (Chinese)
- bok choy
- choy sum
- Brussels sprouts
- kohlrabi
- potatoes: russet (Idaho), waxy red, Yukon Gold, purple

WINTER AND SPRING

- purple kohlrabi
- mushrooms: morel, chanterelle, shiitake, cremini, oyster, King, wood ear
- baby kale
- baby mizuna

acknowledgments

Thank you to my editor at Stewart, Tabori & Chang, Elinor Hutton, who, as she always does, made this book infinitely better and more interesting. I was lucky again to be on the receiving end of Ellie's warm, thoughtful encouragement. Thank you to Ivy McFadden, this book's copyeditor, and Ann Martin Rolke and Elizabeth Norment, its proofreaders, for their excellent work cleaning up and calling out my many mistakes and oversights. I'd also like to thank the book's designer, Chin-Yee Lai, for somehow channeling and beautifully representing, in graphic form, my beloved front porch. Again, I feel very fortunate to have had all of these talented professionals working long hours to make my book into something that seems like it was written by an intelligent person with good taste.

I would also like to acknowledge the role that Lincoln, Nebraska, has played in the making of this book. Not just the people I've met since moving here just as I was starting to write—Nicholas and Michelle Shellhaas, ace recipe testers, in particular—but the city itself. I was expecting very fine steaks; I was expecting fruit pies that were as good as or better than any I could make myself. What I wasn't expecting was the 27th Street corridor. It's a beautiful mess, a dozen or so maddening-to-navigate blocks—plus some side-street action—featuring Asian markets as well stocked in fresh produce as any back east, Middle Eastern and Indian grocery stores with friendly, helpful proprietors, African stores, eastern European markets, hole-in-the-wall restaurants, and taco trucks. And just a few blocks west, a Burmese grocery store, another Indian place or two, and a micro-scale tortilla factory/Mexican market. Thank you to all of these shop owners and their employees for opening their doors and welcoming Lincoln inside.

The thrill of discovering the richness of Lincoln's new-immigrant food culture made leaving Athens, Georgia, a little easier, but what really helped ease the transition was the fact that Athenian Rinne Allen was able to come all the way out to Nebraska to make the pictures you see here. Once again Rinne managed to capture the spirit of this food—easygoing, simple, with a sense of humor and a sense of place. It was an immeasurable pleasure working with her, and I can't thank her enough for taking on this project. I'd also like to thank our hardworking, enthusiastic intern on the photo shoot, Tomas Olsen.

Thank you to dear Leda Scheintaub, Regan Huff, Mary Jessica Hammes, Amy Trauger, and Dean Neff for being so generous with their ideas, their conversation, and their recipes. I'd also like to acknowledge that this book was written very much in memory of my daughter's teacher and friend Johnny Johnson. His abiding love of children—and all other animals—has been truly inspiring.

Finally, thank you, Mom and Dad, for all your help but especially your support throughout the rutabaga and cabbage phases. And thank you, Derek and Thalia, for being such fun and loving companions—in the kitchen and out.